Human relations in education

Human relations in education

Eric Hall and Carol Hall

London and New York

For our parents and children —
Louise, Sara, Cassie and William

First published in 1988 by
Routledge
11 New Fetter Lane, London EC4P 4EE

Published in the USA by
Routledge, Chapman and Hall, Inc.
29 West 35th Street, New York, NY 10001

Reprinted 1992

Set in Monophoto Baskerville
and printed in Great Britain
by Butler & Tanner Ltd, Frome and London

British Library Cataloguing in Publication Data

Hall, E. (Eric), 1936–
    Human relations in education.
    1. Schools, Teachers, Interpersonal
    relationships with students
    I. Title   II. Hall, Carol
    371.1′02

Library of Congress Cataloging-in-Publication Data

Hall, Eric
    Human relations in education/Eric and Carol Hall.
    p.   cm.
Bibliography: p.
    Includes index.
    1. Teacher-student relationships. 2. Communication in education. 3. Interpersonal
    relations. I. Hall, Carol. II. Title.
    LB1033.H219 1988
    371.1′02—dc19

ISBN 0–415–025311 (Hb)
ISBN 0–415–02532X (Pb)

Contents

Introduction

The issues raised in this book generalize so widely that they are relevant to every area of the education system, from a tutor with a group of university students to a nursery teacher talking to parents. But it can serve a more specific purpose for three particular groups:

1   Students involved in initial teacher training. It would be particularly useful in general education courses rather than subject method courses, though we would regret the separation of human relations concerns from the teaching of a subject. It would also provide practical and theoretical material for courses based on personal and social education and the pastoral curriculum.
2   Experienced teachers taking part in in-service training; on extended award-bearing courses, on short intensive courses or as part of school based in-service training.
3   Any practising teacher.

The book provides an integration of theory and practical activities. One without the other by definition must be a limited experience. Theory presented on its own has been a problem of teacher training for many years and a cause for complaint from student teachers who feel that more directly relevant material is needed. Concentrating entirely on practical activities can result in the mechanical application of technique.

The theory, ideas and issues raised in the book are illustrated by experiential exercises. The exercises have been deliberately kept low-key in case they are used with groups of non-volunteers, but nevertheless, they are still likely to generate a degree of self-disclosure and emotional involvement. More advanced forms of experiential learning are probably best done with groups of volunteers on optional courses.

The exercises in this book can provide the basis for a comprehensive course in human relations. They do seem to apply to all the categories of teacher described above. The same exercises can also be used with students in school, though this may require some creative modification on the part of the teacher. Parts of these exercises can be done by the solitary reader, but a great deal of potential for learning is lost without the shared experience of the group.

The exercises read cold from the book have little potency. It requires the involvement of direct experience to bring them to life. Many experiential exercises bear repetition. This applies to both exercises done by the individual, such as fantasy journeys and relaxation, and to group exercises such as those designed to give insight into interpersonal, interactive skills.

1 Human relations in education

Creating a congenial classroom atmosphere is something that some teachers do as if by magic, giving rise to the adage that teachers are born and not made. Although the 'magic' defies analysis, there are in fact a number of specific skills that can be learned, developed and practised, which will promote a positive climate for learning – not only about academic subjects, but about ourselves and the groups and communities in which we live.

Unless the process of education becomes entirely electronic, it must be acknowledged that, in order for institutions like schools and colleges to function effectively, the human relations have to be attended to. Schools can no longer keep up the pretence that relationships do not affect performance, either academic or professional. There are a wide range of attitudes to this issue. Some teachers claim that their prime task is to organize their students' intellectual development, whereas others argue that the major source of difficulty in their work is the problem of relating to their students and their colleagues, and that once this has been sorted out the academic issues are relatively simple.

It would seem sensible that the main thrust of teacher training should be divided between content, which involves the organization of the material to be taught, and the process, which refers to the set of relationships within which the learning takes place. Historically, however, this has never been the case and the power in teacher training has always been in the hands of educators largely concerned with content. This is probably due to an ongoing emphasis on teaching fixed bodies of knowledge using a formal approach. There have been interesting developments in approaches such as discovery learning, but the bulk of the practice has involved the teaching of traditional subjects in order to meet the requirements of formal examinations.

In teacher training, the emphasis has traditionally been shared between theory and teaching practice, preparing the subject teacher to teach specific subjects. This is just as true of aspiring teachers of younger children, where the content is divided among several subjects with the addition of teaching basic literacy and numeracy skills.

There are two factors which are forcing a change in the education system in the UK.

Firstly, both the schools themselves and the teachers' unions are reporting that relationships within some schools are deteriorating dramatically. It may be the pernicious effects of widespread unemployment, which is even beginning to filter down and affect the attitudes of primary school children. Certainly, a situation is developing in schools where relationships are breaking down and there appear to be high levels of confrontation between teachers and students and even between teachers and their colleagues following a long period of bitter industrial action.

Teaching also appears to be becoming a more stressful activity. Research in the UK (Dunham, 1976; Kyriacou and Sutcliffe, 1978) suggests that the increase in teacher stress is largely due to poor relationships with students and, to some extent, to poor relationships with other staff. The research into teacher stress is far more advanced in the USA where recommendations for reducing stress include many of the activities suggested in this book.

Much of the data on teacher stress is in the form of responses to questionnaires sent out to teachers without any form of personal contact with the researcher. It is possible that this data is misleading as teachers may perceive reporting stress as an admission of weakness. Hall, Woodhouse and Wooster (1984) collected data on stress during a one-hour interview conducted following a course in which teachers were encouraged to be more open about their professional and personal relationships. In the interview, it emerged that the teachers placed a much stronger emphasis on problems with colleagues rather than with students; this provides justification for the equal emphasis we intend to give to both relationships with colleagues and students.

Secondly, there is now some convincing evidence to show that improving the quality of human relations in an institution also improves the quality and amount of academic work produced and the attendance of the students. There is also an improvement in less definable qualities such as motivation and classroom climate. The health of the teachers improves. This research is clearly summed up in Carl Rogers' inspiring book *Freedom to Learn for the 80s* (1983). This is an update of an earlier book which made a powerful argument for a move away from an emphasis on teaching, to one on learning. The teacher was seen as a facilitator of learning who should demonstrate Rogers' core conditions of empathy, congruence and positive regard. A great many educators were inspired by this early book, but it was criticized on the grounds that there was no hard research evidence to support his views. Rogers provides us with this evidence in his later book, both with a series of case histories and a review of the work of Aspy and Roebuck (1977).

These researchers, using the traditional tools of the social scientist, established a relationship between the core conditions of empathy, congruence and positive regard with a range of factors such as attitudes to self, school and others, discipline problems, physical health, attendance, IQ changes, and cognitive growth. They used a sample of over two thousand teachers and twenty thousand students in elementary, secondary and college institutions. Their results were all in a positive direction and have been corroborated by research carried out in Germany.

So, there is evidence that putting the emphasis on the quality of human relations in educational institutions can have a positive effect on the one area which is normally held sacrosanct – namely academic achievement. Wooster and Carson (1982) provide an interesting report of how a difficult class of eight-year-olds who were taught social and communication skills over two terms showed dramatic improvements in self-concept and reading ability.

The focus of this book will be on human relations in educational settings. The ideas and activities included generalize to most interpersonal situations and the exercises can be used over a wide age-range. Indeed it might be a salutary experience for trainee teachers to try out some of these exercises partnered by students. Consider the following simple listening exercise:

* Invite the group members to choose a partner and sit with them. Suggest a topic for the pairs (see Appendix) to discuss.
  Instruct members of the pair not to say anything until two seconds after the other person has finished what they want to say.
  Discuss the experience.

There are no guarantees as to exactly what any individual will learn from this experience, but most people find it difficult to even comply with the instructions if the topic is an involving one. It does appear to work with experienced teachers, teachers in training and students in school with a wide range of age and ability. 'Work' here means that the people concerned are involved in the activity and often claim to have learned something in the subsequent discussion. This usually includes learning something about themselves.

In a later section, we will argue that experiential learning is the most productive way of dealing with issues of human relations. The main thrust of the argument is the assumption that we all interpret situations differently because of the uniqueness of our past experience. For this reason, no one can predict what is 'right for you'. These differences in the perception of experience will be considered in the next section.

The nature of experience

Many people behave and talk as if there were a fixed external reality which can be absorbed through the senses and that therefore everyone perceives the world as they do. Society is organized on the assumption that we all have a shared perceptual experience and that those who deviate from those shared experiences are, in some way, mentally ill.

William James (1890) describes the new-born child's experience as being 'blooming, buzzing, confusion'. With our present knowledge, there is no way we can be sure of the nature of the infant's experience, though there is indirect evidence to suggest that we have to learn to 'see', that is to organize incoming sense data into a meaningful pattern. Patients who gained their sight later in life, after cataract operations (Von Sendon – see Dember, 1969), were unable to 'see' simple geometrical shapes and had to learn to see them. Simple perceptual skills which we take for granted had to be learned slowly.

The reality of what we 'see' is an array of shapes and colours bounded by a hazy dark area. With experience we learn to organize this array into trees, tables, houses, people and so on and by moving into it, we learn that it has a three-dimensional quality. Integrated with this learning is the experience of the other senses. Hearing and touch are clearly important for human beings and other senses such as smell may be more important than we think in our total appraisal of an experience. Certainly the bodily experience of feelings and emotions play an important part in our experience of a situation.

In order to develop the discussion, let us go back to simple visual examples. If the visual cues are cleverly manipulated, we can see things that are not 'really' there. A carefully arranged collection of sticks viewed through a peephole will be seen as a chair. Looking through a peephole into a distorted room will make an adult appear to be smaller than a toddler. In reality, the adult is much further away than the toddler, but because we have years of experience of rooms with right angles, the room is readjusted perceptually to match our expectations and the people become distorted. It is interesting to note that it was not possible to obtain the same results from people who came from a culture that built round huts.

These are just two of the elegant demonstrations designed by Adelbart Ames. There is no way that a description of these experiments can match the experience of seeing them. Even pictures of them (Ittleson and Kilpatrick, 1951) do not provide the same disturbing effect on our habitual ways of seeing the world. Bateson (1979) describes how a visit to a warehouse full of these demonstrations left him disorientated and confused about the true nature of reality.

The psychologists who developed this area called themselves transactional psychologists, as they argued that perception was based on a transaction between the individual and the environment. The individual is predisposed to see things in certain ways because of her past experience.

Our experience of square rooms also affects our visual perception of certain simple line drawings. The Neckar Cube, illustrated below, is usually seen as a cube standing on a flat surface, viewed from above.

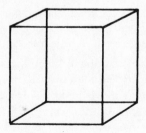

By staring at it for a while, it may change into a cube attached to a wall, viewed from below. It may later reverse every time you blink. By naming the diagram as a cube predisposes the observer. It could be seen as a series of flat triangles and four-sided figures, but it is usually difficult not to see it as three-dimensional. What is the reality?

These simple visual illustrations are relatively easy to comprehend and have been developed by Ihde (1979) into a strong argument for a phenomenological view of perception. Words like phenomenological tend to be off-putting, but this is the technical term for the area of enquiry which accepts that we are all unique in the way that we make sense of our experience. Social scientists and educators pay lip-service to this point of view, but fail to take it seriously, since its assumptions undermine much of what has passed as research in the social sciences and in education.

Much of this research involves the replies to questionnaires and the objective observations of the researcher. The phenomenological view would question the assumption that similar responses to a question reflect the same experience; that the observations of the researcher cannot be separated from her expectations (Rosenthal, 1976) and that the presence of a researcher with her expectations can affect the way people will behave.

Another reason for not paying too much attention to this point of view is that it is difficult to retain a position of power and accept that there are differing possible interpretations of the same events. It militates against the possibility of 'right answers'; it demands negotiation in management situations; it undermines the justification of fixed moral rules.

We have, however, taken a large leap from simple visual illustrations to ethical decision-making. So, let us return to the visual problems and build up to more complex situations. In spite of these individual differences in perception, we tend to make our way round the world in a competent manner. Only occasionally do we realize that our perceptions are totally wrong. Sitting in one of two trains standing side-by-side in a station, it is not always clear which train is beginning to start off. If you are expecting your train to leave, you may assume that you are moving and then get a shock to realize you are still standing at the platform. Reality suddenly changes. Perhaps you have had the experience of starting to speak to someone, thinking mistakenly that you know them. In a situation like this, when you realize the mistake, the features of the other person may appear to change in front of you. Again reality changes.

When it comes to social situations the problems of differences in perception become more acute. Our perceptions of people often remain the same, even though they have changed their behaviour in a way which contradicts the original perception. The image of our parents that we carry around is often from our early childhood. We see our fathers as being very tall and only reluctantly admit they are of average height when we grow up. Changes in behaviour are either not noted, or resented. There seems to be a vested interest keeping people in their pigeon-holes. Too much change in the environment is disturbing.

Now consider the following example of a tutor talking to some of the twelve-year-olds in his group. When Stephen talks about the other children in the class, he often uses the words 'clever' and 'stupid'. When pressed about the use of these words, it turns out that the 'clever' pupils are the ones who work hard and the 'stupid' ones are those who mess around. For Kevin, the 'clever' ones are those who are good at playing up the teacher and the 'stupid' ones are those who get on with their classwork. For Susan, the 'clever' ones are those who are well-dressed and speak politely, and the 'stupid' ones are those who are scruffy and coarse, but for Jane, all the boys are 'stupid' and all the girls are 'clever'.

These children appear to be using the same words in entirely different ways and are probably unaware of this themselves. The teacher too is often not aware that the children are construing words and experiences in different ways. This produces problems in communication that continue into adult life, as we rarely make any attempt to find out if we are using words in the same ways as other people. In any culture there is a great deal of shared experience as we meet people in our daily lives which helps to smooth out some of these differences. On the other hand, long periods of shared experience can still be fraught with misunderstanding, as is demonstrated by many marriages.

The same problems are found in the staffroom. The headteacher thinks the head of geography is soft and sees the metalwork teacher as a good disciplinarian. The head of geography perceives herself as radical and the metalwork teacher as authoritarian. The metalwork teacher sees himself as controlled and the head of geography as relaxed. All of these individuals are basing these judgments on a fairly limited set of experiences.

These differences in construing experiences are given a useful conceptual framework in Kelly's (1955) psychology of personal constructs which will be considered in a later section.

The phenomenologists suggest that we perceive what we 'intend' to perceive and the word 'intentionality' appears frequently in their writing (Wilson, 1966). The term is confusing because this 'intention' is invariably not part of our awareness. The term is used to describe the way in which we are disposed to perceive and experience situations in certain ways. We do, however, feel that the term is useful since it suggests that, at some level, we are making an active choice to perceive things in a certain way – or not to perceive things that are there. Accepting this point of view makes us much more responsible for what happens in our lives and suggests that we might be able to do something about situations that are normally seen to be out of our control.

Consider the following examples in which the wording has been deliberately manipulated to fit the point of view we are advancing. Consider them in the wording given, as they illustrate the idea of intentionality in a variety of situations:

1   Jackie believes that science and maths are not appropriate for girls. She intends to fail.
2   John, at fourteen years old, sees all male adults as being like his father who beat him viciously. He intends to react to all male teachers with fear.
3   Bill, the biology teacher, reacts with anger to anything his head of department says. He intends to argue with her every time they meet. He also intends to reduce their interactions to a minimum. He intends always to react to women in authority in this manner.
4   Jane feels tired, dull and full of apathy when she is teaching. She intends to give up teaching.
5   Towards the end of every term, Malcolm, the deputy head, has a week off school with a genuine illness. He intends not to let the stress of work wear him out.

These examples suggest that the individuals concerned intend to be fearful, unintelligent, angry, apathetic and ill. The popular view is that we are not normally in control of these processes. The notion of intentionality implies that perhaps we can actively intervene in reactions that appear to be automatic.

* Ask the members of the group to choose a partner and sit with them.
  Give out a copy of the five examples listed above.
  Spend fifteen minutes with one member of the pair to identify any aspects of her behaviour which resemble the examples given.
  Change roles for a further fifteen minutes.
* Try to identify a fixed way you have of relating to another person which you may see as negative and would like to change.
  Just once, try and change your habitual way of responding to that person.

Our experience of considering the phenomenological approach to experience and, indeed, education, is very inspiring and adds a new dimension to everyday living. This does, however, seem to be very short-lived. We quickly slide back into old habits, assuming that our perception of the world is the 'right one'. Life may seem easier and more comfortable going along with the old habitual ways of behaving, but in the long term these patterns may be inadequate to meet subtle changes that are going on all the time.

A technique which is offered to minimize the process of sliding back into old habits is the suggestion to keep your awareness in the 'here and now'. Here the aim is to try to drop any analysis or interpretation of a situation and to try to be aware of the immediate experience.

Consider the following fictitious example:

James, the biology teacher, goes into one of his most difficult classes worrying that he is not going to be able to control the class. Two of the problem girls are laughing in the corner of the room and his immediate assumption is that they must be messing about. He shouts at them to stop causing trouble. They shout back and an ugly confrontation develops.

He has created perceptions to meet his expectations.

James is allowing his own construction of the situation to control his behaviour. If he had been attending more closely to his experience, he may have been aware that

as he entered the room, he had a queasy feeling in his stomach and visual images of how the lesson was likely to develop kept coming into his mind. The students were scattered around the room and two girls were laughing in the corner. As they laughed, the feelings in his stomach became much more intense. Instead of making premature accusations, he asks them what was going on and they tell him they were sharing a joke. He tells them to settle down to get ready for the lesson and the feelings in his stomach subside.

Clearly, this is not a panacea for all discipline problems and yet many problems arise because a situation has been totally misrepresented. In some islands in the Caribbean, it is a form of defiance to look the teacher in the eye while being told off. The injunction 'Look at me when I am talking to you' will only cause confusion. Ironically it may be a good thing that non-verbal communication is misinterpreted in some cases as the teacher will be missing gestures of contempt.

In the case of James, the biology teacher, he was hearing sounds. That it was the two girls making the noise, that it was laughing and that the laughing was not in his interests are all different levels of interpretation of the experience of sound. At least James could have checked out his interpretation before acting. Effective ways of doing this will be developed in later sections.

Turning attention to immediate experience provides a space between the experience and the reaction to it. The space provides an opportunity to make a more realistic appraisal of a situation before launching into habitual and possibly harmful patterns of behaviour. The space also provides an opportunity to choose between a range of possible choices. The injunction to first develop awareness and then break habits bears a close resemblance to many forms of mystical training such as meditation and hatha yoga.

Experiential learning

The process of developing awareness and changing habits is central to the activities that come under the general heading of experiential learning. In spite of some brave attempts to define this term (Torbert, 1972; Boydell, 1976; Walter and Marks, 1981; Kolb, 1984), there is still a great deal of confusion in the way the term is used.

Here, we will define experiential learning as that which takes place in a laboratory or work-shop situation in which the participants can actively explore the choices available to them in the way they relate to themselves and to other people.

This definition could apply to a wide variety of situations, and the exercises given in this book will provide a representative sample.

* Choose a partner. Sit with them and have a conversation on a chosen topic for five minutes. Never make eye contact.
  Afterwards, discuss what it felt like.

This is one example where the research evidence provides clear guidelines regarding optimal behaviour – that is that eye contact is important in communication, but that a continuous stare, just as a lack of eye contact, can be disturbing. However, without an exercise of this kind, it is often difficult to know exactly how you are behaving and what effect it has on the other person.

* Write down a list of routine questions you ask children at the beginning of a lesson, such as 'Will you get your books out?' Read them to a partner and after each sentence, change them to a statement, such as 'I want you to get your books out'. Change roles. Then discuss how it felt to change the words.

This exercise allows the participants to explore the practical effects of different language structures. Questions and statements are neither right nor wrong, though some teachers operate entirely with questions, as if it were impossible to make a clear statement.

* Ask a group of students to have a pen and paper to hand and then ask them to jot down the first thought that comes in response to the question 'What kind of weather am I?' ('I' being the group leader.)

Invariably, this question brings out a wide range of responses, such as 'sunny', 'stormy', 'cold' and so on. This illustrates how different individuals perceive the same person in totally different ways.

After each of the last three exercises, some indication of what could have been learned has been given. In the practical situation, this is not necessary and in the writers' view is undesirable. Individuals, in pairs or larger groups, can draw their own conclusions from the experiences they have undergone. They are learning how to learn from their experience.

Each of the last three examples illustrates one of the main sensory modes through which experiential learning can take place, through bodily experience, through words and through imagery. The use of each of these sensory modalities for developing awareness and skills in relating to yourself and other people will be developed in later sections.

An important part of experiential learning is feedback. That is, to get some indication of the results of what you are doing. Learning inter-personal skills is in some ways similar to learning a physical skill. In order to learn to ride a bicycle, it is important to get on it and have a go. Reading a book on a skill will have little or no effect on performance, and verbalizing what has to be done may even interfere with performance. As with bike riding, learning inter-personal skills depends a great deal on being able to learn from visual and bodily cues. Similarly, the young child learns social skills, using these cues, long before she can begin to articulate them.

Some quite complex models of feedback have been developed, but we see no need to go further than the elegant model developed by Miller, Galanter and Pribram (1960) which simply states: try something, see what happens, change what you do, see what happens and keep this process going until you are satisfied with the end product. In their words, 'test – operate – test – operate – test – exit'.

Feedback can be obtained from other people without their knowing about it. You can use statements instead of questions and see if it has any effect on the other person's behaviour. You avoid eye contact with another person and see how it affects your relationship. Both these examples illustrate how it is better to experiment with changes in behaviour in a safe classroom environment. Changing the way you relate to your spouse might wreck the marriage. Avoiding eye contact with your headteacher could give him a prejudiced opinion of you.

Another form of feedback involves comments which are invited from other people. It is easy to be unaware of your own behaviour in an inter-personal situation, and feedback from an observer can be illuminating and sometimes shocking. It is important to acknowledge that the feedback is the observer's construction of reality and that it will be coloured by her intentionality.

However, it is clear that giving what might be perceived as negative feedback can be both unhelpful and damaging to self-esteem in some situations. The skill of giving helpful feedback will be developed in a later chapter. A useful general rule is to say what effect the other person's behaviour has on you – so in effect you are talking about your own reaction to the other person's behaviour, not just presenting a damning picture of what you thought you saw her doing.

A statement such as, 'When you talk to me, you launch into a long lecture and you don't listen to what I want to say', becomes, 'When you go on talking for so long, I get angry inside and just want to walk away.'

In an extensive review of experiential learning, Walter and Marks (1981) do include activities such as listening to a lecture and reading a book as aspects of experiential learning. Obviously, these activities are an experience and a source of learning, but to include every form of learning under the heading of experiential learning dilutes the meaning of the term. In this book, we will limit the term to situations which directly involve the content of the area of enquiry. Reading a book about being more assertive is a second-hand experience, even though it may inspire the reader, stimulate thoughts, memories and feelings. There is no way that the experience of reading the book can recreate the involvement of attempting assertive behaviour in a real situation; facing the feelings of anxiety that contribute to the blocking of behaviour and the flush of exhilaration that goes with success.

We will, however, also exclude those activities which, traditionally, have been described as discovery learning (Silberman, 1973), where the pupil is learning through experience in order to develop concepts within a subject area such as mathematics or geography. We are making this distinction because of the way in which the words are used in practice. Experiential learning does have a subject matter, namely yourself and how you go about your life. Here, it applies to how you go about your life in educational settings, whether as a teacher, student teacher or pupil.

It is important to point out that experiential learning usually takes place in concentrated workshop conditions. Here we learn to look at our behaviour as though under a microscope. This is very different from normal everyday experience. Our daily activities and inter-actions can be a very potent source of learning about ourselves and how we relate to others. However, there does seem to be a law of diminishing returns, because much of this everyday experience happens at a low level of awareness, old habits are run off without any reflection and trying out new ways of behaving can be fraught with anxiety. A young teacher starting in a new staffroom has a lot of choices about who to talk to and how to talk to them. She may find that she quickly settles down to a pattern of relating to the other staff which is very difficult to break out of later on. It may become extremely difficult to sit in a group of chairs when certain staff are there. It may become difficult to address certain colleagues by their first names once a more formal pattern has been established. A teacher who went from school to school as a supply teacher was asked by the head if she liked the school. She replied that it looked and smelt like a urinal. The head appeared to be amused by this response, but it would probably be much more difficult for an established member of staff to reply in the same honest way.

The same process appears to take place with the teachers' relationship with their classes. Initially there seem to be many choices, which decrease as patterns of relationships are established. Perhaps the risks are too high in everyday inter-personal situations. It is hard to experiment with changes in behaviour with spouses, children, friends, shop assistants, colleagues, students and so on, because the experiment might prejudice the relationship.

The development of curricular material using experiential learning for use in schools is now well developed in the United States (Brown, 1972; Castillo, 1974; Canfield and Wells, 1976). Similar schemes are being developed in Britain such as Active Tutorial Work (Baldwin and Wells, 1979), Developmental Group Work (Button, 1982) and Lifeskills (Hopson and Scally, 1980). These sources provide well-planned sequential programmes of activities. The best programmes, however, do appear to be those designed by the individual teacher to meet the needs of a particular group of students, modifying the material to deal with issues that arise as the group develops. An added possibility is to involve the students in the design of the activities and exercises.

Clearly, this book is a contradiction, since it is concerned with learning about issues that are not generally accessible from books. It is, however, seen as an accompaniment to experiential learning in educational settings. The contents of the book are designed as a reflection on experiential learning. This is again a contradiction, in that as we suggest above, an essential quality of experiential learning is that the learner draws his or her own conclusions and that these conclusions will not be the same for everyone. For the inexperienced reader the exercises woven into the text can be done with individuals or in groups. The book will provide a map of the territory, but as Korzybski (1958) suggests, the map is not the territory. This map is an interpretation of the territory.

Humanistic education

Humanistic education is an approach to learning which places a strong emphasis on establishing good relationships. Experiential learning is used as an important tool for the training of teachers in developing relationships and establishing a positive climate.

Again, humanistic education is a difficult area to define. It certainly has close connections with humanistic psychology, which developed out of the writing of individuals such as Rogers (1951) and Maslow (1962) and was seen as a third force in psychology. This was a reaction against the mechanistic theories of behaviourism and psycho-analysis. Behaviourism emphasized conditioned learning and psycho-analysis emphasized the effect of early experiences stored in the unconscious. Humanistic psychology implied that there is more to human beings than blind reactions to rewards and punishments or the effects of events in the first five years of life.

In humanistic education, individuals are seen as having choice, rather than as the victims of heredity or past experience. If we can choose, it seems reasonable that we should have some choice about what we are going to learn and how it should be learned. Rogers (1983) provides some inspiring case histories of teachers handing over responsibility for learning to their students. Experience is dealt with from the point of view of the learner, which means that the teacher may have to find out ways of individualizing the learning.

Humanistic education is concerned with the whole person. For example, equal emphasis is placed on the intellect and the emotions. By focusing on the experience of the learner, issues will be raised which have personal relevance to them. Freire (1972) demonstrated that illiterate people could be taught to read more quickly using emotional issues, such as the conditions in which they lived. Material which is personally relevant generates the feeling or motivation to learn. Without this, learning, we would contend, becomes an arid intellectual exercise.

Many teachers know that the issues that get a group of children talking are those most closely related to their personal lives. Sharing hopes, fears, fantasies, dreams, feelings and so on are almost certain to stimulate an involving discussion. Affective education is a term which is used to describe learning which has a strong emotional component. Many of the exercises offered in this book produce feeling changes in the participants.

Finally, humanistic education, with the emphasis on developing choices and being concerned with the whole person, aims for the full development of the individual. Rogers (1961) writes about the 'fully functioning person', Maslow (1962) writes about 'self-actualisation'. These ideas have led to a strong interest in personal growth, which could be defined as maximizing the choices available to the individual.

Summary

In this chapter we have stressed the need for increasing the emphasis on human relations in educational settings and in teacher training. We suggest that training in this area is best done by working through direct experience rather than in an abstract propositional form. The examination of experience requires accepting the phenomenological point of view that we all make sense of experience in different ways – a basic understanding for developing skills in human relations.

Experiential learning is a useful form for exploring our own experience and the differences in experience. We limit our definition of experiential learning to laboratory situations where changes in behaviour can be explored without prejudicing ongoing relationships. Humanistic education is a wider area which incorporates experiential learning and takes account of the emotional component of learning about yourself and how you relate to other people.

Connections

In this chapter, we have argued that human relations are made complex because individuals make sense of their experience in different ways. Communication in educational settings is often ineffective because no attempt is made to explore the nature of these differences. Experiential learning is offered as a technology for helping the individual, whether student or teacher, to understand themselves better and to gain insights into what is happening when they are relating to others. Hopefully, this will enable the individual to have more choices in life, particularly in the way she relates to others.

Increasing choices is made easier given an understanding of the way behaviour is limited by the rewards and punishments that impinge on the individual and by emotional experiences. This is discussed in the second chapter on conditioning, which explores the way that these processes affect our behaviour when we are relating to other people. This is developed into a consideration of the extent to which we think we control our behaviour and the ways in which this sense of control can be extended. Experiential learning can provide a means of transcending our conditioning and this enables us to break out of old habits in our patterns of relationship which may be unhelpful in the long term.

The sense of what we are capable of doing is an important part of our 'self-concept'. Chapter three provides an examination of three different approaches to the 'self'. Firstly a short review of the research that has been done on the 'self-concept' as it applies to education. Secondly an examination of how the 'self' is expressed through the individual's personal constructs, like the children who were considering each other in terms of 'cleverness' and 'stupidity' earlier in this chapter. Followed, thirdly, by a description of the ways we defend our 'selves' from threat, processes which are well explained in terms of conditioning.

These three theoretical chapters prepare the ground for the exploration in fine detail of what is happening when people are relating to each other in schools and how this communication can be made more effective. In the fourth chapter, relationships are explored within the framework of counselling and inter-personal skills. We will argue that these skills can be used in all of the interactions in educational settings and can even be taught to the students. In order to develop these skills effectively, old habits have to be put aside and new skills developed, which may seem uncomfortable at first.

In the fifth chapter, we will explore three important modes of communication – through language, through imagery and through non-verbal cues. With regard to language, we will explore how different forms of language can have different practical outcomes in the behaviour of the listeners. The use of appropriate forms can have a definite effect on what are described as discipline problems. The discussion of the use of imagery and non-verbal communication will demonstrate that there is far more to human relations than talking.

Poor communication is an important source of teacher stress. Bad habits, lack of a sense of control over events, a poor self-concept and long-term conditioned emotional reactions all exacerbate a stressful construction of reality. The sixth chapter looks at how improved human relations can reduce stress. The reader is given some suggestions on how to relax and how this, in turn, can improve communication.

The seventh chapter argues that all of these processes are best explored in a group format, which is encouraged by the exercises in this book. The use of experiential learning in a group, whether a class in a school, or a group of experienced teachers, appears to result in more co-operation, more friendliness, better self-concepts and increased productivity in the learning goals of the group. This chapter also examines the use of low structure groups as an experiential training situation for learning about human relations.

This range of topics is often dealt with in separate books. As we develop the various sections we will demonstrate how they all provide insight into different aspects of human relations and contribute to the process of experiential learning. At the end of each chapter, the section headed 'Connections' will outline the relationships with the other chapters and show how they combine to form a holistic view of human relations.

We continue with a leap from the optimism of a humanistic/phenomenological approach to a pessimistic examination of how the ways in which we relate to other people are constrained by conditioned emotional reactions and habitual ways of behaving.

2 Taking control of conditioning

This chapter may seem a stark contrast to the earlier discussion of phenomenology, experiential learning and humanistic education, all of which have a great deal to do with increasing the choices available to the individual. However, notions of conditioning give an indication of the extent to which our choices are limited. It is difficult to explore your choices until you have developed some awareness of what you are already doing.

Humanistic considerations and conditioning are often presented as conflicting sets of ideas. The real differences are in the technologies for behaviour change which have grown out of them. Experiments on conditioning have been developed into behaviour modification, which involves the manipulation of rewards and punishments to encourage desirable behaviour. As we shall argue later in this chapter, behaviour modifications can be humanized if the control of the situation is given to the person whose behaviour is being modified.

Most of our behaviour is controlled by the rewards and punishments provided by other people and the environment.

Many of these patterns of behaviour are run off with little awareness and become habits which continue to be run off even though the original rewards and punishments no longer arrive. The reward for the behaviour seems to have something to do with the fact that it is familiar and therefore not threatening.

Conditioning is a technical psychological term which is normally associated with animal behaviour, such as dogs salivating, rats pressing bars to obtain food and a large number of variations on these themes. These notions have often been dealt with in educational textbooks, and have been criticized for having little relevance to human learning. This may be correct in relation to the cognitive processes involved in learning normal school subjects. We will argue, however, that conditioning processes play an important part in the way people relate to each other and in what are often seen as discipline problems.

We will take a simple view of conditioning processes describing the two main forms of conditioning and then relating these processes to human relations in educational settings.

Classical conditioning is the term which is normally applied to the processes originally researched by the Russian physiologist, Ivan Pavlov. Initially, Pavlov was concerned with the digestive system, but he discovered, by chance, that if something happened while a dog was salivating as a result of a stimulus that normally produces saliva, such as dried meat, the dog might salivate when that 'something' occurred at a later time. This simple observation changed the course of Pavlov's life and he devoted a large part of his life to the study of simple learned associations of this nature.

A typical experiment would involve a dog strapped in a harness in a room where every other possible distracting stimulus was reduced to a minimum. Dried meat, which normally produces salivation, would be puffed into the dog's mouth at the same time as a stimulus such as a bell, flash of light or a buzzer. It would only take a few such pairings for bell, flash or buzzer to produce salivation without the dried meat. In effect, the dog had learned something new, namely, to salivate to a stimulus which didn't previously produce salivation.

If the dog learns to salivate to the sound of a buzzer and then hears a buzzer of a slightly different tone, the dog will usually still salivate, but not to the same extent. This is described as generalization. The dog does not have to have an identical stimulus to produce the conditioned response. However, if the dog always gets meat when it hears one tone of buzzer, but never for the other tone, it learns to respond with salivation to one tone and not to the other. The dog can learn to discriminate between two similar stimuli. If the dog hears the buzzer over a long period of time without ever getting dried meat, the salivation response will eventually disappear. The term used to describe this process is extinction; the response has been extinguished.

This is clearly a very primitive form of learning, but it occurs in a wide range of organisms from the lowly flatworm to human beings. Pavlov repeated these experiments with adolescents from a local orphanage, even to the extent of attaching a phial to the cheek to catch the drops of saliva as they flowed. Any natural autonomic response made by the organism can be conditioned in this way. This is important from our point of view, because it applies to the bodily responses that are associated with emotions and, in particular, fear. Emotions play a central part in the way we relate to ourselves and other people. Generally, these inner emotional responses are beyond our control, unless we are familiar with bio-feedback techniques, or are yoga adepts. You may be certain that you will not fall off the 'Big Wheel' and yet to ride on it is still a terrifying experience.

Classical conditioning is a passive form of learning. Events happen to the human or animal and something new is learned. However, before we apply these notions on the importance of classical conditioning to the way we relate to each other, we will compare this form of learning to the other main form of conditioning, namely operant conditioning.

This form of learning has been described under different names, but it has been developed most comprehensively by Skinner (1974), so we will use his term. A typical example of operant conditioning involves a rat in a cage. The cage has a lever which can be pressed to obtain a pellet of food. The rat is starved for a period of time and placed in the cage. Being hungry, the rat thrashes around and may eventually, by chance, press the lever and obtain a pellet of food. If the process is repeated, the rat thrashes around in a similar way, until it again, by chance, presses the lever. This contrasts with the behaviour of an adult human, who would remember the previous experience and go straight to the lever to obtain the food reward. What tends to happen with the rat is that the time taken to press the lever gradually reduces until, eventually, it is able to go straight to the lever to obtain the food. If it is a hoarding species, it will go on pressing the lever and heap up food pellets in the corner of a cage.

The same learning process occurs in relation to a punishing experience. If the lever cuts off an electric current passing through the floor of the cage, the rat learns to press the lever in the same way.

The processes of generalization, discrimination and extinction also apply to this form of learning. The response might generalize to any protruding object in the cage; the rat might learn to discriminate between a round lever and a square lever and if the pellet of food stopped coming, the rat might stop pressing it altogether. The effects of punishment are not that easy to extinguish, but that is an issue we will deal with later in the section.

Operant conditioning is a more active form of learning. The rat has to do something to obtain the reward or avoid the punishment.

Classical and operant conditioning are interconnected processes. If there is a reward or a punishment in a situation, it is reasonable to suppose that the reward will be associated with good feelings and the punishment will be associated with bad feelings, so any example of operant conditioning will include elements of classical conditioning.

So, let us return to classical conditioning and make a large inferential leap from the experimental evidence and suggest that each of us has a unique repertoire of emotional responses to specific situations, people and events which we have learned as a result of past experience. The most dramatic of these responses are called phobias. Fear of heights, dogs, snakes, enclosed spaces, water, spiders, and so on. Just to say the word 'spider' will have an effect on some individuals. They might be able to control the external expression of the feeling of fear, but they are unable to stop the internal feelings.

Some of these phobias can be related to early experiences. One of the writers was bitten and snapped at by a dog at the age of four and always feels a little uneasy with dogs around forty years later. A man we knew trod on a live electrified rail and though knocked unconscious, miraculously survived. However, whenever he treads on cold steel, even through shoes, a spasm of fear goes through him. He will probably retain this response for the rest of his life. Some phobias are not so easily explained and seem to develop for no apparent reason. Vertigo is an example, and may be to do with problems of orientation and balance, and naturally generates anxiety if there is a chance of falling. Some emotional responses seem to be passed on from our parents, particularly mothers. Perhaps, for most of us it is rewarding to be like our mothers and so feel good if we take on their characteristics, even if these are not to our advantage.

Some phobias are extremely inconvenient and other people are often intolerant of them. If the person you are with is unable to use lifts or escalators, it can be extremely inconvenient in places like airports and shopping centres. It is easy to suggest that the phobic person pulls herself together. However, this is underestimating the power of the conditioned emotional response. An examination of the life of the intolerant person would show that there are many situations that make him anxious, but he never permits himself to get into the position of making the anxiety public. Crying in public, saying something loving, expressing anger to a colleague might be examples of fear experienced by an otherwise competent adult. Most of us have an Achilles heel somewhere.

* A discussion of 'the things that make me afraid' always generates
  a great deal of involvement with groups of any age and ability.
  Having established the individual fears in a group, a useful
  technique is to split up into smaller groups of individuals who
  share the same fears. Later, a spokesperson can report back to the
  whole group.

Some classical experiments carried out under the supervision of American psychologist John Watson, who is often described as the founder of behaviourism, provided demonstrations of these conditioned fearful reactions being established. One of his most notorious experiments involved eleven-month-old Albert, who was placed with a white rat. A loud noise was made as Albert reached for the rat and he reacted with obvious fright. The pairing of the noise with the white rat was enough to establish a fearful reaction, not only to the white rat, but to anything white and furry. The response had generalized. Later experiments were designed to demonstrate the removal of fear developed in this way. The infant would be fed chocolate as the feared animal was slowly brought nearer. But the outcome of these experiments demonstrates how difficult it is to control this form of learning. Sometimes the child learned not to be afraid of the rat, sometimes the child learned to dislike chocolate.

Some emotional reactions appear to have been passed on from our parents even though we have not had the appropriate experiences. It is impossible to explain how any particular emotional reaction has developed, but perhaps the process goes something like this. Our parents, particularly mothers, are usually the source of most of the good things in life – food, warmth, shelter, affection, entertainment and so on. Thus, most of us associate good feelings with our parents. To be like them might also produce good feelings, so we take on the actions, the opinions and perhaps even the feelings of our parents. To do so makes us feel good, which is rewarding, even though the behaviour, opinion or feeling may not be very helpful. These emotional reactions which we have taken from our parents probably play an important part in our religious beliefs, our political opinions and our feelings towards people of different races. The suggestion is being made here that our emotional reaction to these important issues is of the same order as one of Pavlov's dogs salivating to the taste of dried meat.

This suggestion is not unreasonable if we also accept that much of what we do is at a low level of awareness. There are many subtle aspects of our behaviour which may be controlled by these learned emotional reactions and which also have a marked effect on the way we relate to ourselves and other people.

What we call conscience usually has a strong emotional component. If we do something which we feel is right, we experience good feelings. If we do something which we think is bad, we experience bad feelings which we might choose to label guilt.

In the days when there were conductors to collect the fares on buses, one of the writers carried out an experiment into his emotional reactions to deliberately not paying the fare. It was not difficult to dodge the conductor, but at the first attempt, there was a grip of panic in the stomach which worsened as he approached the door. Walking away from the bus, there was a tense feeling between the shoulder blades, which seemed to be anticipating an angry shout. The second and third attempts were not much better, though the emotional reactions did seem marginally less. He was never able to avoid paying the fare without feeling uncomfortable. Once the experiment was over, he was relieved to go back to paying the fare. On a rational level, the writer is convinced of the importance of public transport and that passengers should pay their fares. It is a matter of opinion as to whether it is rational processes or the emotional reactions that are exerting the most control.

Some readers might have had the same experience regarding paying fares. Others may find it difficult to understand because they do not have the same emotional conditioning. Presumably, their learned emotional reactions are different.

Here are some examples of differences in behaviour between the two writers. The examples may seem trivial, but the habits are strong and at least one of each pair of examples is maintained by the avoidance of negative emotional reactions.

A	B
Has to scrape the margarine off the lid of the plastic tub.	Would happily throw away the lid with the margarine on it.
Has to carefully unwrap a parcel to save the paper for later use.	Tears open parcels and destroys paper.

Squeezes toothpaste from the bottom to avoid waste.	Squeezes toothpaste in the middle.
Wears clothes for days on end.	Washes clothes after one day.
Never locks the door at night.	Always locks door.
Doesn't want to spend money on Xmas cards.	Has to send Xmas cards.

Appropriate sex-role behaviour is probably controlled in the same way. Most of us feel embarrassed or ashamed when we behave in a manner which doesn't fit the conventions for our sex. Despite a breakdown in some of the conventional attitudes towards sex-roles, it would still be difficult for most men to go to work in a skirt.

This form of emotional control extends into virtually every aspect of our lives, in particular the way we relate to other people. Some of us have difficulty in expressing negative feeling, in expressing warm feeling, in saying 'no' to people. Student teachers have often reported being disgusted with themselves for shouting at their pupils. Perhaps they ought to be grateful to the children concerned for helping them to try out a new pattern of behaviour and to change an aspect of their conditioning.

Many of these limitations on the range of behaviour available to us are not even the result of social pressures. Giving a spontaneous compliment is a perfectly acceptable form of behaviour, but some of us find it extremely difficult to permit a compliment to pass our lips. Emotional reactions do appear to be controlling our behaviour in situations such as this. Often the behaviour established by our fears is particularly unhelpful. If, as a teacher, you find it difficult to make eye contact with your class, there is evidence (Rogers, 1983) that you will be less efficient than a teacher who makes eye contact with ease.

* Ask the individual members of a group of students to circle one of the letters E (easy), A (average), D (difficult) for each of the following statements:

1	Paying a compliment	E A D
2	Expressing anger to a colleague	E A D
3	Telling a joke	E A D
4	Initiating conversation	E A D
5	Telling someone you like them	E A D
6	Complaining in a restaurant	E A D

7	Being late for an appointment	E A D
8	Taking goods back to a shop	E A D
9	Stealing a book from a library	E A D
10	Going shoplifting	E A D

Then ask the students to form groups of four or five and share how they have responded and to share how they would feel if they tried some of the items they found difficult.

There are several ways in which our behaviour is controlled. More extreme forms of anti-social behaviour are controlled by law. A much more restricting control is imposed by social convention. The man who goes to work in a skirt is not breaking the law, but social pressures can be so strong that he may even lose his job if he doesn't conform. This still leaves a wide range of possible behaviours open to us, but our emotional conditioning provides an even more severely restricting form of control, which reduces our potential repertoire of ways of relating to others to almost pitiful proportions. Often we have rational explanations for the limitations we put on our behaviour, but these are probably 'rationalizations' in the sense used in the later section on defence mechanisms.

It is operant conditioning which is usually discussed in relation to education because it seems to be closely related to rewards and punishments. Students in school responding to traditional rewards and punishments, however, are not behaving like one of Skinner's rats. Unlike the rat, they have insight into the situations that relate to rewards and punishments. They know that if they behave in certain ways they will be rewarded or punished, even if they have not had the appropriate experience.

The notion of operant conditioning does apply to humans when they are not aware of what is going on. This is also true of infants who, it is assumed, do not have any rational insight into what is happening around them and have their behaviour manipulated by trial and error responses to the rewards and punishments in their environment. This is also true of adult behaviour when the adult is unaware of what is going on. A strong theme of this book is that both pupils and teachers are not aware of much of what they do, particularly when relating to other people. These processes are beautifully illustrated in John Holt's (1964) anthropological studies of schools in the United States. He describes how subtle forms of reward and punishment manipulate the pupils into providing what the teacher wants. Adult students often report the same process going on at college or university.

The subtle nature of these processes is dramatically illustrated by some early experiments by Greenspoon (1962). In a typical experiment, the experimenter sits opposite a subject and conducts a normal conversation. Every time the subject produces a plural noun, the experimenter says 'uhhum' in a pleasant manner and smiles. As a result of this procedure, the incidence of plural nouns can be increased. The same effects can be produced with nervous habits. If the experimenter smiles every time the subject strokes his nose, the incidence of nose stroking will increase. If the results of these simple experiments generalize to everyday behaviour, which seems likely, then we are influencing each other in our interactions all of the time, encouraging some aspects of behaviour, and discouraging others.

There is an apocryphal story of students in a psychology class who were being lectured on these processes. The lecturer tended to wander around the podium, so the class colluded in smiling when he was on one side and not to smile when he was on the other side. He began to spend more and more time on the smiling side and eventually gave the last part of his lecture in the corner!

This type of evidence suggests that it is possible for an individual to have a powerful effect on another person's behaviour. Imagine a complete school staff deciding to consistently reward every positive act performed by a pupil who was having serious problems of social adjustment in the school. An ongoing experience of punishment is changed to a continuous experience of reward. It seems inevitable that the pupil concerned would change in some way. Unfortunately, it is rare for a staff group to work together so effectively. It is probably more common for patterns of relationships to be established without either pupils or teachers being aware of the rewards and punishments involved.

Indeed, the rewards and punishments in a given situation may work to produce the opposite of what is wanted, because of lack of insight into what is rewarding in a given situation. Consider the following domestic example. Sara, at nearly three years old, usually went through the night without wetting the bed, but occasionally had an accident. She also liked to come into the warm, comforting parental bed. If she woke up in the night and was dry, it was a simple matter to put her back into her bed. If she was wet there would be a lot of trouble changing her clothes and sheets and then getting her back to sleep after all the disturbance. A pattern was set up that every time she was dry, she was put back to bed. Every time she was wet, she was allowed to stay in the parental bed. In effect, wetting the bed was being rewarded and being dry was being punished. One of the parents decided he was going to be consistent and that he would always put her back when she was wet. Unfortunately, Sara quickly learned that if she went to her father's side of the bed, she was punished and if she went round to her mother's side she was rewarded. Dad never had the chance to find out if his theory was correct.

Self-defeating patterns of behaviour are often set up because the individual is responding to a short-term reward rather than a long-term reward. The research into conditioning demonstrated clearly that an immediate reward was far more effective in developing learned conditioned responses than long-term rewards. This may explain a great deal of defensive behaviour. The shy person is rewarded by escaping from a source of anxiety, even though the long-term effects are deeply disturbing. The shy person comes into a social situation and experiences anxiety. By withdrawing, he gets relief from the anxiety and is rewarded. If he then worries about the long-term effects on his life, he will probably experience more anxiety the next time, thus increasing the chance that he will withdraw again. Because of the increased anxiety the sense of relief and reward will increase. Thus a vicious circle is set up, establishing the shy behaviour very effectively.

It is hard to know which specific aspects of behaviour are rewarding for individual teachers, students or children. Certainly, some teachers repeat the same behaviour over and over again, even though it does not appear to produce the desired results. In his first year of teaching, one of the writers developed the habit of shouting when the pupils became unruly and though it had no more than a brief impact on the class, the habit soon became established. Again, the sudden but brief reduction of noise probably played an important part in reinforcing the shouting. There was also an immediate release of tension, which may also have had a reinforcing effect.

Another feature of operant conditioning described by Skinner is that the effects of a reward appear to be much more potent if the reward is not given every time the appropriate behaviour is produced. If Skinner's rats were rewarded every so often, rather than every time they pressed the bar, they may have taken a little longer to learn to press the bar, but the bar pressing went on long after the reward stopped altogether. Presumably, the aim of most rewards and punishments is to establish patterns of behaviour which will continue after the administration of the rewards and punishments has ceased. This would suggest that a 'partial schedule of reinforcement' (to use Skinner's term) would be the most effective way of achieving this aim.

This highly efficient form of learning can also work to the teacher's disadvantage. You might decide that a difficult member of your class is shouting out in order to get attention and that any response on your part is rewarding. So you make a determined effort not to respond to any shouting out behaviour. After a period of being consistent, you might respond without thinking and so you resolve to be consistent from then on. Periodic lapses of this nature are only natural, but unfortunately, they are reinforcing shouting out behaviour in the worst possible way. The unwanted behaviour is firmly fixed.

A common piece of advice given to teachers is to ignore the unwanted behaviour so that it is never rewarded. But, as we have seen, just one or two lapses can produce an even greater problem. Try and assess for yourself if, realistically, in a busy classroom, you can be consistent. Alternative solutions may lie outside the classroom. One idea may be to try to establish a special relationship with the child in another situation, such as a school disco or club.

We have had the experience of teaching our children to whine for sweets. Having decided that a continuous supply of sweets was bad for them, demands would be met with a pompous statement about their health. Of course there would be periodic lapses and the whining for sweets behaviour was being reinforced in the worst possible way. There is a slight whine in their voices now they are young adults.

It is these unplanned patterns of reward and punishment that cause most of the trouble preventing teachers and pupils from establishing productive patterns of behaviour. Because they are often out of our awareness, then our behaviour is of the same order as one of Skinner's rats and it may need careful observation and planning in order to change these patterns. In the hurly-burly of a working school there is rarely time to examine ongoing processes of this nature.

Learned helplessness

One aspect of conditioning research which has received a great deal of attention in recent years is the work on learned helplessness. The notion developed out of work reported by Seligman (1975) whose co-workers gave painful electric shocks to dogs who were restrained so that there was nothing they could do to avoid the shock. The dogs were then placed in a shuttle box. A shuttle box is a piece of apparatus in which an animal learns to avoid an electric shock by jumping over a barrier into a different part of the box. The dogs who had been traumatized by their earlier painful experience were unable to learn this avoidance task, which normal dogs learn quickly and easily. They appear to have learned helplessness.

This concept has been applied to human behaviour, suggesting that prolonged experiences of failure, punishment or pain can produce apathy, depression and even speed up the onset of death in the individual. This generalization has an immediate appeal and we can all think of individuals in educational settings who appear to fit this model, such as teachers who are having trouble with their classes and children who are having difficulties with their social relations or their academic work.

However, humans are different from animals in that some of us respond to life experience with learned helplessness, whereas others rise above difficulties such as illness, failure, disadvantaged background and so on, and use those experiences as a spur to even greater effort. These differences have been explained (Garber and Seligman, 1980) in terms of what the individual perceives to be the cause of the failure or difficulty. The individual's perception of the causation of events is usually called 'attribution' in the psychological literature, and attribution theory has become very complex, suggesting that several variables can contribute to a specific attribution. Another complication is the fact that it is impossible to unravel the years of experience that go towards the formulation of a specific attribution.

For the moment, we will examine three dimensions of attribution and illustrate them with two practical examples. Firstly, a teacher who is having problems in controlling classes and secondly, a child who is having difficulty making new friends having moved to a new school.

(a)   The problem might be seen as due to factors within the individual, or due to factors inherent in the situation. The attributions are varying along a dimension of 'internal', that is, the cause is seen to lie within the individual, to 'external', that is, the cause is seen to be outside the individual.

(i) The teacher might blame his own qualities, or he may blame his head of department for giving him all the worst classes.

(ii) The child might perceive himself as being too shy or he may blame the other children for what he sees as ganging up against him.

(b) The problem might be seen as 'global'; applying to all situations, or it may be seen as 'specific'; limited to this particular situation. Global attributions represent a very pessimistic view of an issue.

(i) The problem might be seen as applying to all teachers, and as insoluble, that is 'No one can control inner-city adolescents (even though there might be plenty of evidence to the contrary)'. Alternatively, he might see himself as having difficulties in this particular school, whereas he was successful in his previous school.

(ii) The child might persuade himself that no one can break into established cliques in the school. Alternatively, he might see himself as getting on badly with the children in his class, but relating well to other groups in the playground.

(c) The problem might be seen in terms of whether the situation is 'stable' or 'unstable'.

(i) The teacher may have had bad experiences with his classes ever since he started teaching and feel that things are unlikely to ever change. On the other hand, he might think he is going through a bad patch because of personal problems and when these have been cleared up, the problems of class management will disappear.

(ii) The child may feel that he will never make friends with the children in his class, because he is the only person of a different group. On the other hand he might be aware that it will take time for him to settle down in the class and for the class to get used to him.

These dimensions can help us to describe attributions and give some indication of to what extent a person is in control of his life. An internal, specific, unstable attribution leaves scope for potential change, whereas an external, global, stable attribution implies a fixed view of the world.

Thus, some attributions leave the individual thinking that there is nothing that can be done to alter the situation. Sometimes this gener-alizes to a wide variety of situations and persists over a long period of time. If you perceive yourself as not being very bright, as not being particularly good at anything, and have experienced many years of failure, then it seems reasonable not to have any high expectations in the future, irrespective of any potential ability. Perhaps a high proportion of children in our schools go through this sort of experience and that learned helplessness is epidemic. It is not relevant that these attributions do not match those of other people. The way a situation is perceived is 'reality' for that person.

Dweck and Licht (Garber and Seligman, 1980) draw some interesting conclusions about the differences in the development of learned helplessness between boys and girls and how this relates to performance in different academic subjects. Their evidence suggests that even though boys receive more negative feedback than girls, a high proportion of it is about non-intellectual aspects of their behaviour in class. For girls, on the other hand, virtually all of the negative feedback they receive does relate to the specific intellectual task. Thus the criticisms directed at girls are a reflection of their intellectual ability whereas the criticisms directed at boys are much more ambiguous, so that it is not altogether clear that negative criticism is a reflection of lack of intellectual ability or about bad behaviour.

Also, teachers ascribed academic failure to lack of motivation eight times more often with boys than with girls. They use this data to explain the findings that girls appear to present more learned helplessness than boys. The girls explained their academic failure as being the result of lack of ability. Boys, on the other hand, were much more likely to explain their failures as being due to lack of motivation.

They go on to develop this argument and explain why boys are generally better at maths and girls are better at verbal skills. Since maths usually involves specific solutions and failure is clear cut, it is here that the unambiguous message contained in the feedback for girls will be most precise. The boys who receive much more ambiguous feedback will be more resilient to the criticisms because they don't see it as a direct comment on their ability, and if the teacher ascribes their failure to lack of motivation, then it might even be a spur to greater effort.

In the subjects involving verbal skills, there is not the same emphasis on right and wrong answers, which may explain why girls appear to do better in these areas.

There are other explanations for the differences between the sexes in these subjects, such as differences in the development of lateralization of the brain. Probably no single explanation is adequate. However, the research into helplessness does suggest strongly that some individuals respond to failure with a helpless reaction, blaming stable factors such as their lack of ability, whereas others respond with what has been described as a 'mastery orientation' blaming less stable factors, such as lack of motivation. This has profound implications for education and the ways in which feedback is given to children. Dweck (1975) showed that children improved in their reactions to failure when they were taught to attribute it to lack of effort rather than lack of ability.

In spite of success in some areas of life, most of us can find examples of helplessness which have grown out of earlier experiences of failure. Repairing cars, singing in tune, telling jokes in public and expressing anger are a few examples we can offer from our own experience.

* Try to think of some examples of learned helplessness from your own experience and then enter them into the following sheet with the additional information asked for.

Example of learned helplessness	What experiences brought this about?	What could you do about it?
1.		
2.		
3.		
4.		
5.		
6.		

Counsel a partner for twenty minutes on what they have written. Then change roles for a further twenty minutes.

A further difficulty with the notion of helplessness is the possibility that the individual is pretending to be helpless. This could well be a common reaction in secondary schools in the UK. With little hope of a qualification or a job, there is no incentive to work at tasks which are not intrinsically interesting. 'I can't do it Miss,' is a stock response, which is often given even before the task has been seen. This is not, however, just a response from recalcitrant adolescents. One of the writers had long experience of changing nappies and, being faced with the same task several years later, soon found that if he stood by looking helpless, the job would be done for him. Similarly, in a team teaching situation with a large number of pupils, it is easy to stand back and allow the teacher with the strongest reputation for maintaining order to do all the work. If this type of behaviour becomes a habit, there is a danger that the person concerned may eventually become convinced that he cannot perform the task of maintaining discipline, thus acquiring a form of learned helplessness which is different from the notion we have been discussing.

Locus of control

In the previous section, it was suggested that an important dimension of learned helplessness was the attribution made by the individual as to what was responsible for success or failure in a given situation. Individuals who perceived themselves as responsible for their success or failure were less likely to experience helplessness.

These types of attribution are clearly related to the idea of locus of control. This notion grew out of a simple experiment by Phares (1957) who showed that subjects changed their expectations about how well they would do in a simple task significantly if they believed that their performance was due to skill rather than chance. Research into this area was given a boost by the development of a questionnaire to measure locus of control by Rotter (1966) and his associates. This I–E Scale places the respondent on a continuum from 'internality' to 'externality'. A person who scores high on 'internality' takes responsibility for what happens in life. The person who scores high on 'externality' perceives more of life's happenings 'as the result of luck, chance, fate, as under the control of powerful others, or as unpredictable because of the great complexity of the forces surrounding him', to use Rotter's words.

When things go wrong in school, do you find yourself blaming the headteacher, or the fact that you happen to have been given the worst classes, or the chaos of working in a large institution? On the other hand, do you look to your own behaviour to see if there are changes you can make to produce the results that you want? In your studies, did you blame poor teaching, or bad luck in question spotting, or the scarcity of books for lack of success? In the next exercise, try some of the questions which have been designed to resemble the I–E Scale, but have been modified to apply to teaching situations.

* For each of the following pairs of statements, circle either (a) or
  (b) according to which most matches your experience of teaching:

1 (a) My lack of success has been largely due to bad luck.
  (b) The development of my teaching has been the result of my own actions and decisions.
2 (a) I try to make the best use of my day, in spite of organizational problems.
  (b) The timetable is so badly planned, it is impossible to teach a meaningful sequence of lessons.
3 (a) The exam results of the classes I teach depend on how hard they have worked.
  (b) I modify what I do to meet the individual needs and abilities of my students.
4 (a) No one can effectively teach inner-city children.
  (b) The skilful teacher can produce good results from children of any social background.
5 (a) My head of department blocks all of my creative ideas.
  (b) I must try to work at the part I play in the failures of communication in my department.

Pair off with another person and discuss the extent to which you feel you are in control of the events that happen to you in teaching situations.

Later, change the discussion to consider to what extent a questionnaire of this nature can provide a score which makes a meaningful statement about your personality.

A number of questionnaires have been designed to measure locus of control; these have played a central part in a large number of research studies. Some questionnaires have been designed to investigate particular areas, such as responsibility for academic success (Crandall, Katkovsky and Crandall, 1965) and many of the questionnaires distinguish between taking responsibility for the good and bad things that happen. A scale has been developed at the Child Health Research Unit at Bristol called the Children's Attribution of Responsibility and

Locus of Control Scale (see Gammage, 1982) for use with English school children.

We are not happy about the validity of the scores obtained by self-report questionnaires. Responses are easily distorted by the need to produce an answer that will please the investigator. Respondents may have a grandiose opinion of the extent to which they are in control of their lives. An accurate external view is probably far healthier than a deluded internal view. In any society there are groups, like the ethnic minorities in this country, who have the odds stacked against them in terms of acquiring wealth and opportunities available to the majority group.

However, in spite of the potential limitations of the measures, the research has come up with some fairly consistent findings. These are summed by Phares (1984). From the point of view of human relations in education, the most important of these are:

1   Externals tend to be more conforming, compliant and more easily persuadable individuals. They are the people in staff meetings who are happy to go along with the wishes of the majority or an authoritarian leader. On the other hand, a person with an internal orientation may find it hard to fit into an authoritarian regime because they prefer to be independent and self-reliant.
2   Internals and externals tend to see other people as having the same views about responsibility as themselves. Thus, a person with an internal orientation will be more willing to delegate authority because she believes colleagues can be trusted. This approach provides, in our view, a more efficient working climate. The same may be true about permitting students to take responsibility for their own learning.
3   Internals tend to be better adjusted, less anxious and have fewer psychiatric symptoms. It seems reasonable to assume that these characteristics, or rather the lack of them, will contribute to improved human relations.

The assumptions made in relation to each of these three findings probably reflect the writers' own presumed internal orientation. It could be argued by a person with an external viewpoint that it is good to have a firm chain of command and that authority should not be questioned. This applies to the relations between staff and children and between superior and subordinate within the staff hierarchy. You will have to make decisions on these issues for yourself, but the results of Milgram's (1974) research and the lessons of history suggest that most individuals will perform horrific acts if given an order by a powerful other – demonstrating a high degree of externality.

These processes may begin in infancy. It was once fashionable not to go to a baby when he cried. When this happens, he is likely to learn that he is not in control of the attention given to him by his parents; a pattern which may continue into adult life. It may be worth putting up with the difficulties created by going to a baby when he cries, in order to develop an internal locus of control.

Summaries of the research on the relationship between scores on tests of locus of control and academic achievement (Stipek and Weisz, 1981) show a consistent relationship between internality and high achievement. This is not to say that one in some way causes the other, and research which merely correlates the results of tests is usually not very helpful. However, interest in the notion of locus of control is maintained partly because there are several well-developed tests which give a score, providing a quick and efficient research tool.

A much more complex, and in our view more appropriate model of the way a person perceives himself to be in control of his life, is provided by psychologists in the general area of attribution theory. This has already been related to the notion of learned helplessness. Their writing is very complex and justifiably so, since the everyday events of our life are also complex and the extent to which we perceive ourselves to be in control of these events will vary from situation to situation. To avoid the maze of terminology, we will consider one approach, namely De Charms' (1981) ideas on personal causation.

Personal causation

De Charms rightly points out that locus of control theory refers to the extent that an individual perceives himself to be responsible for successes and failures, and rewards and punishments in his life. But this ignores the fact that the parameters are often set by outside agencies.

Let us take the example of John who knows that if he makes careful notes in his lessons, reads the required textbooks and plans a careful programme of revision at home, he is certain to earn a good set of grades at the end of the year. In this situation John sees himself as being in control of, or responsible for, the rewards he gets from his educational experience, but he is not in control of the lessons he attends and the subjects he studies.

De Charms' notion of personal causation refers to situations where the person not only controls the rewards and punishments, but also controls the parameters.

Take the example of Susan. Susan is not so keen on the work she is being asked to do at school. She is fascinated by the electric synthesizer, and this interest has taken her deeply into the theory of harmonics and composition. She plays in a semi-professional band and earns good money playing in local clubs. At the age of eighteen, after two years of self-directed study, she has become an expert in programming computerized music and lands a plum job with a recording company. She never attended a music lesson at school.

This is an extreme example of a person who is in control of what she does as well as the rewards she earns. De Charms refers to being in control of what you do as 'personal causation', which he suggests is different from 'locus of control'. We would argue that personal causation subsumes locus of control. If you make an active choice in what you do, then you are also responsible for the outcomes or rewards for that behaviour. De Charms uses the term 'origin' for a person who is in control of what he does and the term 'pawn' for a person who does not have this experience. These are colourful terms, and most of us would place ourselves somewhere on a continuum between these two extremes. Our experience of being 'origins' or 'pawns' will probably vary from situation to situation. See how you respond to the exercise on page 39.

In order to permit the exercise of personal causation, a classroom would have to be organized in a manner that allows students to be directly involved in the decision-making process. The case histories included by Rogers (1983) are of this nature, and range from working with a class of difficult sixth graders to a neurophysiology class at a university. In these situations, the students were not allowed total freedom of choice, but the teacher was used as a resource in the process of negotiating the content of the curriculum. This is not a common event in English schools.

However, personal causation may not be so much to do with what is actually happening in schools, but the extent to which the pupils perceive themselves to be in control of what they do. De Charms (1972) involved students in grades 6–8 in programmes which gave

* Write down what you consider to be three important achievements in your life and then rate each one on the three scales provided.

Achievements	I did this for:	Not at all 1	A little 2	Half and half 3	A great deal 4	Totally 5
1	Other people					
	A tangible reward					
	For myself					
2	Other people					
	A tangible reward					
	For myself					
3	Other people					
	A tangible reward					
	For myself					

them greater responsibility and control over what they did in the classroom. These students changed their attributions to those of greater control and also made gains in academic achievement.

The same issues are relevant to decision-making in the school within the staff group. The headteacher can take an authoritarian role and dictate policy to the staff. Alternatively she can use decision-making structures that permit power to be shared. Lloyd (1984) provides a fascinating case-history of taking over the headship of a secondary school and changing from an autocratic to a democratic style of leadership. As with most forms of change, she met with initial resistance, but does appear to have succeeded in the long term. She took a pragmatic stance and chose to be autocratic when it appeared to be appropriate. The overall effect, however, was to give the staff a greater sense of control over what was happening in the school.

She uses the term self-empowerment to describe this sense of increased control. This notion is developed strongly by Hopson and

Scally (1981), who suggest that a great deal of what happens in society, and in particular in education, is a 'depowering' process. They argue the need for reversing these processes, which is one of the aims of their Lifeskills programmes. These are designed to empower the individual, and make considerable use of experiential learning.

This discussion begs the philosophical question as to whether or not we have any control over our lives at all. This is not an issue we can resolve here, or that we are aiming to deal with. However, most people lead their lives, talk and behave as if they do have choices, however real they may be.

Training for greater control

The issues of learned helplessness, locus of control and personal causation are important to the practising teacher because a series of studies have shown that it is possible to change children's perception of their degree of control in each of these areas. In several of these studies, the sense of greater control was accompanied by an increase in academic achievement. Work by De Charms and Dweck has already been mentioned. Similar results were obtained in three studies reviewed by Stipek and Weisz (1981).

The notion of permitting pupils to have a choice in what and how they study is not one which would be readily accepted in many secondary schools in this country. Apart from the constraints of the examination system, most of us have been brought up in, and are used to, a highly authoritarian regime. This is just as true for the relationships between staff as for the relations between teachers and students.

An experimenter can work with a class of children and give them a greater sense of personal control over their educational experience. This does not, however, do much to change the education system, and an experimental class will quickly change its behaviour with a change of teacher. A more potent source of change is in in-service training or initial training, where teachers could be given the experience of taking control of their own learning. This requires finding a way out of the paradox of telling people to take responsibility for their own learning.

If you tell people to take responsibility for their own learning, they can either refuse to do it, or agree to do it, in which case they are doing what you say and hence not taking responsibility for their own learning. One way out of this paradox in teacher training is through the use of experiential learning. Setting up learning structures like the exercises in this book, and not providing the 'right' answers seems to set up a sense of frustration, which forces individuals to draw conclusions for themselves. A more intense form of experiential learning involves a group sitting in a circle who are invited to explore inter-personal relations using the behaviour generated by the group itself. Carl Rogers (1969) calls this type of learning situation an encounter group, though it goes by many other names. Hall, Wood-house and Wooster (1984) evaluated the effects of six days intensive training for teachers using a combination of these two forms of experiential learning and found many examples of an increased sense of responsibility both during the course and at work a term later.

Unfortunately, in our view, a majority of people involved in the teaching profession would not agree with the idea that there should be more sharing of responsibility in educational settings. They may agree with our views in a statement of their aims of education, but their actual behaviour involves a reinforcement of existing patterns of authority. By their deeds shall ye know them. Rogers (1983) and Curle (1973) provide similar explanations as to why individuals are not given responsibility for their own learning. Simply put, a person in a teaching situation who gives students responsibility for their own learning, or an administrator who gives staff greater responsibility for running the institution, is giving away power. Giving away power seems to cause a great deal of disturbance in the wider institution and forces are mobilized to destroy those situations which may be genuinely empowering for the individual.

From the management of behaviour to self-control

In the first part of this chapter, we considered the way in which random rewards and punishments can affect our behaviour in every-day life, and how events established patterns of good and bad feelings. We went on to see how we learned ways of behaving which enabled us to produce the good feelings and avoid the bad. In this section we will consider the deliberate manipulation of the environment in order to get what we want or to get other people to do what we want.

The question of control is a prime concern not only for teachers working in difficult schools, but also experienced teachers who often report that they still have terrifying dreams about their classes getting out of control.

First we will consider techniques which have been developed for controlling behaviour by the teacher directly manipulating rewards and punishments. Later we will describe how the management of these techniques can be passed on to the pupils themselves, thus changing a behaviouristic approach into a humanistic one.

As an extreme example of control by the teacher, imagine a class of pupils, each of whom is wired to a control panel on the teacher's desk. Every time a pupil steps out of line, he receives a sharp but safe electric shock. There is no doubt that this will be a very well-behaved class, apart from the occasional students who will compete to see how much shock they can take. There would probably be an outcry against such an inhuman system, even though it would probably be physically less dangerous than the cane or the tawse.

When presented with a fantasy of this nature, a wistful glaze often passes over the faces of teachers, which does suggest that they would like to be more in control of their classes. The technology for the management of rewards and punishments in classroom settings has been around for some time (Skinner, 1968; Axelrod, 1983), but the practical implementation of the techniques has been largely limited to very young children, or children with special needs such as severely subnormal or disruptive students.

Wheldall (1981) explains the slow development of behavioural techniques in the UK as being partly due to ignorance, and partly due to ethical considerations. Should a human being be treated in the same way as a rat or a pigeon? If a child is unable to keep his tongue in his mouth, it may be possible to 'shape' his behaviour using a food reward, so that the tongue stays in. Does the end justify the means? If the pupils involved decide for themselves the changes they would like to make in their behaviour and also decide what the rewards will be, then most of these ethical considerations melt away. Aside from the ethical considerations, Thorenson and Mahoney (1974) provide some evidence to show that if you are in control of your own behaviour management programme, then the learning is more effective.

Most programmes which are deliberately designed to modify behaviour involve giving a reward in order to increase the probability of the desired behaviour. There are other possibilities, such as punishing undesirable behaviour, ending a punishment when the desired behaviour is produced and removing a reward for undesirable behaviour.

Behaviour modification programmes using punishments tend not to be suggested by educational psychologists for use in schools. Although there is no reason why punishment should not be effective for eliminating specific undesirable behaviour, there is a good chance that a programme of this nature would establish a negative conditioned emotional response to the teacher involved and to the whole process of schooling.

The technology was originally developed as a form of treatment in the psychiatric clinic. Methods were developed to 'cure' patients of patterns of behaviour that were seen as unhelpful to them. These could be habits which are immediately gratifying, such as drinking, taking drugs and indulging in sexually deviant behaviour. This is behaviour which is difficult to eliminate, because of the immediate reward; the punishment, that is a hangover or social stigma, comes some time later. Changes have been attempted by inserting a punishment between the activity and the reward. The alcoholic is made to vomit as soon as drink touches his lips. A person who wishes to change his sexual preferences is given a sharp electric shock as he looks at a picture depicting this preference.

Aversion therapy is not used by behaviour modifiers in educational settings for the reasons given. It is, however, attempted inefficiently by teachers who use punishment but have no evidence for its long-term success. This inefficient behaviour is probably maintained because of the immediate short-term gratification provided by the infliction of physical or emotional pain on a person who is making life difficult. Indeed, Rutter et al (1979) found that in schools where punishment was having an effect, the effect was to make the situation worse.

* Invite a group of students to divide into fours. Suggest that they range over the whole of their school experience and recall specific incidents when they were punished by teachers and discuss:

  (a) How they felt at the time
  (b) What were the long-term effects.

  Spend 20 minutes on this part of the exercise and then ask them to discuss for ten minutes what it felt like to reminisce in this way.

A second set of undesirable behaviours involves having an intense emotional reaction which makes it difficult to cope with a situation. A phobia is a good example of this. As we suggested earlier in this chapter it is not just the popular phobias such as fear of heights, water, enclosed spaces and so on that affect our behaviour. Most of us can think of forms of inter-personal situations where the emotions involved are debilitating. Some children become too emotional even to go to school. Most of us developed aversions to particular teachers and lessons. At the age of eight, one of the writers was caned for getting a sum wrong three times. From then on, that teacher produced a fearful response and there has continued to be an uneasiness about maths, which may be related to that incident. Children are frightened of exams, of talking in front of the whole class, of speaking to teachers, of getting undressed for PE and many other situations which might surprise adults who did not share the same experiences as children.

Desensitization is the name given to the clinical technique used to attempt to remove these unwanted fears by the use of fantasy. A patient negotiates with his therapist a graduated series of imaginary scenes which are likely to generate an increasing amount of anxiety. The patient is taught to relax and in the relaxed state he is invited to imagine the least stressful scene. If there is no experience of anxiety, he moves on to the next scene, and so on, and the session is ended as soon as there is the slightest indication of anxiety. Another technique, flooding, involves forcing the person to stay in the anxiety provoking situation until the fear subsides. Techniques of this nature are not normally easy to slot into the busy timetable of a pastoral care Head of Year in a comprehensive school.

Unintentional flooding may take place in the most unfortunate ways, such as the PE teacher holding a child under a shower or an English teacher who makes a shy child talk or read to the whole class.

However, there are many other ways in which desensitization processes can be helped to take place. Just to sit and talk gently to a pupil who is clearly scared of you is a mild form of flooding. Many of the experiential exercises described in this book are designed to provide a safe environment for trying out ways of behaving which might be too scary in a real-life situation. If a child is shy of social contacts, it might be possible to negotiate a series of tasks to work through, ranging from very simple to difficult. One of the writers managed to dive off the three metre board, but never made it from the five metre. One of his fantasies was of having a series of boards between three and five, each one an inch higher than the first. Unfortunately this was never tested out in reality.

Some complex forms of changing emotional associations are

described by Bandler and Grinder (1979) as part of a system they call neuro-linguistic programming. They use hypnotic techniques to help a person to relax and then associate the relaxed state with a simple physical response. It may be that the wrist is squeezed at the same time that a phrase is used in the relaxation procedure, such as 'relax and let go'. The person whose eyes are closed, is asked to imagine a situation in which an unwanted emotion is invariably generated. As the scene is imagined, the wrist is again gently squeezed, assuming that an association between the squeeze and relaxation will inhibit the unwanted emotional reaction. The process may have to be repeated several times before emotion is inhibited in the real situation by a squeeze of the wrist. Some people, however, report a definite change after one training session. It may be that paying attention to the task interferes with the habitual routine.

* Try the following exercise with another person.

Decide who is A and who is B. A chooses a situation which occurs fairly frequently with a pupil or colleague which produces unwanted feelings.

B helps A, who is seated on a chair, to relax, using one of the procedures described in the later section on relaxation. As he says the phrase 'relax and let go', he gently squeezes B on the left wrist. Repeat the squeeze each of the three times the phrase is used.

After a pause, B asks A to close his eyes and gently hold the left wrist with the right hand. B then reads the following script:

'I want you to summon up a mental image of the situation you have chosen. Do not see yourself in the image, but be in the image. Be aware of what you can see. (pause) Be aware of what you can hear. (pause) Be aware of what you are feeling. Now gently squeeze your left wrist.'

After a pause, A repeats the process with B.

When, in future, the situation occurs in real life they may choose to gently squeeze the left wrist while the interaction is taking place. At a later date, A and B could get together to share their experience.

A similar sense of relaxation can be learned simply by slowing and deepening the breathing. By deepening the breathing in a situation that normally induces unpleasant emotions, a sense of relaxation may come to be associated with that situation. Unfortunately, it is often difficult to think of using a simple technique when you are angry or afraid.

A unique application of conditioning procedures to remove an unwanted spontaneous activity is the use of the 'bell and blanket' technique to cure enuresis. Some children find it difficult to acquire bladder control through the night; a problem which is embarrassing for the child and highly inconvenient for the parents. To deal with this problem, a device is placed under the sheet, which, if soaked with liquid, completes a circuit and makes a disturbing noise which is fairly certain to wake the child. Invariably, there is an initial emission of urine or the flow stops on awakening. When the child wakes, there is still a feeling of having a full bladder. Thus the child learns to associate a full bladder with waking up, and by the process of generalization, will wake up with the early feeling of pressure on the bladder, hopefully, before the bed gets wet. This is a likely explanation, but whether it is true or not, the apparatus does have a high success rate.

By far the most common techniques applied in school settings are those that involve giving a reward for behaviour that you specifically want to increase, or in order to encourage activity which prohibits the possibility of undesirable activity. Simply, you might reward a child with praise every time he gets a sum right. More deviously, you might reward a child for spending time in his seat when you are trying to stop him from wandering around the class.

It is not, however, an easy task to establish what is rewarding for another person. To be praised by a teacher might be a punishing event in an anti-social peer group. Similarly, to be told off in the same group might result in an increase in status. The effects of rewards may change over time. A class may be highly enthusiastic about being given merit marks when the scheme is first set up, but later treat the system with disdain. If the reward is an experience that the child often receives in other situations, then the reward value will be low.

A general principle which is often suggested is that an effective reward is something that a person normally chooses to do a great deal (high-frequency behaviour). This can be used as a reward for something that the person rarely does (low-frequency behaviour). A child may spend all her break times in the biology lab watching the fish in their tanks, but never completes her biology homework assignments. To become an effective reward, the fish-watching has to be reduced considerably, so there is a sense in which the child is being punished for not doing her homework. The business of identifying activities which will act as a reward for a low frequency, but desirable behaviour is not easy, but see how you get on with the following exercise.

* Complete two lists, one of low-frequency behaviours you would like to increase, and another of high-frequency behaviours that could be used as a reward.

low-frequency behaviour	*high-frequency behaviour*
1 Completing biology homework.	Watching fish.
2 Taking exercise.	Eating chocolate.
3	
4	
5	
6	

Pair off with another person and share:
(a) What you have written on your list.
(b) Which pairings of low-frequency and high-frequency behaviours would you be willing to use to modify your behaviour.
(c) Which high-frequency behaviours do you see as undesirable and feel that to use them as rewards might create further problems.

The suggestion at the end of the last exercise that some high-frequency behaviours can also be seen as problems, adds to the complexity of deciding on appropriate rewards. Sweets are not necessarily the best form of reward to give to children, and in one study, adolescents were given cigarettes for co-operative behaviour in a youth club.

It is a difficult enough task to identify appropriate rewards for individuals, but it is even more so for a group such as a class of children. An alternative procedure with such groups is the token system. Here, individuals within the group are given a token immediately the target behaviour is produced and the accumulated tokens can be cashed in at the end of the day or week for a more tangible reward.

The application of token economies to classes in schools is well documented (O'Leary and O'Leary, 1977; Axelrod, 1983) and does seem to be effective in changing specific target behaviours in a group, even though it may fail for some individuals. Giving a token provides the minimum disruption to the ongoing activities of the class and the token can be cashed in at a later date for a reward specifically chosen by the individual child. It is curious that there are rarely references to tokens being stolen.

The extensive application of behaviour modification techniques is largely an American phenomenon. Wheldall (1981) provided a useful survey of the use of these approaches in this country. He suggested that the teaching profession in this country is dragging its feet in the development of behavioural approaches and blamed the current state of teacher training for maintaining ignorance among teachers on these techniques. Behavioural modification is often seen as having opposite aims to humanistic education as described in the first chapter, because the behaviour modifier is in control of the learning and decides what the learning outcomes should be. Some behaviour modifiers take total control of the situation and may not even explain to the children what they are doing. This is the tone of books by Herbert (1981) and Westmacott and Cameron (1981) which are excellent manuals but barely mention involving the children in the decision-making. Others are willing to hand over the technology to their clients or students, acting more as consultants than as experts. Thorenson and Mahoney (1974) used the term 'behavioural humanism' to describe the processes whereby the control of a behaviour modification programme is put into the hands of the person whose behaviour is being modified.

Self-management

We will now examine the procedures necessary for implementing an effective self-managed behaviour modification programme. The same principles apply to a programme that is being imposed on an individual or a group. The procedures can be applied to the teacher's behaviour, as well as the child's. If you are experiencing difficulties with a particular class, it may be preferable for you to change your behaviour. Indeed, your responses may be the main source of difficulty.

Whether you are working with a child, or on your own behaviour, the first stage is to make a thorough analysis of the situation. Try to make a clear description of the behaviour that is the target for change. What are the resources available to you in the situation and what would be appropriate rewards for the individuals concerned?

Next, simply observe the incidence of the target behaviour. This might be done using a simple counting procedure. As a teacher, you might be concerned about the number of times you raise your voice in lessons and may wish to reduce the incidence of shouting behaviour. Identifying a shout may be an arbitrary decision, but having made the decision, the incidences can be counted unobtrusively on a knitting counter, which can be held in the hand. If you have a good relationship with the class, the children could make the observations for you. Or, you might be concerned that you are paying more attention to the boys than the girls. By raising these issues with the class, you are adding a new dimension to the learning process, and by making the project public may increase your own commitment to change.

When the data has been collected it can be presented in a simple visual form such as a graph. You may wish to display it publicly. Going through this procedure can have an effect on the target behaviour and may even eliminate it altogether. There may be an aversive quality to having clear information about aspects of your behaviour that you do not like. This is similar to the processes involved in some forms of meditation; when unwanted thoughts and images emerge, merely noting them helps them to disappear. There may be a distinct pattern in the data. Your shouting might increase at certain times of the day with a particular class, or for some women just before they menstruate. This sort of information will be useful in the next stage of planning a course of action.

It is possible to work out a plan of action on your own, but from personal experience it is easy to set up a project which is bound to fail. Probably because the behaviour you are trying to eliminate has an important pay-off. Negotiating with another person, or better still with a group who are all involved in some form of behaviour changes, makes the process public and less easy to abandon. The proposed behaviour change needs to be defined precisely and not be too ambitious. Success with simple changes can be built upon.

Having defined the target behaviour to be achieved or avoided and an appropriate pattern of reward established, it is useful to formalize the programme into a contract, which is signed and countersigned by a witness. Again, a public commitment. Some adults are very resistant to signing a contract, objecting to its formal, legalistic nature. They seem to be unwilling to put their money where their mouths are as it were. This sort of objection is usually a precursor to failure.

Once the programme is under way, the recording process needs to continue. Apart from any tangible reward you may be giving yourself, success is a reward in its own right. Again the recordings can be displayed visually and publicly. The public display of failure probably has a strong punishing effect.

After a period of time the programme can be assessed. The project might be abandoned, because new successful behaviour has been established. Alternatively, the programme might be developed to enlarge the repertoire of new skills.

It is important to remember that changes in behaviour produced in this way may not always be welcomed either by family or colleagues. Try to be aware of this and be sensitive to the issues as they arise.

These same procedures for self-management can be worked through with a group of student teachers, or with a group of students. By taking part in the negotiating process, the students may develop an increased sense of control over their lives.

Summary

In this chapter, we have taken the notions of classical and operant conditioning and have shown how they can be used to explain some of the processes that are going on in inter-personal situations. We suggest that classical conditioning processes explain how we develop a repertoire of emotional responses to situations. It is claimed that these emotional responses are not under our control and affect our behaviour, even though we may control the outward expression of these emotions. In terms of the bodily experience of emotion, our responses can be likened to the responses of animals, such as Pavlov's dogs.

Regarding operant conditioning, that is working to obtain rewards and avoid punishments, our behaviour is different from that of animals, unless we are at a low level of cognitive development or, as adults, not aware of what we are doing. Often we have insight into what behaviour will produce a reward or avoid a punishment. In inter-personal situations, rewards and punishments are often meted out with little awareness by either participant. By developing some minimal awareness of these processes, it is possible to exert considerable influence over the other person.

The issue of control over your own life is dealt with in relation to learned helplessness, locus of control and locus of causality. Research in these areas deals with the extent to which an individual sees himself as being in control of the rewards and punishments he gains in life, or in control of what he does. Generally, it would seem to be a good thing to have this control. Also, it is possible to learn to believe that you have more control and that this change will have a positive effect on academic outcomes.

To be able to change your own behaviour will give you an increased sense of control over your life. This is also true for a group such as a class of children. This would support the idea of passing the decision-making in behaviour modification programmes over to the client group.

Connections

In the introduction, there was an emphasis on humanistic approaches in education, whereas this chapter has focused on conditioning processes. Behavioural and humanistic thinking are often seen as contradictory. However, being able to transcend your conditioning and habits is in the best of humanistic traditions. Before you can develop as a person, it is important to become aware of old, unhelpful patterns.

Learned emotional associations probably play an important part in the development of 'intentionality' which helped to determine our perception of reality. This is particularly true of our perception of ourselves, which is developed in the next chapter. Good feelings and bad feelings about ourselves appear to have a significant effect on the things we try to do, particularly academic achievement. The same seems to be true of our performance as teachers.

Learned emotional responses and habits play an important part in the way that we defend ourselves from threat. This notion is developed at the end of the next chapter. These defence mechanisms interfere with effective communication.

Working through the anxiety generated in experiential learning situations can help to reduce these anxious reactions in the future, thus increasing the number of choices we have available to us in interpersonal situations. This in turn leads to a sense of greater control over our lives and a reduction of stress in inter-personal situations, particularly in teaching. If we can become more relaxed in the ways suggested in chapter six, then unwanted anxiety reactions are likely to be inhibited. This can result in an improvement in the way we relate to other people.

We have used the word 'self' several times in this connecting section. In the next section, notions about the self are developed and related to problems of human relations.

3 The self in human relations

The way we relate to each other is affected by the way we relate to ourselves and particularly how we perceive ourselves.

> 'I couldn't possibly do the academic work to get a degree.'
> 'I'm hopeless at maths.'
> 'When I have done my GCSE, I shall concentrate on science subjects, with a view to doing microbiology at university and then go on to do research.'
> 'I can't draw.'
> 'Achieving something is just a matter of wanting to do it.'

Attitudes to the self tend to have a feeling component which has developed out of emotional experiences in the past. As we recounted in the previous chapter, one of the writers, at the age of eight, was caned for getting a sum wrong three times. From then on, meeting that teacher always produced a wave of fear, and doing maths became an anxiety-provoking activity. Thus, conditioning provides part of the explanation of how the self-concept and future performance are affected by interactions with other people.

The notion of the self is an interesting one. From a philosophical viewpoint, the concept of 'self' is as elusive as 'mind', and like mind, the word self fits easily into our everyday vocabulary. This suggests that it is somehow a meaningful concept.

The experience of self appears to vary from culture to culture, and it is not easy for us to understand how people from radically different cultures perceive themselves. Dorothy Lee (1976) described how in some so-called primitive cultures such as the Sioux, the Arapesh and the Eskimo, the self is developed for the benefit of the community. This seems to produce a high level of personal and physical development as well as an intense community involvement. The more self-centred approach to personal development encouraged in western society compares badly. As a culture we seem to be intent on a more destructive course than equipping ourselves for survival.

In this chapter we will examine the self from three points of view which will relate to the main themes developed in the book as a whole. Firstly, the effects of educational experience on the self-concepts of both students and teachers, secondly, expression of the self through the individual's personal constructs and thirdly, the ways in which the self defends against threat.

Educational experience and the self-concept

The self-concept can only have meaning in terms of how a person perceives herself, and this is inevitably dependent on feedback about other people's perception of her. The importance of their perceptions will depend on how significant they are in her life. For most of us, our parents are the most significant people in our lives and they play a crucial part in the development of our self-concept. Often, this is so well established that contradictory perceptions from teachers have little impact.

Research into the self-concept is made difficult by the problem of measurement. This is normally done using self-report questionnaires which require the respondent to answer questions such as, 'Do you succeed in most of the things you attempt?' A score is then obtained by adding together the number of items marked in the appropriate direction. A problem with this sort of test is that often the individuals who have a strong self-concept are more likely to admit to deficiencies, whereas those who have a low self-concept understand what the test is about and provide an answer which they feel is socially acceptable, rather than reveal the truth about how they perceive themselves. Thus the tests are hardly a true indicator of the extent to which the students' self-concepts have been damaged by their experiences in school. If the analysis by Hargreaves (1982) of the damage done to the majority of students by their experiences in comprehensive schools is correct, then the negative effect of these experiences is not being revealed by the standard tests.

A group of children arrive at their special school on the bus, having been to the swimming baths. As the bus drives through the school gates, the students, unaware of the teacher sitting in the back, start making comments like, 'Who goes to this nutters' school?' 'This is the school for dafties'. It would seem that their self-concept is so low that they have to pretend that it is someone else who goes to the school. Back in the school an angry teacher refers to the same group as 'The scum of the earth'. These are real events and it is difficult for experienced teachers whose lives have been relatively successful to have any idea of what it must be like to have a continuous school experience of failure and what effect this must have on the way the self is perceived.

Burns (1982) provided a thorough review of the statistical relationship between scores on tests of self-concept and academic achievement. Where tests of general self-concept are used, most studies find a consistent relationship of about 9 per cent of the variance common to the two measures. When a measure of academic self-concept is used, about 30 per cent of the variance is common to both measures (correlations of between 0.5 and 0.6). This does not prove that low self-concept is causing low academic achievement or that high self-concept is causing high academic achievement. It does, however, seem reasonable that they affect each other in a cyclical fashion, so that a high self-concept stimulates higher achievement, which in turn boosts the self-concept. Conversely, both a low self-concept and low academic achievement can contribute to a downward spiral.

We have suggested that the self-concept scores used in studies of this nature are not accurate, because students with high self-concepts will tend to be modest, and students with low self-concepts will hide their inadequacies. If these distortions are generally true, then the underlying reality will reflect a much stronger relationship between these two variables. This may explain why the differences between students becomes wider as they grow older, to the extent that many adolescents are operating at a lower level of academic achievement than they were in the top class of primary school.

So what aspects of a teacher's behaviour might be contributing to the lowering of their students' self-concepts? One process which has received a great deal of research attention is teacher expectation. Most of us who have visited classrooms in schools have had the experience of the children in the class being described in terms of their potential ability, often within earshot of the students. 'All of my best readers are on this table' (usually close to the teacher's desk). 'I am afraid you can't expect much from this group, they don't have much up top' (often distant from the teacher's desk and looking scruffier and less well socialized than the other group). This teacher has clear expectations of how well these children are likely to succeed in academic terms and in this case is telling them so. Hopefully, these direct statements are rare. However, a body of research has been carried out to establish whether these expectations are having an effect in much more subtle ways.

This was triggered off by the now notorious study by Rosenthal and Jacobson (1968) described in their book *Pygmalion in the Classroom*. In this study teachers in the first five grades of a school were fed false information that a small number of students were 'bloomers' and were likely to make considerable academic gains in the coming year. They claimed that a significant proportion of these students did, indeed, make such gains. There has since been a wealth of writing in the area, criticizing the original design and describing studies that either confirm or contradict the original research. Reviews of this research seem to reflect those writers' own expectations. Hamacheck (1978) suggested that, on balance, the research did confirm the original hypothesis, whereas Burns (1982) was much more cautious and implied that no clear conclusions could be drawn from this kind of research.

It is interesting to read Rosenthal's (1976) own comments on this issue in his later book *Experimenter Effects in Behavioural Research*. The book gives many fascinating examples of how researchers, even in the physical sciences, have supported hypotheses because their observations were distorted to see what they wanted to see. His research in this area probably stimulated the hypothesis for the Pygmalion research. He then goes on to review the research on expectation in the classroom without mentioning that his comments on bias in scientific research also apply to his own work.

Giving teachers false information is not typical of school experience, and there are enough naturalistic studies to convince the sceptic that teacher expectation does have a powerful effect on student achievement. A moving account is provided by Rist (1970), who observed a class in the United States going through kindergarten and the first two grades. They were assigned by the teacher to three separate tables. It was found that she had placed most of the children with higher socio-economic status together on one table and they were labelled the 'fast learners'. These differences seemed to become fixed and continued into the subsequent grades. The teacher consistently saw herself as instructing the higher status children and controlling and disciplining the lower status children. She spent more time with the higher status children. It would appear that these children's educational future was established in the first weeks of kindergarten, because of the preferential treatment they had received. The teacher involved was seen as a normal competent professional, and though the study involved only one group of children, it rings true as typical of much educational experience in this country.

Another intriguing study was carried out by Rubovits and Maehr (1973) with white women student teachers who were assigned to teach groups of four students, two white and two black. The children concerned were of similar ability but the student teachers were misled by being informed that one black and one white were 'gifted' and the remaining two were 'ungifted'. The white children were generally treated more favourably than the black children. The gifted whites received more attention than the ungifted whites. The gifted blacks received more negative criticism than any other category. If this finding generalizes to multicultural classrooms in the UK, and this seems likely to the writers, then the problems of differential expectation apply to racial differences as well as socio-economic ones.

The depressing catalogue continues in the reviews by Brophy and Good (1974) and Burns (1982). They both make suggestions for alleviating the pernicious effects of expectation. Burns sensibly advised increasing the number of individual conversations with children, praising all children realistically and setting tasks to suit individuals. The hard-pressed classroom teacher could well argue that it is not easy to maintain this sort of vigilance given the normal pressures of a teaching day. These problems are compounded by the possibility that expectations are being conveyed non-verbally and the teacher is unaware of what she is doing. A count of the different interactions that take place in a lesson will show whether the teacher is ignoring some students, giving nothing but criticism to others or only inter-acting with the students sitting directly in front of her. However, as we shall see in chapter five, the nature and impact of non-verbal communication in the classroom is still poorly understood and unavailable to an external observer. If, as we suggest, the impact of non-verbal communication is potentially much greater than that of verbal communication, then important aspects of the effects of a teacher's behaviour and expectations are still not even being considered.

A partial solution might be for teachers to have a better awareness of themselves and their own behaviour. Another important contribution by Burns (1982) was to emphasize the relationship between the teacher's self-concept and the experience of working in classrooms. His review suggested a clear relationship between effective teaching and a high level of self-esteem on the part of the teacher and that those teachers with a negative view of themselves had a negative effect on students' achievement and self-concept.

It is probably unhelpful to look for a cause and effect relationship between student self-concept and the relationship between teachers and students. If you were to ask the teachers themselves, they would probably claim that the students' behaviour was having a destructive effect on their self-esteem and that they had to become more punitive and negative in order to combat the students' behaviour. The students would probably claim that they behaved badly because the teacher was always telling them off and being critical, and that their behaviour was just a form of retaliation. Thus all the individuals concerned are trapped in a downward spiral. The general pattern of relationships stays the same but deteriorates steadily.

These problems were discussed by Short (1985), in terms of the relationship between the expectations of UK teachers and the behaviour of Afro-Caribbean students. He argued that expectation is not a one-way process and that the behaviour of the students plays a real part in the development of the teacher's expectations.

The teacher, in a professional leadership role, has to take responsibility for initiating positive change in a no-win situation. It is of no constructive use blaming the students, or expecting them to change their behaviour as if by a miracle. The power and the authority for change lies in the hands of the teacher. These changes will inevitably take time to become established.

If solutions can be found, then the spiral could develop in a positive direction. As the teacher behaves in a more positive manner, the behaviour of the students will in turn become more positive. The experienced teacher could be forgiven for responding to the previous statement with cynicism. In the first place it is difficult to change habitual patterns of behaviour, particularly in stressful situations. Secondly, other people do not always notice changes in behaviour in the short term and it is understandable if the teacher falls back on familiar habits, accepting the short-term reward of the comfort habit rather than the possible long-term rewards.

Changing behaviour does not necessarily mean lurching from one pattern to another. There is no point in trying to be a totally different person for one lesson and then complaining, 'I tried being nice to them and they walked all over me'.

Examples of simple changes which would not disrupt existing patterns could include:

1.   Choose the pupil who causes the most trouble and have a short personal conversation with him during, or at the end of each lesson. Later, try to increase the number of personal contacts you make with other members of the class.
2.   Try to take an interest in all the students' work, whatever you may think of it. Textbooks make a big issue of praise, but there is no point in being complimentary when it is not justified. Just to pay attention to what a student is doing is a reward in its own right. We all know that tiny babies need attention. If we examine our needs as adults it will become clear that we need attention as well. There is no reason to believe that the children in between do not need the same sort of attention.
3.   Try to avoid making a public show of the weaker students' deficiencies. Once again, as an adult you must be aware of how painful it can be to be shown that you are wrong, or be made to look foolish. For the student who has experienced less of the successes in life, it must be even more painful. Even if the student concerned has built up a wall of defence against the external expression of these concerns, there is a good chance that the feelings are registering at some level. This is a difficult suggestion to follow because of the conventions of classroom management, where students are often asked questions or asked to read aloud. One of the writers remembers blundering into a class of thirteen-year-olds and asking a non-reader to read in front of the class. This is an extreme example, but similar demands of a more subtle nature are being made in classrooms all the time.

These suggestions all involve giving the student positive forms of attention. If you hate yourself or hate the students, and the two appear to go together, then it is going to involve more personal effort to give positive attention. However, you may find that making the effort will help to diminish your general sense of low self-esteem and begin to start the upward spiral that we described earlier.

If, as Burns (1982) suggested, the most effective teachers have positive self-concepts and they tend to encourage positive self-concepts in their students, it would make sense to include self-concept enhancement into teacher training programmes. The actual effect of initial training appears to result in a reduction in positive self-concept, particularly during teaching practice. Burns suggested that this was due to the marginality of the role of student teacher – not yet a proper teacher – and the undermining of their idealistic notions about education by experienced teachers. We would guess that a further contributory factor is the fact that young children do not readily do as they are told and problems of discipline inevitably damage self-esteem.

If high self-esteem is an important variable in effective teaching it would seem sensible to include aspects of personal development in teacher training programmes. This was advocated in the 1950s by Jersild (1955), who conducted in-service courses which encouraged experienced teachers to examine themselves through discussion. This idea has rarely been taken seriously because the emphasis in teacher training has always been on the skills of teaching a subject rather than the personal growth of the teacher.

Exceptions to this are provided by Combs (1965), who stressed the importance of the development of the self in the professional training of teachers. Carkhuff (1969) and Rogers (1983) were essentially putting forward a similar viewpoint and offered forms of inter-personal skills training as a means of improving effectiveness in the helping professions in general and teaching in particular. The training procedures they advocate are experiential and inevitably enable the individual to become more aware of himself and how he relates to others. If this is successful, it is bound to have an effect on the student teacher's self-concept. It seems reasonable to assume that improved personal effectiveness will result in a more positive self-concept.

Classroom activities have been developed for enhancing the self-concepts of students (Canfield and Wells, 1976; Hopson and Scally, 1980). These often involved encouraging the students to emphasize their positive qualities and to make positive statements to each other. There is no guarantee that activities of this nature will necessarily produce an improvement in self-concept. However, with a reasonable relationship between a teacher and class, most forms of experiential learning appear to contribute to a more positive self-concept in students. These issues are raised again in chapter seven on working in groups.

* Ask the members of the group to write down three things they do really well and three things they do badly. Then invite each of them to make a public statement in the group, with three sentences beginning, 'I am the best person in the world at ...' and three sentences beginning, 'I am the worst person in the world at ...'

   Then invite the group to share what it feels like to make these statements.

* Ask the members of the group to think of an activity that they used to be very good at, but have not done for at least two years. Then divide the group into threes and give each person six minutes to talk about their involvement in this activity.

* Provide the members of a group with a large sheet of paper and a thick felt-tip pen.

   Then invite the group members to pair off and to take turns in drawing a large outline of each other's head and shoulders, and to write their first names in large letters underneath.

   When everyone has completed their outlines, place them on view around the room. Invite all the group members to make a positive comment about that person on the outline. It is important to stress that these personal comments must be positive. When everyone has finished writing up their comments, pin up the completed outlines and give the group time to read what has been written.

The last exercise, which involves the public display of positive statements about the group, does depend on the facilitator or teacher being able to prevent the exercise being abused, and this would be a reflection of the established relationship with the group. The power of the exercise, both with young children and with experienced teachers, is indicated by the silence which settles when people read the comments on the outlines. Wooster and Carson (1982) reported the effect of the exercise on a child from an itinerant family, who was having difficulty integrating into his junior school class. He appeared to be drawn into the class group by the experience and kept going to look at what had been written about him over and over again. Even his mother was impressed when she saw what had been written and began to co-operate with the school.

One problem with exercises which only emphasize the positive aspects of a student's behaviour is that they represent an unbalanced form of feedback. An accurate self-picture is a better basis for development than an unrealistically positive one. On the other hand, if a student has had a long history of experience which is depressing his self-concept, then some positive experience is likely to be therapeutic.

Expression of self through personal constructs

The way we perceive other people has a strong effect on the way we relate to them. The significant dimensions we have for perceiving others are invariably important with regard to the way we perceive ourselves. If you are critical of people whom you perceive as untidy, there is a good chance that you are concerned not to be untidy yourself. If you regard caring as an important attribute for teachers, then it is likely that you try to be caring yourself.

Alternatively, you might admire qualities in other people that you think are lacking in yourself. One of the writers is particularly concerned about the qualities of generosity and meanness. He sees himself as being mean in both a psychological and a financial sense. He admires people who are generous and sees this as an important quality in his interactions with other people.

Another variation of the same theme is the person who is highly critical of a certain trait in other people, but seems to be unaware that the same trait is typical of his own behaviour. A head teacher might indulge in long diatribes about politeness and consideration for others during morning assembly and yet consistently treat both staff and students in an overbearing and ill-mannered fashion. This is a form of the defence mechanism known as projection, which will be dealt with in more detail in the next section.

* Invite the group to identify the qualities that are important to them in relation to both staff and students.

Write down three of the characteristics you like to see, and three of the characteristics you do not like to see in both students and staff:

Students		Staff	
like	do not like	like	do not like
1	1	1	1
2	2	2	2
3	3	3	3

Now form groups of three and examine, in your group, the way in which all of these characteristics relate to you.

In the first chapter, we examined the ways in which the children in a junior school class were using the same words to describe totally different aspects of their peers' behaviour. Similarly, we gave an example of how staff used totally different words to describe the same behaviour in their colleagues. If differences of this nature exist and the people concerned are unaware of them, then it is inevitable that attempts to communicate using these words are bound to be problematic. A psychologist who specifically worked on this problem was George Kelly (1955), and the rest of this section will be devoted to his ideas and the development of his ideas.

Kelly was an American clinical psychologist working in the mid-west of the United States who felt that it was important to come to an understanding of how his patients perceived their experience, in particular their experience of important people in their lives. He preferred to work with their theories about the world, rather than the current orthodoxies of psycho-analysis and behaviourism. He developed these ideas as an academic at Ohio State University. His colleagues and students remember him with a warmth and affection which reflects the humanity of his approach to the person.

Kelly suggests that man behaves like a scientist and develops his own representation of the world so that he can predict and control events. This representation of the world consists of a limited number of categories, which are called constructs.

An important part of the theory is that these constructs are expressed in terms of similarity and contrast. A personal construct will say how two people are the same but different from a third. Thus all constructs are bi-polar, such as 'generous–mean'. 'Generosity' would have no meaning if there were no 'meanness'. It would be difficult for either pole to have any meaning if they did not apply to more than one person.

This idea of bi-polarity is central to Kelly's theory. A construct is similar to some primitive and classical uses of words, where a single word is used to express both ends of a continuum. The Latin 'sacer' can mean both 'sacred' and 'accursed'; 'altus' can mean both 'high' and 'deep'.

The main idea contained in the theory is that each individual builds up a unique repertoire of constructs based on his experience. These constructs help him to predict events and order his life. The experiences referred to by the constructs are called elements. The elements could be virtually anything such as people, cars, books, homes or teaching situations. Constructs can be generated which are relevant to the universe of elements which is being studied.

Originally, Kelly suggested that his theory applied only to personality and inter-personal relations. The constructs are the ways in which a person views other people. The elements which have contributed to the development of any individual's personal constructs will consist of people from the past, people in the present, the person himself and even imagined individuals such as the person you would like to be, or an ideal self.

So is it possible to come to an understanding of how a person construes other people? There are several techniques for eliciting constructs, such as the repertory test (Fransella and Bannister, 1977), which for research purposes have been developed into complex forms. We will start with a simplified version of this test and would strongly recommend that you work through it with a friend and then ask them to work through it with you. It is important to go through both processes; firstly to develop an awareness of your own construing, and secondly to come to a realization of the dramatic differences between your construing and that of the other person. You might by chance share the experience with a person who construes other people in ways that are very similar to yours. In our experience this is highly unlikely.

* Working with a partner, take six small cards and ask the other
  person to write a name on each one. Include parents, partner
  and/or close friend, a colleague or fellow student that they like and
  at least one that they do not like. Some people like to use initials
  or pseudonyms to make the process anonymous. These are the
  elements. Turn the cards over, shuffle them and then turn three
  of them face upwards in front of the other person. Ask the question:
  'I would like you to tell me something about these three people.

In what important way are two of them alike, but different from the third?'

Invariably the person will produce a word to describe how two of the people whose names are written on the cards are the same. This is called the emergent pole of the construct. He may have to be asked again to supply the contrasting or implicit pole. This may produce two contrasting words such as 'attractive–repulsive'. Sometimes the implicit pole can only be defined by the absence of the emergent pole, such as 'religious–not religious'. Some constructs can only be expressed as phrases such as 'the sort of person I avoid at social functions'.

When the person is satisfied with the words he has chosen to describe the poles of his constructs, three more cards are laid on the table and the procedure is repeated. In this way a list of bi-polar constructs can be generated:

strong – weak
attractive – repulsive
religious – not religious
kind – cruel
the sort of person I avoid at social functions – the sort of person I talk to at social functions.

This is often called the triadic technique.

This procedure is usually carried out with a larger number of elements, as many as twenty-four, which are presented systematically in different combinations. In our experience a smaller number presented randomly will provide the same information. Although the procedure be time-consuming, most people exhaust their repertoire of personal constructs after about twenty presentations. It is surprising that even very intelligent people with a high level of verbal skill often begin to dry up after ten constructs and rarely go beyond twenty-five.

The description of the procedure is easy to understand, but actually doing it is not always so simple. Some people find it difficult to verbalize how they perceive people, and there may be long silences as the cards are shuffled around. Having produced an emergent pole there may be some difficulty in finding the appropriate implicit pole, and it is important to resist the temptation to supply one. On the other hand, it may be useful to help the person reduce a long phrase to a single word or a short phrase.

A combination of words may be produced which is so much at variance with the investigator's own construct system, that he may want to object. Obviously these differences are the basis of personal construct theory and the temptation must be resisted strongly.

Often constructs are produced which appear on the surface to be concrete descriptions of sex, age, occupation or physical appearance. When these occur, it is often worth questioning further to see if the meaning goes beyond mere physical appearance. If the construct 'male–female' is produced, it might be worth asking what is important about being male and female. Maleness may be a quality that is applied to some females and vice versa.

Constructs such as 'old–young' often go beyond strict chronological age, in that some of the 'old' people are chronologically younger than some of the 'young' people. The construct 'close family–not close family' may be an important emotional dimension for one person but not for another.

Questioning an apparently concrete construct may elicit a more important underlying construct. A person might produce the comparison 'red-haired–blonde'. On being asked what is important about being 'red-haired', it may turn out that this person sees all 'red-haired' people as 'bad-tempered'.

Going through the business of eliciting constructs for the first time can be a salutary experience and really brings home the importance of individual differences in construing. It may create problems for the researcher when the constructs that are important to him are not generated. Constructs that are central to his system of construing just may not occur to other people.

There is no need to stick to the triadic technique described above, but it does seem to work. Constructs can be elicited in many ways, such as presenting the cards in pairs, or by laying all the cards out in front of the person, or by asking him which cards he would have liked to have come up and why. Young children and less able adults seem to have difficulty with the triadic technique. Young children particularly seem to be put off by a formal interview situation. It has been shown that children will make more complex judgments of other people in written essays compared with those elicited from triads.

The following comments were taken from a fifteen-year-old girl

talking about her teachers. They demonstrate that it is possible to
elicit constructs using an informal technique.

Mrs B. takes no notice of messing around and just carries on
teaching. Mrs C. is quite good – she doesn't stand any lip. She
has everyone quiet and you really learn something. Mrs H. is nice
because she is one of those who always gets sidetracked. Mr H. is
a 'suck' because he thinks everything you say is gospel. He is nice
to you if you do your homework. There is not much to say about
Mr O. Miss C. is about twenty years ahead of the other teachers
in the school. Miss G. is nice – a nice person. She teaches fairly
and doesn't give too much homework. Teachers should keep to
homework schedules. Mrs O. is nice because she lets you talk in
maths and is nice to talk to.

Games teachers are generally nice – they tend to be more up to
date – more liberal-minded – more willing to accept change. One
bad thing is that they have favourites. Mr E. is okay as a teacher,
but you don't talk to him. He never says the whole lot of you are
terrible. He doesn't threaten you with the exam.

As it stands, this series of statements is somewhat confusing, but at
least five constructs seem to be emerging:

fair – unfair
can talk to – can't talk to
up-to-date – old-fashioned
keeps order – doesn't keep order
teaches you – doesn't teach you

This analysis was checked out with her and she agreed with most of
it, except 'can't talk to', which should have been 'don't want to know'.
This is a good example of how easy it is to make assumptions about
other people's constructs.

Nash (1976) asked twelve- to thirteen-year-olds to discuss teachers
they had previously divided into teachers they 'got on with' and
teachers they 'did not get on with'. From these interviews, he extracted
six constructs that were common to most of the pupils:

1   keeps order – unable to keep order
2   teaches you – doesn't teach you

3   explains – doesn't explain
4   interesting – boring
5   fair – unfair
6   friendly – unfriendly

This result will probably come as no surprise to the perceptive teacher and has been confirmed by many teachers trying their hand at generating constructs from children in schools. Indeed, the construct 'boring' came up over and over again when students were talking about their experience in secondary school. It may be that the students concerned are applying the concept out of habit, without really thinking it through. However, the development of the construct must be based on earlier experience and would suggest that a large part of the average secondary student's life in school is extremely boring.

Perhaps the most important consideration for eliciting constructs from another person is to listen to what they have to say. It is possible to obtain a reasonable picture of a person's construct system by attending carefully to the conversation and exploring the ideas that are generated. This must be done without feeding the person with your own constructs, and perhaps the mode of questioning described in Gestalt therapy (see chapter five) is most appropriate here – using questions such as 'How do you feel about . . .?', 'What is your attitude to . . .?'

Techniques for eliciting constructs have been described as an extended conversation and accept the inevitability of the effects of interaction between experimenter and subject (Rowe, 1978). There is room for a great deal of creativity in developing techniques for eliciting constructs. Fransella and Bannister (1977) report an unpublished study by Baillie-Grohman, who elicited constructs from deaf children using mime.

Constructs can be generated from a class of children. The elements can be written on the board and the exact categories can be negotiated with the teacher.

Once the process of eliciting constructs has begun, there can still be a two-way interaction over the words being produced and the investigator can wander round to check that the instructions have been understood.

Probably there will have to be some short individual interviews to sort out any anomalies in the constructs that have been elicited, bearing in mind that what appear to be anomalies for the investigator, may not be anomalies for the person providing the constructs.

The following description is of a much more informal approach to eliciting constructs from a group.

One of the writers, teaching a top band class in a comprehensive school, managed to generate meaningful constructs from a class of thirty-four thirteen- to fourteen-year-old children at the same time. The children were instructed in the following manner. 'Think of your father. Now think of Mr B.' (a teacher they knew well). 'How are they different from your cousin?' It was then explained how they were to write down the two poles of the construct.

The questioning continued in the same way. 'Think of your mother. Think of me. How are both of us different from the headteacher?' Subsequent role titles included specific people and also suggestions like 'someone you really fancy', 'your best friend', 'someone you dislike intensely', 'someone you have respect for', 'someone you are jealous of', and so on.

When individual children complained that the role titles were not appropriate to them, alternatives were given. When they complained that they could not think of anything, they were prompted with statements like 'When you think of ..., what is the first thing that comes to mind?' Most of this was done while the teacher was wandering round to check that they understood what they were doing.

Active co-operation in a task of this nature probably requires a good relationship with the group concerned. This group appeared to be highly involved, and each produced between ten and sixteen meaningful constructs. It was an absorbing task because it was close to their experience and emotionally charged.

An indication of the amount of involvement in the task comes from one girl in the class who went home and repeated the process with her mother and came back with a meaningful set of constructs that she had helped her mother to generate.

A common complaint from adults who have generated a list of personal constructs is that given a different mood or context, they would probably have generated a different set of constructs. The reality is that the person would probably have produced a different set of words, but the underlying constructs and the organization of the constructs would have been more or less the same. Teachers on in-service courses who have repeated the process of generating constructs after a gap of two years have been shocked at the similarities between the two sets.

A technique for exploring the underlying meaning of constructs designed by Hinckle (1965) is called laddering. This simple technique can produce some profound insights for the person whose constructs are being laddered. It involves selecting a single construct from a person's repertoire and asking three simple questions. The following is a real example using the construct 'belonging–non belonging'.

First question: 'Which would you rather be, "belonging" or "non belonging"?'
Response: 'Belonging'.
Second question: 'What's good about being "belonging"?'
Response: 'It means that you are not lonely.'
Third question: 'If you are not, "not lonely", what are you?'
Response: 'Lonely'.

This last response produces a new construct 'not lonely–lonely'. The same process can be repeated with the new construct and then with a third and so on. The responses can be recorded in the following way, which illustrate the laddering of two constructs from the same person:

(a)   belonging – non belonging
      not lonely – lonely
      get more things you want – don't get things you want
      more needs fulfilled – less needs fulfilled
(b)   realistic – unrealistic
      don't try to do the impossible – try to do the impossible
                                achieve more
                                more needs fulfilled

It is interesting that the laddering of both constructs ended up with the same construct. This suggests that this is an important construct for that person and yet was not generated in the original list. In the second laddering the preferred pole changed from one side to the other. The laddering used in this example came to a natural conclusion quickly. Sometimes the process has to be repeated many times before the person concerned feels that it is appropriate to stop.

The process of laddering can open out the original construct to point up important existential issues for the person such as 'gives meaning to life' or 'make me happy'. This has happened to some extent in the example given. At other times the laddering narrows the focus of the construct, perhaps giving the person a more precise understanding of the issue that is being raised.

Laddering is a technique which is used by clinical psychologists who are sympathetic to Kelly's ideas. It has been used by a number of educational psychologists in this country. Working with children in English schools was pioneered by Ravenette (1977). One of the writers has used it as a classroom exercise with adolescents in a comprehensive school. The process was first demonstrated with an individual, and then the students were led through the stages with a little more explanation than would be required for an adult. Individual assistance was given moving around the class and most of the students produced meaningful results. The exercise produced considerable involvement and, subsequently, a lively discussion (naturally so, since they were dealing with important issues in their lives).

* Demonstrate the process of laddering to the whole group and then ask them to form pairs and try it out for themselves. Insist that they experience both sides of the process and change roles. Again the results may highlight individual differences in the construction of experience.

What we have said about personal constructs so far has been concerned with eliciting individual constructs, or lists of constructs. These notions are made more complex when we consider the relationships between the constructs. This can be another source of confusion in communication. A simple fictitious staffroom example involves the geography teacher for whom the construct 'radical–traditional' is important in his assessment of his colleagues. He is also concerned about 'professionalism' and 'inefficiency', and this is an important related construct. He perceives his 'radical' colleagues as 'professional' and his 'traditional' colleagues as 'inefficient'. The headteacher uses the same pairs of constructs, but perceives the 'radical' teachers as 'inefficient' and the 'traditional' teachers as 'efficient'. Just to complicate matters, if they were asked to categorize the staff into 'radical' and 'traditional', their choices would be totally different. It is little wonder that they have given up trying to communicate with each other and, understandably, gravitate towards colleagues who have similar ways of construing.

The relationships between the constructs can also be examined by the repertory grid technique devised by Kelly. Forms of grid analysis can involve complex statistical techniques, and the interested reader is referred to Fransella and Bannister (1977). For our purposes, we will generate a fictitious grid and show how the relationships between the constructs can be checked visually.

The children described in the Nash study could have been asked to tick the teachers to whom the emergent poles of the construct applied. Young children can be asked to divide cards, with the names of the teachers on them, into two piles according to how they were perceived. The following diagram is a possible grid produced by one child.

	Mrs J	Mr C	Mr X	Miss Y	Mrs B	Mr K
keeps order	√		√		√	
teaches you	√	√	√		√	
explains	√				√	
interesting			√	√		√
fair	√			√		√
friendly	√			√		√

A quick visual inspection would suggest that this pupil associates 'keeping order' with 'teaches you', and possibly this says something about how he construes his experience of school. 'Fair' and 'friendly' are used in the same way, but differently from 'keeps order' and 'teaches you'.

It is curious that he doesn't construe Mrs J. as interesting, considering all the other positive qualities she appears to have. However, seeing this as an anomaly is really a function of the writer's construct system, and what has been given should be accepted. It could be possible to ask the child about this, but this would have to be done in a neutral way, in case the respondent changes his mind because he thinks he has done something 'wrong'.

The grid given is a small one, but may be appropriate to a particular investigation. Most grids, however, have more elements and constructs and it is not so easy to extract information just by a visual inspection. A quick method of establishing the relationship between constructs on a larger grid is to line up a piece of paper along the first construct and mark off the ticks. The paper can then be moved down the constructs. A measure of the relationship between each of the constructs can be obtained simply by counting the similarities and subtracting the number of dissimilarities. Similarities will include blanks as well as ticks.

Having completed this procedure with the first construct, the piece of paper can be folded over and the procedure can be repeated with the second construct. Thus, the degree of similarity between all of the constructs can be estimated, without using complex statistical techniques.

It is possible to see the relationships between your own constructs without using a grid. If you have completed the earlier exercise in which you were asked to generate a list of constructs, you may wish to develop it in the following way:

* Invite the group to look down their lists of constructs and they will probably find that a large proportion of them are really referring to the same quality. Take the list we used as an example.

  strong – weak
  attractive – repulsive
  religious – not religious
  kind – cruel
  the sort of person I avoid at social functions – the sort of person I talk to at social functions

  If all the people you know who are 'strong' are also 'attractive', then the two constructs are not discriminating, and even though the words appear to have different meanings they are being used in essentially the same way. Now cluster your constructs into groups that have similar meanings. See how many groups you end up with.

Most adults find that more than half of their constructs are being used in similar ways. This dominant grouping has an over-riding influence on how they perceive other people. Depressingly, it is rare for more than two further clusters to emerge. Thus even though a person has produced a long list of varied words to describe people, the way these words are used in practice is essentially very limited, and probably pre-empts the way they relate to other people. Among groups of teachers who attend human relations courses, the construct 'caring–uncaring' seems to predominate.

With a normal cross-section of teachers other constructs predominate, such as 'efficient–inefficient'. These major constructs which subsume large numbers of other constructs are called super-ordinate constructs. In a sense it does not matter what the super-ordinate construct is called, but usually the individual concerned can provide a label. Initially, the notion that we only have about three major ways of seeing other people is rejected. However, after undergoing the process of generating constructs and then comparing them, these limitations do become clear. It isn't that we don't have the vocabulary to describe people in different ways, but that when we meet someone, our experience of them is filtered by the constructs which are important to us and their other qualities may be ignored.

If a student perceives all adults at the negative end of a 'can trust–can't trust' construct, then it will be difficult for you as a teacher to gain his confidence whatever you try to do. If as a teacher you are concerned that both colleagues and students should not look untidy, then it will be hard for you to see good qualities in those who are not well dressed.

* Split the group up into pairs and ask them to take turns to examine their lists of constructs and decide on a label for the main super-ordinate construct.

    Then ask each pair to consider to what extent the negative end of their main super-ordinate construct plays a part in their lives. Is there a part of them that wants to be like that?

    Then bring the group together and ask them in turn to complete the statement, 'The main way that I perceive other people is along the dimension "   " to "   ", and then encourage them to elaborate on this.

An exercise of this nature should bring out the importance of individual differences, and underline the need to take a phenomenological approach to communication. It is not easy to accept that the negative poles of our constructs apply to ourselves. If this is true, then in construing the world, we are projecting our own internal structures onto people and events. How he organizes his experience reflects his own internal organization.

This would suggest that a person's personal constructs are saying more about himself than the people and events he is construing. Thus the repertory test can be seen as a projection test.

Projection tests are often criticized for their lack of objectivity, but if the data obtained are closer to reality than the standardized test, then this criticism loses its force.

Personal construct psychology was developed to help the clinician working with individuals. The development of grids as a research tool has been disappointing when applied to education (Pope and Keen, 1981; Adams-Webber, 1979). For the working teacher, or the teacher in training, it is important to come to some understanding of these complex individual differences. This is perhaps best achieved by going through exercises similar to the ones given here. This can help to give insight into the person's own internal processes and also into serious breakdowns in communication.

Kelly's approach can be contrasted with personality tests which give a score on a standardized questionnaire. These are sometimes inappropriately described as more 'rigorous' approaches. Working with personal constructs brings out material that would be difficult to obtain using a standardized technique. Slang and idiom often help to provide shades of meaning which are not expressed by more conventional words. In the study of fourteen-year-olds previously described, the constructs 'sucky' and 'magic' came up several times. 'Sucky' is a local slang word for immature, and 'magic' is a superlative taken from a TV show. Once they were used as the opposite poles of a construct, but for everyone else, they had different opposite poles. Possibly these construct labels will disappear soon.

It could be that the more 'rigorous' approaches are taking the easy option in trying to understand human behaviour. Easy, in the sense that they have taken a model of man that is inappropriate, but one from which it is easy to derive consistent measures. The examination of personal constructs provides looser, changing, dynamic information which is difficult to generalize across subjects. Possibly the choice of method says more about the tester than the problem being investigated.

Defending the self from threat

Teaching in most State schools is not an easy job. The first teaching practice for student teachers is usually a chastening experience.

Women who have had a break from teaching to bring up young children often dread the prospect of going back when their own children have started school. Teachers commonly report having dreams where they are in a classroom and are unable to control the students, or of being inadequately prepared; in the case of one teacher, fifteen years after last holding a permanent teaching post. In chapter seven we will discuss the evidence suggesing that teaching is a highly stressful activity for a high proportion of teachers, and that to be anxious about teaching is actually quite understandable.

In fact much of this anxiety is perfectly reasonable. A teacher is expected to have a degree of control over the students in classes and to maintain a high standard of academic achievement. If the students conspire to defeat these ends, then this is likely to be a blow both to self-esteem and to his standing among his peers, which is certain to generate anxiety.

Other forms of anxiety are more specific to individuals. You might become anxious every time the headteacher comes into your classroom, even though he has never done anything to threaten you. These feelings may come up every time you are in the presence of an authority figure. You may find a group of mature adolescents threatening, even though they have always been friendly and co-operative. Some adults have vague feelings of anxiety which they do not understand and which probably relate to events that happened in early childhood. Sometimes these feelings of anxiety become so strong that the person concerned is unable to go to work and the symptoms might be described as anxiety attacks.

Anxiety in the individual is usually generated by a threat to self-esteem – though sometimes there is a real threat of physical attack. Sometimes the threat seems to be irrational, as when a colleague complains that the head is plotting to ruin his career when there is no evidence that this is the case. Often a distinction is made between real and imagined threat, but as Smail (1984) argued, the threat and the anxiety are both real for the person concerned, irrespective of what an external observer might think.

The degree of threat in a given situation will depend on how that situation is perceived. One teacher might perceive a specific class as an exciting challenge because it includes several interesting, independent characters. Another teacher might perceive the same class as difficult to control and a threat to his authority. One teacher might perceive a noisy class as a sign of involved activity, whereas another might see the same situation as being out of control. This again fits in with the phenomenological view put forward in the introduction, and it is both inappropriate and unhelpful to advise a person to change the way she perceives a situation. A far more helpful approach is the use of experiential exercises to facilitate changes in awareness and to practise new ways of responding to situations. Hopefully this will produce changes in perception.

* Ask the members of the group to fill in the following sheet:

Critical Incident Record Sheet

Write down three incidents in your experience of teaching which made you anxious.	What exactly did you feel in your body?	How did you respond to the anxiety?	What alternative action could you have taken?
1			
2			
3			

The same issues of anxiety and threat apply to the students in school. In the first part of this chapter we reviewed the evidence which suggested that the experience of school is an affront to the self-esteem of a high proportion of students. Teachers tend to come from the more successful proportion of the school population, and it is difficult for them to understand the lives of students who are having a continuous experience of failure and the threat that this must impose. The more successful students will have their own problems of pressure to succeed and to live up to the expectations of both parents and teachers. Relations within the peer group pose further threats with problems of being rejected, ridiculed and even bullied physically.

Some children feel threatened every time an adult speaks to them, and some are so excruciatingly shy that they spend all their free time standing on their own in a corner of the playground. Some children are worried about the appearance of their bodies, and changing for PE is a painful activity. Related to physical problems are the problems of burgeoning sexuality and sexual attraction.

The natural response to threat is to defend oneself. This can be done by either attacking the source of threat and trying to neutralize it, or by escaping from it. If the threat is from a relationship then neither attack nor flight provide an adequate long-term solution to the problem. When the anxiety of teaching a difficult class becomes too much, you might break out in a violent verbal outburst. In the long-term, this may result in your dealing with all discipline problems by shouting and eventually this will have little effect. Alternatively, you might escape to the staffroom in tears, which is clearly not a useful way of dealing with classroom problems. Unfortunately, responses of this nature provide an immediate relief from the stress of anxiety and, as we suggested in the chapter on conditioning, short-term rewards can be very powerful. The development of more appropriate patterns of behaviour may require a considerable effort of will.

Ways of coping with threat are learned in early childhood and usually continue on into adult life. These ways of coping are often called defence mechanisms, and a large part of this section will be devoted to an examination of the mechanisms of defence. If we are honest about our behaviour, then we will be aware that we often use various ways of defending ourselves against threat. These are not symptoms of a disturbed personality, and individuals who are willing to discuss their defences are probably better adjusted than those who deny that they are defended at all.

A criticism of the notion of defence mechanisms is that they have not been investigated under controlled experimental conditions. This is not correct, and the interested reader is referred to writers such as Murphy (1975), Laughlin (1970) and Tucker (1970). However, perhaps the best source of evidence is to refer to your own experience and your observations of colleagues and students.

Different writers produce different lists and categories of defence mechanisms. Here we will deal with them individually and provide examples from educational settings.

Fantasy and day-dreaming

This is perhaps one of the most innocent forms of defence. The survey by Singer (1966) suggested that most of us day-dream most of the time, and that it even intrudes into complex mental activities. It is not merely an indulgence by bored adolescents. Day-dreams usually intrude most strongly when we are faced with dull repetitive tasks. As we pointed out in the previous section, most adolescents experience secondary education as boring and it is not surprising that many students sitting in class seem to drift off into a fantasy world of their own. Both of the writers experienced drifting off into fantasy when involved in routine teaching activities, even when reading a story out loud or giving a lecture to a large number of people.

The effect of fantasy is to put right those aspects of our lives which are going wrong in reality. If you have failed to confront a colleague on some issue because you were afraid, or it was inappropriate, you may find yourself rehearsing what you would have liked to have said as you are walking along the road a few days later. Sometimes the words might actually pop out of your mouth, to your embarrassment if there are any passers-by.

Adolescents are not alone in dealing with their unresolved sexual needs in fantasy. Many adults of both sexes will admit to having frequent sexual fantasies. Each of us will have a unique fantasy world which provides useful indicators of some of the important, unresolved issues in life. Unfortunately, our culture does not encourage a close examination of our fantasy lives and both teachers and parents make negative comments about the process.

* Divide the group into sixes and invite them to share their main
  fantasy themes and the situations in which they tend to emerge.
  It is usually helpful for the person facilitating the whole group to
  model the process with examples from her own fantasy life.

Some people are frightened by the themes in their fantasies, and the process of discovering that others share the same themes and that they are not uncommon, is reassuring. A colleague reported that he often had a fantasy of smashing his fist into the faces of students who made his life difficult. Other members of the group expressed relief that this was a common fantasy theme. Another common theme is that people who are very close to you die. Invariably the people who are close to you provide considerable rewards in life, but are also seen as a source of frustration. Thinking of a parent, partner or child being killed, usually produces too much guilt to cope with, so the notion might pop up in a fantasy accident. Thus the process of sharing fantasies can help to dispel the idea that your fantasy life is in some way a sign of disturbance.

Indulgence in fantasy can become dangerous if individuals spend most of their time locked in a fantasy world. For some children, and even adults, the real world is such an unpleasant place that they remain locked in a fantasy world for long periods of time. This may be what is happening to some autistic children. Another danger is that the boundary between fantasy and reality may become blurred. This has been portrayed in fiction by such characters as Walter Mitty and Billy Liar.

Some children tell lies and make excuses which appear to become the truth as the words are being uttered, and no amount of persuasion can make them change their minds. If this is the case, then to describe them as liars could be inappropriate. However, it is difficult for the teacher not to be affronted when he has seen the events involved. One of the writers remembers teaching a student who would come to school in the morning and recount the exciting adventures he had had the night before. The stories usually culminated in being picked up by the police and taken home in a police car. His friends said he never went out. His fantasies provided means of competing for status in his delinquent peer group.

Here we have dealt with fantasy as a means of defending against unpleasant situations such as boredom, and for dealing with the frustration of unresolved needs and unfinished business. This form of defence is used by all of us to some degree and probably provides a healthy outlet for issues that cannot be resolved immediately. In chapter five we will examine more constructive approaches to the use of fantasy.

Denial

Sometimes our actions and our feelings do not fit in with our internalized set of values. To cope with this, we deny them. This is not to say that we are lying, but somehow close off our awareness of them. This is probably done by the process which Freud described as repression, which may be an unconscious process. We do something or have feelings that are unacceptable, so in some way it is not permitted to be a part of our awareness. Spender (1982) demonstrated that both male and female teachers paid more attention to boys than to girls, reinforcing the cultural stereotype that the education of girls was not worthwhile. Most teachers would deny they were doing this.

Teachers will also deny not being able to control a class when there is plenty of evidence that their discipline is poor. Parents are often blind to their children's inadequacies and seem unable to 'see' the evidence that the child is unlikely to succeed. Adolescents often develop the habit of denying that they can do any work that they are given, with the phrase, 'Can't do it, Sir'. Often the denial is reinforced by not even looking at the work.

A more prevalent form of denial is to deny feelings which you have learned are unacceptable. Anger and fear are the emotions that are most often denied, and the skills for repressing these feelings are probably learned as part of early childhood socialization. This denial of feeling takes place at both conscious and unconscious levels. It is difficult to admit to a colleague that you are afraid of going to teach a difficult class so you might pretend to be confident and calm. When a student is threatened by a teacher, he may say 'I'm not afraid of you', and at the same time give off a number of cues that indicate he is experiencing considerable anxiety. For the teacher it is probably inappropriate to express fear or anger every time these feelings arise during a lesson, but the denial or repression of these feelings does take its toll. Sitting down to relax in the staffroom, the feelings will often well up. If they have been repressed more effectively then they might erupt as you drive home or as you relax in the evening. As we will suggest in the chapter on stress, the long-term denial of feeling can result in serious illness.

Byrne (see Tucker, 1970) made an interesting distinction between repressors who tend to avoid or deny threat, and sensitizers who deal with threat by admitting and discussing it. The repressors tend to do well in their careers which suggests that the denial of feeling is encouraged in our culture, but they suffer by having a significantly higher incidence of psychosomatic illness.

The more you examine your own life, and those of people around you, the more evidence emerges of the ubiquitous nature of denial. We deny our racism, sexism, evidence about the dangers of smoking, drinking, lack of exercise and over-eating. We deny the evidence of starvation, poverty, injustice and perhaps the most massive denial in our culture is the denial of death (Becker, 1973).

Similarly, denial pervades our educational institutions. A small minority of headteachers, faced with the threat of their grammar schools becoming comprehensive, pretended that their schools had never changed, and even continued to refer to the school by its old name. At the other end of the spectrum, many teachers have had the experience of coming across a student in tears who will only say that there is nothing wrong, because the threat of saying what really happened is greater than anything the teacher might do.

Rationalization

'I had to resort to corporal punishment. It was the only thing that would keep him under control. It was for his own good.'

'I couldn't do my homework assignment because my friend needed me to play in the football team and then there was an important programme on TV so there just wasn't time.'

When we do things that are objectionable to ourselves or other people, we often produce elaborate explanations as to why we behaved in the way that we did. Basically, they are excuses, but often they are so subtle or well-used that we fool ourselves. The words used in a denial are often a rationalization. Politicians are past masters at explaining why their current behaviour is the opposite of promises made prior to election. 'I can't get on in maths because Mrs Sharples had got a down on me.' 'Discipline is falling apart in this school because of the changeover to comprehensive education.' Since discipline has not fallen apart in some schools that have changed over, it would seem reasonable that there may be other reasons for discipline problems.

A distinction is often made between 'sweet lemon' rationalization and 'sour grapes' rationalization. In the case of 'sweet lemon' rationalization, the explanation makes the subject out to be better than it is. This is one of the problems of asking experienced teachers to give feedback on extended courses they have attended. If a year's secondment and a great deal of effort are put into a course and it turns out to be a dud, it is difficult to admit that all the time and effort has been wasted. 'Oh yes, it was very interesting. I learned some useful things.' If pressed for how it was useful, it may be difficult to be specific.

In the case of 'sour grapes' rationalization, if you have spent a great deal of time and effort on an extended course and then fail it, it is easy to argue that it was not a good course, that the teaching was bad and that the marking was unfair. This is a common reaction from students in school to activities they do not do well. Fail in maths and 'maths is lousy'. No good at games and 'football is a waste of time'.

With the development of courses in social and personal education, students are being invited to examine both their feelings and behaviour and then to try out new ways of relating. There is, inevitably, some degree of anxiety and threat in these activities, which is often dealt with by rationalization. 'This is stupid.' 'Why can't we do some proper work?' Similar responses come from experienced teachers when they are asked to undergo the same type of activities in in-service training. 'I've done this sort of exercise before.' 'I didn't come here to play silly games.' 'I have to relate to people all day, there's no point in me coming on a course to practise it.' This type of comment often comes from the people who are least skilled in inter-personal relations, which may explain in some measure why the exercises are threatening to them.

In any staffroom in the country, rationalizations can be heard which often provide a block to effective problem solving.

'With children from this sort of home background and lack of parental support, you can't expect to teach them anything.'

A defence mechanism, which is similar to a rationalization, occurs when a person deals with social and emotional problems on a purely theoretical, academic or intellectual plane. Predictably, this is called intellectualization.

This is not to say that it is wrong to consider issues intellectually, but if this is the only mode in which a person can operate, then essential aspects of communication are being missed out. 'My job is to teach my subject and not to sort out kids' emotional problems.' In staffroom discussions, the intellectualizer will see any emotional statement as 'irrational', and it would appear that his own emotions are so dangerously near to the surface, that statements of feeling have to be denigrated. When such a person is taken on in rational argument and loses, he may, paradoxically, have a temper tantrum.

Compensation and substitution

Most of us are threatened by our own inadequacies and usually we behave in ways which prevent other people being aware of them. A more constructive approach to inadequacy is to work hard at becoming better than average in the particular area in which you feel inadequate. Thus, compensation, which is described as a defence mechanism, can produce highly positive results for the person concerned. The classical example usually quoted is of Demosthenes, the ancient Greek, who stammered as a child. He would go down to the beach, fill his mouth with pebbles and speak against the noise of the sea. He went on to become a greater orator. A friend suffered from vertigo, which did not fit his masculine self-image and he would deliberately put himself in situations which involved coping with heights. Some rock climbers also report having suffered from vertigo.

Students of average ability work extremely hard and succeed academically. This becomes a danger if they over-reach themselves and find themselves on a course of higher education which is too difficult for them. Some forms of compensation are seen as undesirable, as when girls who perceive themselves as unattractive become promiscuous, and when children who feel inadequate start to bully younger children. Most of the time, however, forms of compensation are to the advantage of the person concerned. Indeed this process is involved in many forms of personal growth.

Another approach to dealing with the threat of personal inadequacies is to give up on the activity that usually ends in failure and substitute for it something that tends to bring success. A student who is not very good at sport might give up trying and concentrate on academic work. This process could happen in reverse. These forms of substitution may produce good results in the chosen area, but can produce an unbalanced approach to life. This is particularly serious when the individual concerned becomes intensely involved in an introverted activity to cope with fears of social situations.

Simon spent all his spare time near railway lines, recording not only the numbers of trains, but also of carriages and trucks. He rarely even spoke to members of his adolescent peer group. His academic work enabled him to go to university, but a nervous breakdown prevented him from completing the course. One of the writers used the example of men who spent hours working on their model train lay-outs, rather than deal with the problems of their marriages. Unfortunately, in every group of experienced teachers, there were always one or two who confessed, shame-facedly, to having an elaborate lay-out in their garages or lofts.

Reaction formation

This is a defence mechanism in which the threat of unacceptable feelings, thoughts and impulses are dealt with by exaggerating the opposite of them. This may be done so effectively that the offending thoughts and feelings are completely repressed and the person concerned is only aware of the feelings that are acceptable to him.

This process probably begins during the socialization of the young child. The example usually given is of the toddler who acquires a younger brother or sister. Having lost the exclusive attention of his mother, he has strong feelings of hatred and may even wish that his rival were dead. He soon learns from his parents that these feelings are not acceptable and that the offending baby should be loved. The child then expresses feelings of love, but the repressed feelings often leak out. The little boy next door was once seen advancing on his younger brother in the pram. As he went to stroke his hands he said, 'Ah! The lovely little baba!', and then dug his nails into the baby's hand, making them bleed before he could be restrained. Emotional leaks of this nature are much rarer in later life, but they sometimes erupt with deadly violence, usually within families.

One of the writers was once being shown around a comprehensive school by the head of department of a student teacher who had been placed at the school. Turning a corner, we came across two students kissing in an alcove. The head of department directed a torrent of abuse at them, which seemed somewhat excessive at the time. At the end of the term the student teacher complained of the unwanted sexual advances of the head of department. It is probably worth examining closely the issues that make you critical or trigger you into giving moral homilies.

It is particularly worth examining the criticisms that involve considerable emotion. Most honest parents will admit that they tell their own children off for faults that they themselves are guilty of and that these are the ones that they notice. The teacher who confiscates a dirty magazine with a reprimand and then has a quiet read in private is unfortunately a reality.

This mechanism is best understood by people who have given up smoking. Both of us gave up some years ago and now we are highly critical of others who smoke and see it as a dirty, filthy, antisocial habit. Prior to starting smoking, we were not concerned about others indulging. This would suggest that our current criticism is a way of holding down a strong need.

The students in school provide abundant examples of the reaction formations acquired during their upbringing; excessive primness to avoid the guilt of burgeoning sexuality, an exaggerated masculinity to avoid feelings that might be seen as feminine, a quiet nature to hide violent aggressive feelings against authority figures and so on.

Projection

Patterns of behaviour which could be described as reaction formation merge into those which could be described as projection. When a person has thoughts, feelings, impulses and patterns of behaviour which are unacceptable, he may blame other people for having the same patterns, often when there is no evidence for it. We protect ourselves from the threat of the unacceptable side of ourselves by projecting it onto other people. A common projection is to criticize other people for the way they go about furthering their careers when, in fact, most staff tend to be concerned about this. In effect, we see the faults in others that are also true in ourselves.

This process was demonstrated experimentally by Sears (1936), who asked a group of students to rate each other on the traits of stinginess, obstinacy, disorderliness and bashfulness. Students who consistently used higher ratings on any of these traits were judged by most of their peers to be high on those specific characteristics.

In school, the tell-tale is invariably a student who is always getting into trouble. The boy who fails to be selected for the football team may blame the games teacher for having favourites, when he himself would like to be the teacher's favourite. The child who is continually involved in fights invariably comes up with the excuse, 'He hit me first'.

Perhaps the most insidious form of projection in the school setting is where individuals project the negative aspects of themselves onto minority groups, particularly racial minority groups. These projections distort perception so much that it is often impossible to see anything good about a person who is strikingly different from yourself.

A number of clinical tests have been designed to manipulate a person into projecting repressed thoughts and feelings onto what appear to be neutral situations. Perhaps the best known of these is the Rorschach Ink Blot Test. Here the subject is asked to say what images can be seen in a series of random patterns of ink on cards. These are produced by folding over sheets of paper with ink spilled onto them. There are set interpretations for specific responses. The assumption is made that the respondent is projecting unconscious thoughts and feelings onto the ink blots.

Another well known projection test is the Thematic Apperception Test, in which the subject is asked to write a short story about one of several of a series of pictures taken from magazines in the 1930s. The subject is invited to write what he imagines the people in the picture are thinking and feeling before, during and after the event in the picture. When one of the writers was introduced to this test, he hammed up a really exaggerated story as he knew the intention behind the test. On reflection, however, the story still included some of the main themes in his life which he was not normally willing to make public.

Doll play is an approach which is sometimes used with children who have been referred with psychological problems. Here children are invited to play with dolls which match the people in their families. Sometimes the children mete out extreme violence to the dolls which represent their parents or siblings. These feelings may never be expressed in any other way, and the assumption is made that the children are projecting unacceptable and inexpressible feelings onto the dolls.

Violet Oaklander (1978) provided moving accounts of how children of any age seem to project thoughts and feelings into any creative activity, such as drawing, fantasy writing, drama and so on. She takes the point of view, and we would agree with her, that no one can interpret children's creative work. She demonstrates how the possibilities for interpretation can be drawn skilfully from the person concerned. Many children seem to be harbouring feelings of sadness, hurt and anger which are difficult to express publicly. Creative activities in school provide an opportunity for these feelings to be leaked out. We will take up this issue again in the section on fantasy in chapter five. We would stress, however, that it is important for teachers not to project onto children's projections, which is likely to be happening when attempts are made to interpret.

Projection is an extremely common defence mechanism. As with reaction formations, many of the criticisms we level at colleagues and students relate to issues we could be guilty of ourselves. Criticisms of head teachers and heads of departments often reflect the critic's own distorted feelings about authority. We project into our fantasies, daydreams and dreams. We may even project our own state of mind and health in the passing comments that we make to each other when we meet in the morning. 'You look a bit under the weather.' 'You are looking really well today.' Occasionally you may have had the experience of receiving conflicting comments within a very short space of time. Some people even project onto inanimate objects. Having clumsily tripped over a chair and feeling rather stupid, you might complain about the clumsy stupid chair.

* Ask the group to:

'Spend five minutes recalling the behaviour which annoyed you in both colleagues and students in your teaching experience. Write down your three main criticisms of colleagues and your three main criticisms of students.'

'Now form groups of four and share to what extent you feel that the same criticisms apply to yourself. If you feel they don't apply in any way, share how you would feel if you did indulge in that behaviour.'

Our projections onto other people usually contain a degree of truth in them. However, we pick up on the faults in other people that are true for ourselves and get upset because they are issues which are important to us. Most projections are not very helpful because they distort the communication process and prevent us from having a true picture of ourselves. The business of projection becomes really serious when there is no truth in the projection. The person concerned could then be described as deluded and suffering from paranoia. A member of staff might imagine that the senior staff are plotting to ruin his career. Many racist comments are paranoid. Occasionally a head teacher who isolates himself in the staffroom has the time to build up delusions about his staff.

Withdrawal

A simple way of escaping from a threat is to withdraw from it. When the going is rough for some children, they simply run out of the school. Some students find school such a painful experience that they refuse to attend. Some teachers have to retire to the staffroom when the stress of the classroom is too much and may even find it too difficult to go into work each morning.

Forms of withdrawal can take place without leaving the situation. The shy child will go out of her way to avoid social contact and may become invisible to the teacher. The day-dreaming described earlier could be seen as a form of withdrawal. One of the writers had experience of a child who withdrew from all verbal communication for five years of secondary education. She was only heard to utter one monosyllable – 'No'. Yet she talked at home. Running away from problems is not socially acceptable and if it involves not turning up for work, then eventually the person involved will get the sack.

A much more socially acceptable way of escaping is to become ill, to develop a psychosomatic complaint. This is the body's way of dealing with psychological stress. Medical experts have widely differing views regarding psychosomatic illness, some believing that virtually all illness is psychosomatic, while others do not believe that it exists. Most doctors would take a middle view. It is generally accepted that a number of specific complaints are stress-related and this will be taken up again in chapter six.

Both of the writers used to wait until half-term or holiday time before becoming ill with cold or 'flu. It was as if a few days in bed were needed, but over-conditioned consciences would not allow this to happen in term time, and, possibly at an unconscious level, waited until the end of term to succumb to a virus. This is a relatively simple use of psychosomatic illness. Some forms of cancer and heart disease are thought to be stress-related and here the outcome of the defence might be fatal.

The categories of defence mechanisms we have discussed could be extended, but we have chosen those which contribute most to the breakdown of communication in educational institutions. The exact labels are not important and, as we have suggested, a pattern of behaviour could be put into more than one category. It is important to consider these issues, as defence mechanisms are commonplace in educational settings, both among students and staff, and an awareness of what is going on, particularly in your own behaviour, is a necessary condition for change.

Change is difficult because many of these mechanisms are operating at a low level of awareness – some would argue, at an unconscious level. We would prefer the notion of relative levels of awareness, as the unconscious implies a place where things are stored away in an all or nothing fashion. To have the use of a defence mechanism pointed out can be amusing, provided the threat to the self is not too great.

Forms of experiential learning, such as the exercises given in this book, can help a person become more aware of the ways he defends himself. Defensive behaviour is brought to the surface in a powerful way in the type of training group described in chapter seven and in any situation where the participants are open and direct in sharing feedback about each other's behaviour.

If you are asked about the ways in which you defend yourself, you will probably give a fairly accurate reply, even though you may not have been aware of your behaviour at the time.

* Ask the members of the group to read a copy of the following questions and then choose one of the alternatives.

When you find yourself in a difficult social or inter-personal situation do you:

1　Take the first opportunity to leave the situation?
2　Become verbally aggressive and attack the other person/people?
3　Become very calm and rational and explain the situation away?
4　Blame the other person/people for causing the problem?
5　Drift off into a fantasy world of your own?
6　Talk continuously and chatter in a distracting manner?

Divide the group into subgroups of those people who ticked the same category, and ask them to discuss the advantages and disadvantages of behaving in this way. Arrange for each group to have a spokesperson to report back to the whole group at the end of the session.

Working at defence mechanisms in an experiential mode is probably one of the best approaches to becoming less defensive yourself. We would suggest that there is no point in trying to teach or to tell people such as colleagues and students to be less defensive. It is, however, possible to behave in ways which will encourage less defensive behaviour in the other person. This can be brought about by the procedures described in the next two chapters. To conclude this chapter, we will suggest patterns of behaviour which prompt defensive reactions from colleagues and students, and you can decide for yourself to what extent you are able to reduce your use of them. These are adapted from Gordon's (1974) *Teacher Effectiveness Training* and he called them 'roadblocks to communication':

1 Giving orders. 'Just get on with your work and stop arguing with me.'
2 Threatening. 'If you talk once more, I'm going to send you to the Head.'
3 Moralizing. 'A boy of your age should be able to behave in a more mature manner.'
4 Giving advice. 'If I were you, I would keep away from those girls in 5c, they will only lead you into trouble.'
5 Lecturing. 'That sounds reasonable, but let's look at the way it should be. It's important to get it right.'
6 Judging. 'This is the worst class I have ever had to teach.'
7 Labelling. 'He has always been a backward reader, I don't think there is much we can do for him.'
8 Interpreting. 'I can tell you're not telling the truth because you can't look me in the eye.'
9 Praising. 'You've been doing really well recently, I am sure you will be able to do the work if you try.'
10 Using sympathy. 'I can understand that you feel bad about not getting into college, but you'll feel differently once you have been working for a few weeks.'
11 Interrogating. 'What on earth do you think you're doing? Why haven't you done your homework?'
12 Distracting and using sarcasm. 'I don't think we want to hear about that.' 'It's nice to see that you have honoured us with your presence today.'

The content of this list is, in fact, the stock-in-trade of many teachers. It is difficult not to slip into these patterns given the existing conditions and expectations in schools. They are so common in schools and in everyday communication, that it is unlikely that the student teacher will avoid building them into his repertoire. Most of the available models of experienced teaching involve the use of forms of these roadblocks when problem situations arise.

We are involved in a paradox here, because we are giving advice and lecturing in suggesting that these patterns are unhelpful and that the suggestions in the next two chapters involve better ways of communicating. What we would suggest is that you give the alternatives a fair trial and then decide for yourself which way of relating is the most effective. More advice!

Summary

In this chapter, we have examined three contrasting but overlapping approaches to the self. There is now conclusive evidence that a good self-concept is an important variable related to academic achievement and general adjustment to education. There is also some evidence that teachers with a positive self-concept also encourage a positive self-concept in their pupils. This would support the idea that developing a positive self-concept should play an important part in both schooling and teacher training. Forms of humanistic and affective education, using experiential learning, have developed a considerable body of material which is designed to foster a more positive attitude in the self.

Personal construct psychology provides a sophisticated analysis of how the self is reflected in the way other people are perceived. Other people are construed along dimensions that are important to the construer. An examination of ways of construing in a group brings out the unique way we each perceive other people and how limited most of us are in the way we do this.

Defence mechanisms provide a useful model of the way the self is defended from threat. These patterns of defending are extremely common and contribute to distortions and breakdowns in communication.

Connections

A consideration of the self is central to the phenomenological point of view set out in the introduction. The way we construct reality is central to the way we perceive ourselves. Our perception of reality could, indeed, be seen as a projection of ourselves. As we grow up, we internalize our experience, particularly of other people, and later development becomes a transaction between these earlier experiences and our present experience. The extent to which we perceive ourselves to be in control of our lives is an important aspect of our self-concept.

Our individual ways of perceiving other people are the basis of personal construct psychology, which provides strong support for taking a phenomenological approach to human relations. The counselling or communications skills elaborated in the next chapter are based on the premise that it is important to arrive at an understanding of how the other person perceives the world, and also to facilitate their understanding their own perceptions. This approach, developed from the work of Carl Rogers (1951) and Gerard Egan (1975), is also in the humanistic/phenomenological tradition.

Hopefully, the same communication skills will result in a reduction of defensive behaviour and an increase in skilful self-disclosure. Again, this may produce a reduction in the experience of stress.

The next chapter will examine these skills and how they can be put into effect.

4 Communication skills for the classroom and pastoral care

The coffee bar in the School of Education at Nottingham University used to employ a woman who was often seen to be involved in deep conversations with her customers. Almost unawares, the customers would find themselves talking more and more about their lives, sometimes going into intimate personal problems. Her skill was in paying close attention to what the other person was saying, demonstrating that she understood what life was like for this person and did not break in with her own issues. In effect, she was a good listener and was demonstrating the skills of an effective counsellor.

Some individuals seem to be highly effective helpers and communicators without any training at all. Perhaps the only requirement for the successful counsellor is to be fully integrated and to be able to relate empathically to the other person. Concepts such as 'empathy' and 'fully integrated' are difficult to define and yet it does seem that some people can be highly effective helpers and communicators without any training at all. (See Buber, 1947; Rogers, 1961; Brandon, 1976; and Murgatroyd, 1985.) Conversely, some individuals who have had extensive training in counselling skills still fail to make effective human contact with others. We have had the experience of going to conferences of experienced counsellors, most of whom are a delight to be with. There is however the odd exception who does not seem to be able to indulge in a casual conversation and appears to be stuck in a stilted counsellor role.

In this chapter, we will use the terms counselling skills, inter-personal skills, communication skills, helping skills and social skills as overlapping and possibly interchangeable categories. The skills used by the effective counsellor are useful in any inter-personal situation, including teaching and relating to colleagues. This is not to say that these skills are used a great deal by the average teacher. Indeed, most honest practitioners would confess to the excessive use of Gordon's (1974) 'roadblocks to communication' described in the previous chapter. If as a teacher you see your job as largely imparting information to the students, then the skills described here will interfere with that task. You may, justifiably, complain that the teacher's day does not permit the time for extended counselling sessions. We would suggest that the skills can be used in single sentences 'on the run' in the corridor and as part of the normal transactions of classroom teaching.

At the time of writing there are few full-time school counsellors and their numbers are declining. This means that the responsibility for this function falls on the teachers with a pastoral role, which includes all teachers. We will be examining counselling skills to the extent that they are useful to the teacher whether dealing with staff or students on a one-to-one basis or with classroom groups.

There are a large number of theories of counselling (Corey, 1977; Patterson, 1980; Nelson-Jones, 1983) most of which include ideas which are potentially useful to the teacher. We will limit our discussion to the ideas that have developed out of the work of Carl Rogers (1951) which he has related to psychotherapy, counselling and interaction in educational settings. We have limited ourselves to Rogers' ideas because they dominate the practice of counselling and interpersonal skills training.

Rogers stresses three core conditions that are necessary for effective helping. In a recent outline of these conditions (Rogers, 1983) they are described as:

1   Realness or genuineness, where the helper presents herself as a real person, without any front or façade. She is in contact with her feelings and is able to communicate them when it is appropriate. This gives the teacher permission to express a range of emotions: anger, disappointment, joy, excitement, boredom, as they occur. Many teachers present themselves according to their notion of a stereotypical teacher and it is not difficult for students to see through this phony image. Perhaps their inner feelings leak out in non-verbal behaviour.

2   Prizing, acceptance, trust. This involves caring for the other person and accepting them in their own right. Acceptance applies to both the positive and negative aspects of the other person's behaviour.

This is a difficult quality to maintain in the face of insolence, anti-social behaviour or apathy.

3   Empathic understanding, which involves being able to appreciate what life is like for the other person; to be able figuratively to stand in their shoes.

These notions have been criticized because they are difficult to define and in particular, difficult to measure. The concept of empathy has come in for particular criticism (Gladstein, 1977), but the criticisms are largely directed at studies which use dubious scales for measuring empathy.

The best test of these ideas is in practice, and the skills elaborated in the rest of this chapter provide ways of demonstrating the core conditions. Expression of feeling, self-disclosure and confrontation are indications of realness. Reflection of content and feeling are a strong indication of empathy. The fact of supporting a client-centred approach and making the effort to use client-centred skills is an indication of prizing the other person and accepting that she has the resources for her own development. The reader is recommended to try out the skills and then make her own evaluation of the relevance of the core conditions.

Basic attention

The process of attending to another person is often interrupted by your own thoughts, needs, problems and feelings. The research on attention demonstrates the difficulty of concentrating on two complex verbal tasks at the same time. If you are rehearsing what you want to say next, it is difficult to attend to what the other person is saying. In fact, if you have something you are burning to say, you are likely to interrupt the other speaker before she is finished. Similar problems occur if you are trying to intepret the other person's behaviour, thinking about similar problems in your own life, or struggling to cope with your anxiety about the interview.

You may have shared this experience in staff meetings, where you have been concentrating on formulating something really impressive to say on the current issue. Having spoken, you find that the previous speaker had said exactly the same thing, but the words had been blotted out by your earlier concentration.

* This exercise looks at how well a person can cope with two verbal messages at the same time.

   Divide the group into threes. Ask two members to sit on each side of the third and then talk continuously, giving advice to the person in the middle about how to be a better person. What they say doesn't have to be true but it is important to keep talking.

   After five minutes, invite the second member of the trio to go in the middle and give the same instructions, followed by the third.

   After the third five minute session, invite the groups to spend five minutes sharing their experience.

Even when you are motivated to attend to the other person, it is inevitable that your mind will wander from time to time, unless you have extraordinary powers of concentration. The tasks which are set to concentrate the mind for meditation bring this out very clearly. Sit, with a pencil in your hand and try to concentrate on nothing but the feel of the breath passing through the nostrils, and make a mark each time you are aware of your mind wandering. It may be a salutary experience. Bandler and Grinder (1979) wrote about 'going into uptime' when you are with another person. This involved just taking in the other person as a sensory experience, without indulging in any thinking. An impossible ideal, but a delightful image to use when you are relating to another person.

So, it would appear that the conversations going on inside your own head can have a negative effect on attempts to communicate with students, staff and parents. The complaint, 'He never seems to hear what I say', is not uncommon and may literally be true. Your own angry, depressed or worried thoughts can dominate your attention. Because of the redundancy in most of our speech, it is possible to keep a conversation going with minimal attention, but the lack of involvement is usually picked up by the other person. Hopefully, people who know you well will tell you when you are only going through the motions of attending.

Having had this issue brought to your attention, you are unlikely to become a perfect listener overnight, as everyone has lapses of attention. Hopefully, however, you will notice these lapses of attention more often. If you find you cannot concentrate, it is probably better to be honest with the other person. 'I've got too much on my mind at the moment, perhaps it would be better to continue this discussion another time.' This is more likely to engender trust than trying to pretend.

Posture

Many of the postures that we think make us look relaxed are really quite harmful for the body. They seem to be relaxed because we have adopted them for many years and are old habits. A good example is leaning back in a chair with fingers interlaced behind the neck. A colleague manages to fold his legs twice, sitting with his arms folded so that the hands disappear under his armpits. Try this position and see how it feels.

Observations of successful counsellors have produced the following guidelines:

1   Maintain a relaxed alertness, with the body leaning slightly forward. Face the other person squarely with the arms open and unfolded and try to judge an appropriate physical distance.

2   Keep effective eye contact with the other person. A hard stare can be disturbing. Looking away or out of the window for long periods of time implies disinterest. A soft, involved eye contact, with the focus occasionally moving away, appears to be the most helpful. (Henley, 1977; Weitz, 1979.)

3   Move in synchrony with the other person. This is difficult to define, but avoid excessive fidgeting or sitting completely still.

4   Avoid physical barriers such as a desk or the arm or back of a chair.

5   Maintain a relaxed breathing pattern.

Trying this out for the first time can seem to be very uncomfortable and a common complaint is that it is impossible to relax in such a position. It is, however, more important to consider what the other person feels about your posture. Invariably it gives the impression that you are paying more attention to what is being said.

* Divide the group into pairs. Ask them to divide into 'talker' and 'listener'. Then give the 'talker' five minutes to discuss one of the topics in the Appendix. The listener is to respond in any way that seems appropriate.

While the pairs are talking, draw some stick figures on a board showing some of the postures adopted by group members. At the end of five minutes draw the group members' attention to these drawings and describe the optimal posture. Then ask them to continue the discussion with the listener using the optimal posture.

After three minutes ask the listeners to sit at right angles to the talkers and make no eye contact. Continue for a further three minutes.

Reverse roles and spend five minutes with the new listener in the optimal posture, followed by three minutes in the right angled position.

Form fours and spend ten minutes sharing the experience.

Initially, the ideal posture may seem a little stilted and, indeed, moving out of it occasionally may even be an improvement. The open posture can be adapted for a standing position, which is quite a common situation for teachers. However, since teachers are often taller than their students, this can be intimidating and it may be worth trying to arrange a quiet place to sit if delicate issues are being dealt with.

* A useful and often entertaining way of learning about interpersonal skills is to exaggerate bad practice. This exercise can help lighten the heaviness of continual skills practice.

Divide the group into fives. Select one person in each group to spend three minutes telling the rest what a wonderful person he is. The rest of the group have to ignore him in any way they choose, but preferably in ways that they use in their normal lives. The talker can do anything to persuade them to listen. Rotate the role of talker every three minutes.

Minimal encouragement and silence

One caricature of the non-directive counsellor is of a person who says nothing herself, and whenever there is an awkward gap in the conversation goes 'Um-hmmm'. The caricature is unfair, because this can be a highly effective way of demonstrating that you are paying attention to what the other person is saying, so long as this is not the only intervention used. As we discussed in chapter two, the smallest of cues can be rewarding and will tend to encourage the behaviour that is going on at the time. Other cues will have the same effect as is illustrated in the following exercise.

* Divide the group into pairs in which one is the 'listener' and the other is the 'talker'. Give the 'listener' a sheet, which is not to be shown to the 'talker', with the following instructions:

   'Conduct an interview just using minimal encouragement, for example:

   head nodding, smiling, "um-hmmm", "yes", "do go on" or repeating a word or two from the last statement made by the other person.'

   Give the 'talker' a topic which is likely to produce some awkward pauses, such as, 'Talk about some of the mistakes you have made in your life and what you would like to have done instead.'

   Suggest that they talk for six minutes, with the listener following the instructions.

   Then reverse roles, but give the next 'listener' the following new instructions:

   'Conduct an interview, but always wait five seconds before you respond to a pause.

   Then only use minimal encouragement, for example:

   head nodding, smiling, "um-hmmm", "yes", "do go on", or repeating a word or two from the last statement made by the other person.'

   Use the same topic and suggest that they talk for six minutes with the 'listener' following the instructions.

   Then move into fours and spend ten minutes sharing the experience of the two interviewers.

Ivey and Authier (1978) quoted evidence that inexperienced counsellors responded much more quickly than experienced counsellors, often before the other person had completely finished what they wanted to say. The use of minimal encouragement led to longer periods of talking from the other person and if the interviewer always waited five full seconds before responding, then the other person initiated more discussion in 25 per cent of instances.

Some people appear to be fearful of silences in a conversation and have to rush in to fill the gaps. Clearly this is not helpful to the inarticulate student who is struggling to find the words to express himself, and the teacher's ability to tolerate pauses can be a useful skill for facilitating learning in the classroom as well as in inter-personal or counselling situations. Having our sentences completed for us can be a very frustrating experience.

Sometimes the person you are interviewing may be so talkative that it is difficult to get in a single word. Of course, this will not stop you from smiling or nodding. This continuous talking does defeat the purpose of the exercise described above, but it can give the 'listener' the opportunity to discover that you can encourage the other person without saying anything at all. If they do talk continuously, then an intuitive decision will have to be made as to whether or not it is more helpful to break their flow.

Open and closed questions

Many teachers use questions excessively and students have the feeling that they are being 'grilled' or 'interrogated'. It is, however, difficult to take a large class without asking any questions at all. Some teachers complain that they find it difficult to encourage students to join in a discussion and yet they often only ask questions that invite mono-syllabic replies.

We examine the practical outcomes from the use of different forms of question in the next chapter on how language is used. Indeed, a question could be defined as open or closed in terms of its practical outcome. Some questions do invite a 'yes' or 'no' response or a piece of factual information, such as the other person's name.

Open questions often begin with 'what', 'how', 'why', 'could', or 'would'.

'What' questions tend to produce facts and information.

'How' questions tend to generate processes and feelings.

'Why' questions tend to produce reasons, motives and explanations.

'Could' or 'would' questions ask the other person to explore their potential.

An interesting point of view taken from Gestalt therapy is that 'why' questions are potentially embarrassing, in that many people are unaware of the motives and reasons for their behaviour. This is not to say that 'why' questions are not to be used, but they may block the other person from saying much more (Perls, 1969). This notion is developed in the next chapter.

An apparently open question may still produce a short answer, such as 'Don't know', or even silence. The following exercise will enable the examination of the outcomes of different questions. Asking the appropriate question is described by Ivey and Authier (1978) as 'an open invitation to talk'.

* Divide the group into threes, with each person designated as either 'questioner', 'talker' or 'observer'. Invite the 'questioner' to find out as much as possible about the 'talker's' educational experience by asking appropriate questions, while the 'observer' records the exchange on the following sheet:

Exact words used in the question	Outcome in terms of the length and quality of response	Is this an 'open' or 'closed' question?

Reflection of content

One of the indications of accurate empathy (Egan, 1975) is the ability to feed back to the other person the main content of what she has been saying. Rogers (1951) played an important part in the development of this approach, which is a way of responding to the other person without judging or evaluating what has been said. It also provides a clear indication of listening.

Most of the skills training manuals emphasize the reflection of both content and feeling and it is difficult to separate them. It is, however, useful to deal with each in turn as a training exercise.

It is important to avoid merely repeating the exact words spoken by the other person. This is described as 'parroting' and can give the impression of insincerity. An unfair parody of the non-directive counsellor is of a person who simply restates what has just been said. On the other hand repeating the last phrase of what the other person has said can be helpful, as we discussed under minimal encouragement. In fact, after exercises where one member of a pair merely parrots back what the other person has been saying, the person talking often reports the experience as being helpful and gives a useful opportunity to reflect on what is being said.

Student: 'My life is in a mess, I can't settle down to work and I have failed my exams.'

Teacher: 'You feel your life is a mess, you can't settle down to work and you have failed your exams.'

It is certainly worth trying as an exercise in order to get some feedback regarding the effect on the other person.

* Divide the group into pairs of which one is the 'talker' and the other is the 'listener'. Give the 'talker' a topic from the Appendix and suggest that the 'listener' parrots back what is being said.
    Reverse roles after five minutes and after the second session, spend five minutes sharing the experience.

Some people find having their words parroted extremely irritating. Others do not even notice what is going on and feel that the other person had been listening carefully to what they have been saying. Often, too much has been said for every phrase to be fed back, so some form of paraphrase or reflection of content is more appropriate.

Teacher: 'My wife is pregnant again. That's okay, but we need a bigger house and there is no way on my salary I can move unless I get another job. It looks as though the head of department will be here for another twenty years.'

Colleague: 'So you are going to have much heavier financial commitments and you don't anticipate any promotion in the near future.'

Parent: 'James is really making life difficult for me. His father is never at home and I feel I just can't cope.'

Teacher: 'So difficulties at home are getting you down.'

Accurate paraphrase helps to give a better understanding of the other person's experience and the way he views the world. It is, however, important to be aware that different individuals have different meanings for the same words and phrases. We have discussed how Kelly's (1955) work illustrated the idiosyncratic ways that individuals construed their experience. It is easy for the teacher to believe that his way of construing is the 'correct' one.

This leads to the problem of distortion. The person reflecting content may not get the paraphrase quite right. This may confuse the other person, he may go off at a tangent or he may even accept the counsellor's distortion as an accurate reflection of his experience. Often non-verbal cues are given off which indicate that something has gone wrong. Distortion is a difficult problem to deal with and it is important to create a relationship that will permit the other person to correct you.

A person in distress may present himself in a confused and rambling fashion and the teacher may be equally confused about what is being said. It is easy to pretend that you have understood the other person's statement, but at the same time, insincerity may be communicated. An admission of confusion may be a clear indication of honesty and may contribute a great deal to enhancing the relationship.

Reflection of content can bring a degree of order to a long rambling series of statements. This does mean that the teacher is helping to determine which areas will be developed.

Once the skill of reflecting content has been developed, it can become a mechanical affair. Computers have been programmed to reflect content, using fixed formulae to re-order the meaning of what has been said. Interestingly, people do find this computerized approach useful. Indeed, if the process of reflecting content is new to you, it is worth being fairly mechanical in the practice of the skill, such as in the use of the following exercise:

* Divide the group into pairs and give them each copies of the two lists given below. Invite them to take turns reading a statement from the list so that the other person can role-play a teacher reflecting back the content of what has been said. Ask them to discuss how well it was done after each attempt at précis.

For staff

1   'It's impossible to develop group work in my class because we just don't have the resources.'

2   'You know I'm getting pretty tired of being a nobody in this staffroom. I've been here longer than an awful lot of these people, but I never get promotion.'

3   'This child is completely disruptive and I won't have him in my class any more.'

4   'I'm feeling really depressed. Somebody hinted to me today that I'm not pulling my weight. They said there'd been talk about me sloping off early in the afternoon if I have a free period.'

5   'Nothing is being done to help the brighter children in this school. All resources are being given to the lower streams.'

6   'I don't know how to say this, but ... I've fallen for this girl in the sixth form and I ... told her ... the other day. Now I have the feeling that the sixth-form girls are giggling every time I walk past them. The Head's sure to find out.'

7   'It is useless to complain to the Head because he never does anything. All he does is give them a cup of tea and a chat.'

8   'My head of department is a real martinet. He always fixes the time-table so he has the good classes and I get the rotten ones. I feel really resentful.'

9   'Forget the idealism, the important thing in this job is to survive. It's us or them.'

10   'Batten down the hatches, here comes Mr Bloody Self Importance. He should really see what he looks like in a mirror, that man.'

11   (Head to member of staff.) 'I insist on boys wearing ties in my school so I'm damned sure that I'll have members of staff wearing ties too.'

12   'It's taking me a lot to say this, but I have to speak to someone. I can't control my classes ... this morning they had me in tears ... I can't go on.'

For students

1   'Mr Barton is always picking on me. Every time I move or say anything he jumps down my throat. I'm not going to woodwork any more.'

2   'I don't want to talk to you about myself. What happens

between me and my friends is my business. I hardly know you. Why should you have to know anything about my life?'

3   'She's got it in for me. All the other kids mess around and I always get told off.'

4   'All you ever do is tell me off. I can't remember a single time when you did anything but complain about me. Well I couldn't care less what you think.'

5   'I don't like being in Mrs Drew's class, she always makes us work.'

6   'I'm really bored with school. When I wake up in the morning and think about getting up for that, it makes me feel sick and I just turn over and doze off again.'

7   'I won't be able to do my homework because my mum is going to take me to my nan's tonight.'

8   'I have this lad who keeps wanting to take me out. He seems nice, but I keep having this funny feeling that all he wants to do is get me to go to bed with him.'

9   'My dad says I don't have to do homework, because it's a waste of time.'

10   'You're just like all the other teachers, a big phoney. You think you're good, think you can tell me what to do, push me around! Well you can't and you can piss off!'

11   'She always loves to call for me, but she didn't come today. Then in form period, she sat next to somebody else and started passing notes about me saying I went out with her boyfriend.'

12   'I just can't understand the lessons in physics. I try, but I can't. Now the physics teacher is sending me to the Head for wasting time – he says I don't work in his lessons, but I do!'

The teacher's skilful use of reflecting content can be helpful in what are seen as difficult, confrontational or discipline situations. Understandably, this is often the last thing that comes to mind when you are angry, affronted or threatened. The process of reflecting content in a situation like this takes the focus of attention away from the teacher and onto the student. Some of the examples in the previous exercise provide the possibility for a role-play involving a reflecting response to a confrontational situation:

Student: 'What do you keep picking on me for! The rest of them are always messing about and you never tell them off.'

Teacher: 'So Paul, you think I am always telling you off for things that the others get away with?'

Student: 'I hate maths. It's stupid and boring. I can't do it and I'm not doing the homework.'

Teacher: 'You're not getting on with your maths and you want to give up altogether.'

These responses certainly do not fit the conventional reactions of teachers to the students' responses. At least, they open up the possibility of a dialogue, rather than an emotional confrontation.

To conclude this section, we will offer the classical listening skills exercise which is a source of learning even for people who have done it many times.

* Divide the group up into sixes and ask each six to sit in a circle. Ask the group to discuss, 'Acceptable forms of punishment in school'. The rule for the group is that the person who wants to speak next, must first paraphrase what the previous speaker has said, and the previous speaker must agree that it is an accurate paraphrase.

  Allow the groups to discuss in this manner for twenty minutes, and then give them ten minutes to share the experience.

Expression of feeling

We are deliberately including this section between 'reflection of content' and 'reflection of feeling', as it seems a sensible assumption that you must have a good understanding of the expression of feeling before you can accurately reflect it. If as a group, you have been working steadily at skills training, then some exercises designed to encourage the expression of feeling will provide a welcome change. Ivey and Authier (1978) quote research which suggests that the trainee counsellor can help another person to deal with his feelings, to the degree to which he is skilful at expressing his own feelings. The expression of feeling throws you into sharp relief as a person and inevitably will give you more impact in a teaching situation.

Many people find it difficult to put their feelings into words. Most of us have been brought up in an education system that devalues feeling and punishes the expression of it. Johnson and Johnson (1982) pointed out that Sanskrit is reputed to have more than nine hundred words expressing feeling states, but English has fewer than fifty. They go on to list eight ways in which the expression of feeling can become distorted. These are very similar to Gordon's (1974) 'roadblocks to communication', described in the previous chapter. They are so common in teaching situations as to warrant the repetition. In each case, the second statement is offered as an improvement.

1   *Labels:* 'You are silly, irresponsible and a disgrace to your class,' compared with, 'I am angry with the way you keep disrupting the class.'
2   *Commands:* 'Get off my back,' compared with, 'I'm fed up with you criticizing my lessons.'
3   *Questions:* 'Do you do any homework for the other teachers?' compared with, 'I don't like you to miss out on your homework without discussing it with me.'
4   *Accusations:* 'You never give me any help,' compared with, 'I am frustrated that you don't give me any feedback on my teaching.'
5   *Sarcasm:* 'I see you have honoured us with your presence today,' compared with, 'I am disturbed with the number of days you have missed this term.'
6   *Approval:* 'You are fantastic,' compared with, 'I am amazed at the way you get on with your classes.'
7   *Disapproval:* 'You are pathetic,' compared with, 'I am disturbed by the lack of involvement in what we do in the class.'
8   *Name Calling:* 'You're a disgrace to the human race,' compared with, 'I hate the way you bully the younger children.'

These distorted forms of communication slip out without a thought; old habits run off with little awareness. As with most undesirable behaviour, it is best dealt with by first developing awareness, and second by building up a repertoire of alternatives. It may be that there has been a change in awareness simply as a result of working through the exercises provided in this book, and the participants may have been surprised by the feelings they have generated.

*   The difficulty of expressing feelings in words is often due simply to lack of practice. This exercise is designed to provide such practice. Divide the group into pairs and ask the members of each pair

to complete the following sentence stems aloud, with both
members attempting each sentence and alternating who goes first.
Stress that they try to name the feeling and then say how it affects
them in physiological terms – the bodily response.

Example:

When I am about to go into a new class, I feel ... and ...

When I am about to go into a new class, I feel anxious and my
   throat goes dry and my legs feel weak.

When a student refuses to do what I say I feel ... and ...

When a person in authority criticizes my teaching I feel ...
   and ...

When a student tells me about the awful events in his life I feel ...
   and ...

When I get a good response from the students in my lessons I feel
   ... and ...

When I catch a student bullying another I feel ... and ...

When the students say they have enjoyed a lesson I feel ... and ...

When I sit down in the staffroom after a lesson has gone really
   badly I feel.... and ...

When a student cannot understand the work I have set I feel ...
   and ...

When I get up in the morning to go to school I feel ... and ...

When a colleague, who I consider to be a close friend, is in deep
   conversation with someone else I feel ... and ...

   Move the pairs into groups of six and ask them to share their
experience for ten minutes.

Feelings sometimes emerge for no apparent reason. It may be that
these feelings are being experienced now, because other feelings have
been suppressed in the past. At other times there is an obvious cause
for the feelings which are a result of an interpretation of the situation
in which you find yourself. A change in your interpretation of the
situation may result in a change of feeling.

   The car behind you in a queue of traffic may bang into the rear of
your car. This will probably produce an immediate angry reaction.
If you then discover that the driver of the offending car is having a
heart attack then it is likely that the feelings involved will change
dramatically. This does suggest that it is possible to change your
feelings by changing your perception of situations.

   The anger that you feel in difficult situations may be fuelled by unresolved anger that you have failed to express in the past. It is doubly unfortunate if you are unable to express your frustrations at work and then take it out on the people in your private life. And yet colleagues and friends seem to conspire to prevent an open expression of feeling. If a colleague is angry in a staff meeting, he might be asked to calm down and be reasonable. Depressed and upset in the staffroom, you might be told to cheer up and that things are not that bad. Even expressions of joy and happiness can be frozen out by the sort of subtle cues described in chapter two.

Paradoxically, in the privacy of the classroom, there may occur some really extreme outbursts of emotion. This sometimes happens to teachers who have tried to be calm and reasonable for long periods of time and then suddenly erupt. One of the writers remembers in his first year of teaching in Liverpool, reprimanding the students for shouting, 'Shut up, you!' to each other. A few weeks later, he was yelling, 'Shut up!' at the top of his voice.

What, then, is an appropriate expression of feeling? A useful guideline is to avoid statements which condemn the other person out of hand.

'You are a naughty boy.'
'I dislike you intensely.'
'This is the worst class I have ever taught.'

A far more accurate statement involves identifying the specific behaviour in the other person which is being reacted to.

'I get really angry when you mess about with the paints.'
'When you ignore what I say, I get really upset.'
'This continual shouting out is making me very annoyed.'
'I am really pleased about the way you have been helping Paul.'
'I am delighted with the way you have organized the concert.'

It is easy just to consider negative feelings in relation to teaching situations, as a high proportion of the statements made are of a damning nature. A way out of this trap is to practise using positive comments as well as negative comments in the form given above.

* Ask the members of the group to form pairs. Ask both members of the pairs to write down three positive and three negative

statements about their partners, using the form:

'When you ... I feel ...'

Then ask the pairs to read their statements to each other trying to express the appropriate emotion for each of the statements.

Then ask the pairs to form fours and to share their experience for ten minutes.

One problem which may be highlighted by this exercise is that there may be a mismatch between the words that are used and the feeling that goes with them. These problems of incongruence are raised again in chapter five under non-verbal communication, where we suggest that non-verbal cues have more impact than words, particularly for young children.

Intuitively, we are certain that an open expression of feeling, directed to both individuals and groups, can only enhance the quality of relationships in educational settings. Furthermore, a substantial shift towards the expression of positive feelings will improve the school or college ethos even more.

In your next week of teaching or on your next teaching practice, choose the student with whom you experience the most difficulty and at the beginning of a lesson, try to fit in three positive statements of feeling about him in the manner we have described above.

Reflection of feeling

There is a great deal of feeling content in much of what is said in school. A member of staff is complaining about a student who refuses to do as he is told, or a colleague who has let him down. A student may be complaining about being bullied, or about having been physically assaulted by another teacher. Sometimes the feelings are being expressed very clearly. At other times they leak out in the form of subtle non-verbal cues.

Feelings usually play an important part in the problems that are presented to a person in a pastoral or counselling role. Focusing on these feelings and reflecting them back to the other person adds a further dimension to merely reflecting back the content of what has been said. The expression of feeling is often part of the content:

Student: 'I'm really fed up that my parents won't let me stay on at

school. The way they are interfering with my life makes me want
to scream.'
Teacher: 'You sound really upset about the way your parents are
blocking your plans.'

A much more subtle reflection of feeling involves feeding back the
emotions that are behind the content but have not been directly
expressed. Sometimes this is obvious, as when a colleague storms in,
choking with anger about a student who has been insulting. It may
be so obvious that to reflect back the feeling is either trite or ridiculous.
However, you cannot be certain about this until you have tried it out.
In the case of positive feelings, a reflection of that feeling can accentuate it and make it infectious. It is, however, the reflection of implicit
feelings that facilitate the communication and develop understanding.

The reflection of feeling which is implicit in what has been said is
difficult to discuss on the written page since it involves registering
information which is not contained in the spoken word. As we suggest
in the later section on non-verbal communication, the words are
expressed in a digital form, which involves an exact correspondence
between words and meaning. The expression of feelings, on the other
hand, is analogic in that it involves a configuration of aspects of non-
verbal communication such as facial expression, voice tone, posture
and so on (Watzlawic, Beavin and Jackson, 1967).

With these difficulties in mind, the importance of exploring feelings
with great care cannot be overstressed. Your ways of construing
(Kelly, 1955) feelings may differ considerably from those of the other
person, so it is important to try to enter his feeling world as sensitively
as you can.

* Divide the group into pairs and give out copies of the twelve
  statements listed below. Suggest that one member of the pair reads
  out one of the statements, putting in implicit meaning as he feels
  appropriate. Then the other person tries to reflect back what he
  thinks is being implied. Then they can discuss how skilfully it was
  done. Both members of the pair could attempt each statement,
  taking turns to go first. It may be helpful for the person who is
  facilitating the group to give a demonstration.

  1 'No, I'm not being bullied, I'm all right. Don't ask me about
    that, I'm all right.'

2 'Your lessons are fascinating. Why can't we have you all the time?'

3 'Please sir/miss, Sandra's being a right bitch. Get her to give me back my pen.'

4 'There's nothing wrong at home and it's none of your business anyway.'

5 'Lounging around in the staffroom again, eh? While the rest of us do all the work!'

6 'Ooh, sir/miss, I'm not reading this poem – it's rude!'

7 'I haven't got any problems with the girls in 4B, we're all friends.'

8 'I'm not going into Mr Simpson's class again. He's awful!'

9 'Yeah, thanks for your help. I've got everything sorted out now. I should apologize to Miss Jones.'

10 'Sir, I'm scared, there's a big spider on the floor here.'

11 'I'm glad you've found the best armchair in the staffroom. Staying long are you?'

12 'Kick me out of your lesson; see if I care.'

Sometimes, the feelings expressed in the client's words are different from those being expressed non-verbally. Here you may choose to confront the person with the discrepancy.

Teacher to colleague: You say you are upset by being asked to consider early retirement and yet you seem relaxed, at ease and are laughing a lot.

Teacher to student: You asked to see me to talk about what was happening at home and yet you seem tense, closed off and unwilling to talk.

It may be inadvisable to confront a person too early, as you may be threatening an habitual defence for coping with their anxiety, which is necessary for survival.

Sometimes faint indications of feeling are leaked out by the client. There may be a tremor in the voice when dealing with a particular topic, or there may be a hint of pain around the eyes. To comment on this sort of data involves a degree of interpretation on the part of the counsellor and can involve the projection of the counsellor's own feelings.

These perceptions are best checked out with the other person as concretely as possible.

Teacher to student: 'When you started to talk about how you were getting on with the other students in the class, you laughed nervously, shrugged your shoulders and looked away. It looked as though things weren't quite right.'

The person may be encouraged to talk about new issues that relate to the hint that was given. Alternatively, the other person may deny the interpretation that has been made. In this case there is no point in pressing the matter further and, indeed, it may have been a mis-perception on your part. Often an intuition is denied by the client and is brought up in a later session as if it had never been mentioned earlier.

A way of making interpretations begins with the statement:

'What I hear you saying is . . .',

which is followed by a restatement in terms of the unspoken message that is coming across. This can be a very potent intervention, but it is sometimes abused and used to impose a point of view on the client. It is also jargon, which may confuse some individuals.

* The following exercise provides an opportunity to practise several skills at the same time.

    Divide the group into threes with one member of each trio in a counselling role, one talking about 'Good and bad aspects of my relationship with my parents' and the third acting as an observer.

    Give the observer a copy of the following observation sheet.

    As the discussion continues, write down comments on the counsellor's behaviour under the following categories:

1   Body posture.
2   Use of silence.
3   Minimal encouragement.
4   Reflection of content.
5   Reflection of feeling.
6   Any other comment.

Give the 'talker' ten minutes to talk about his parents while the 'counsellor' uses his skills as he sees appropriate. Then allow five minutes for each trio to share the experience. Repeat the exercise twice to give each member of the trio a turn in each role.

Self-disclosure

'What's your first name, Sir?'
'Are you married, Miss!'
'Have you got a boyfriend, Miss?'

These questions are not unusual, particularly for a new or student teacher. Certainly, for the new teacher, questions of this nature may appear to be cheeky, but they do probably reflect a genuine desire to know. Once a good relationship has been established with a class, questions of a personal nature can be asked and responded to without any difficulty.

Jourard (1964) provided evidence that the more effective members of the helping professions were also skilled at self-disclosure. They were not afraid to talk about themselves, their thoughts and feelings in a spontaneous manner. Chelune (1979) summed up a considerable number of studies which suggested that the skilled helper has to find a happy medium between revealing too little and revealing too much. Certainly, he should not over-indulge in self-disclosure too early in a relationship. We are all familiar with the person who pours out intimate details of his life at the first meeting, usually to the embarrassment of his audience. On the other hand, some people seem to be able to keep their private life a complete secret from the people they work with. Teachers have been known to use classes of students as an audience for an outpouring of their personal problems. Other teachers respond with anger at any attempt on the part of the students to find out anything about their personal lives. Both positions are probably inappropriate and reduce their effectiveness as teachers. In our view, there is room for an increase in self-disclosure on the part of teachers in their professional lives and generally they are too aloof from their students.

There are many ways in which teachers can reveal aspects of themselves, both to students and to colleagues. We will discuss two of these.

Firstly, talking about aspects of your personal life outside the school, both past and present. Secondly, being open about thoughts and feelings during ongoing interactions, that is being open about 'here and now' experience. If you have worked through some of the earlier exercises in this book, you will probably have used both of these forms of self-disclosure. If you have worked through the exercises in a group, you will probably find that the members have become much closer and are a more efficient working group. If this is the case, then perhaps exercises involving self-disclosure will improve the working efficiency of any learning group.

1   Disclosing your private life. 'Where do you live?', 'What sort of house have you got?', 'Have you got a car?' As we have suggested, it is probably inadvisable to rush into answering a string of personal questions from a class the first time you take them. On the other hand, there is no reason why this sort of information should not be shared when it is appropriate. If you are involved in teaching social and personal education or forms of the pastoral curriculum which involve self-disclosure on the part of the students, then self-disclosure is a useful thing to model. If you have no previous experience of doing this, then some simple exercises will help to make a start in breaking the habit of being closed off.

* Ask the members of the group to write down something they had done that they were not very proud of.
    Form groups of about eight and invite the group members to talk in turn about what they have written down. Invite the group members to ask each other about what they have disclosed. When every member of the group has had a turn, ask the group to share how they felt about what they had done.

The following exercise can involve much more personal self-disclosure.

* Give each member of the group a large sheet of paper. Ask them to spend five minutes reflecting on which were the high points in their lives and which were the low points. Then invite them to draw a line from one side of the paper to the other, representing their lives from birth to the present time. For the high points allow the line to go up to the top of the page and for the low points allow the line to go down to the bottom of the page. Then invite them

to use crayons or felt-tip pens to draw representations of the events at the highs and the lows. Then ask the group to divide into threes and suggest that one member spends ten minutes talking about the drawing, while the other two use their listening skills to facilitate self-disclosure. When each member has had ten minutes, bring the group back together to discuss the experience for a further ten minutes.

The exercise can be varied and the time span limited to just one day, or a week, or a year.

Thus, having practised and come to some understanding of self-disclosure, the teacher can try using it in the classroom situation. Hopefully, the careful use of this skill will enable the teacher to present himself as an interesting person without becoming self-indulgent and occupying too much lesson time. Self-disclosure has to be used much more sensitively when the teacher finds himself in a one-to-one counselling situation.

The basic listening and attending skills we have described so far, are often sufficient to enable the other person to say more about important issues. Sometimes students will be anxious that talking about their problems will give the impression that they are abnormal or even insane. Sometimes, as with the case of physical disabilities, there is no shared experience which could be disclosed by the teacher. There are, however, developmental problems and problems with relationships that many teachers have been through. To the student, the teacher who has never admitted to any human failings will appear as a person who is unlikely to understand what he, the student, is going through.

We know of teachers who have shared the experience of broken relationships, being intensely angry with their parents, running away from home, thinking about suicide, being hit by parents and so on, and in every case it seemed to lead to a more trusting relationship and a deeper understanding between teacher and student.

It is, however, important that the self-disclosure on the part of the counsellor does not distract the client and draw them both into a discussion of the counsellor's problems. There are teachers who are immature enough to use students in a counselling situation to off-load their own problems.

2   The second form of self-disclosure requires being more open about here-and-now thoughts and feelings. We all have an ongoing stream

of consciousness involving thoughts and feelings, much of which we would like to keep to ourselves. Indeed, much of this activity is so habitual, that we do not notice it happening. It does nevertheless often contain some very useful information, and if it is shared skilfully it can have a potent effect on the interaction.

In the classroom situation, a great deal can be gained by commenting on seemingly ordinary things. 'I like the way you've done your hair.' 'That's a new jacket isn't it?' 'I'm feeling a bit tired today, so don't raise your voices', and so on. This type of comment comes easily to some teachers, whereas others feel quite embarrassed about making a personal statement.

* Divide the group into pairs sitting opposite each other. Invite them to spend five minutes making simple complimentary comments about how the other person looks, about their dress and general appearance. Then move into fours and spend five minutes sharing the experience.

   Then, within the group of four decide on a target person to whom three complimentary comments will be made in a short space of time. Give each person a turn and then share the experience.

Objections to exercises of this nature are often made on the grounds that the compliments are contrived and insincere. These complaints are usually made by people who have difficulties themselves in giving compliments.

This section is not an invitation to rush into your class and self-disclose indiscriminately. If there is not a trusting relationship with the class, you may find your self-disclosures thrown back at you in an insulting manner. This leaves a negative double bind. Self-disclosure without trust can lead to problems, and yet we have suggested that trust can be developed by demonstrating that you are a human being through self-disclosure. The resolution of the bind comes in starting slowly and increasing the degree of self-disclosure as the trust develops.

Confrontation and assertion

Wherever there is a conflict of interest, there is a good chance that a confrontation will develop. Conflict seems to be endemic in schools, particularly when teachers are trying to impose an inappropriate or irrelevant curriculum on their students, many of whom would prefer to be anywhere else but in school. Conflicts also arise between staff themselves, and there is limited evidence that these are more stressful than the conflicts with the students (Woodhouse, Hall and Wooster, 1985).

Situations which involve conflict and confrontation are often taken as a sign that things are going wrong. It is, however, reasonable to expect that there will be conflicts of interest in a complex institution such as a school. These are often turned into negative situations because the confrontations that develop are handled unskilfully by the participants. Avoiding the confrontation is probably the least skilful strategy. This is easy advice to give, but the writers are as guilty as anyone in trying to avoid confrontation. Undoubtedly, those confrontations which remain unresolved tend to fester and produce an unhealthy set of relationships.

Some of the skills we have discussed may prove helpful in confrontation situations. The expression of feeling and self-disclosure both help to bring relevant material out into the open and may even be threatening to another person. Simple reflection of content can be a revelation to the person who does not pay attention to what he is saying. To be confronted with your own words and behaviour can be a painful learning experience.

Assertion training (Lange and Jakubowsky, 1976; Liberman et al, 1975), a popular activity at the time of writing, involves ideas and exercises which are similar to those for developing skills in confrontation. Assertion training is summed up in the title of a popular book in the area, *Don't Say Yes When You Want to Say No* (Feusterheim and Baer, 1975). Women have taken a particular interest in assertion training in order to overcome the cultural stereotype of the passive female (Phelps and Austin, 1975). For our purposes, we will assume that assertion training is an aspect of confrontation; a communication skill.

For a confrontation to be resolved satisfactorily it may be helpful to say how you feel about a situation, what you think of the situation and what you want out of it.

Three main types of unskilful confrontation have been identified in the literature on communication.

1   Aggressive confrontation. Aggression here is seen as an attack reaction to a perceived threat, usually verbal, although sometimes in

* Ask the members of the group to identify three conflict situations in their own lives, which they felt they had not dealt with effectively.

Suggest they include one situation from their personal lives, one in their relationships with other teachers and one with students in school. Briefly, list the incidents on the following form and fill in the subsequent sections about how they felt, thought and what they wanted from those situations.

Description of incident	How did you feel?	What did you think?	What did you want?
1 With teachers			
2 With students			
3 Personal life			

Divide the group into pairs and invite them to discuss to what extent there is a pattern to their responses and what alternative statements they could have made in those situations.

---

schools this can spill over into physical violence. An aggressive response effectively blocks communication and prevents the other person from having a say. This may be an effective short-term expedient to get out of a tricky situation, but in all probability the same conflict will arise again, as the underlying cause has not been dealt with. One common outcome of an aggressive encounter between staff is that they cease to communicate and gingerly circle round each other, sometimes for years.

Aggressive communication is often described as 'hit-and-run', a powerful image for a situation where one of the protagonists has no intention of communicating genuinely, but is just giving vent to anger and frustration which perhaps should have been directed elsewhere.

Direct assertive confrontations are so rare that they are often perceived as being aggressive. This is a particular problem for women, who, having made a confronting statement, might be put down with terms like 'abrasive'. A good model of confronting behaviour is found

in TV soap operas, where the characters often confront each other with enviable clarity. It would be comforting to have a script to work from rather than have to respond creatively to situations as they arise.
2   Passive confrontation. This is a contradiction in terms and involves the avoidance of the confrontation. One of the writers was involved in supervising a student teacher taking a lesson when the students in the class started to make paper aeroplanes and skim them over his head. The only acknowledgment he made that this was going on was to make an occasional grab for a passing 'plane' and stuff it into his pocket. This was the only occasion that the writer concerned interrupted what was going on in a student teacher's lesson. His total avoidance of the situation meant that there was almost no contact between what he was doing and the realities of the classroom situation.

Excessive politeness is often used in situations where a more confronting response would be more appropriate. This is often the case with a person in a subordinate position. An unskilled headteacher may not permit direct forms of confrontation from the staff and react punitively when it occurs. Authoritarian management of this nature is likely to produce a staff who are polite in face-to-face situations, but who give vent to their anger and frustration in other, less appropriate situations. This passive politeness occurs in many other types of relationships involving teachers and students.

Some colleagues will go out of their way to smooth over a potential confrontation whether they are one of the main protagonists or not.

'There's no need to get upset, I am sure it can be settled amicably.'

The real feelings in the situation are not given permission to emerge.
3   Manipulation. Here the teacher uses an indirect approach to gain the upper hand in a conflict of interest. This is done in many different ways. Teachers cajole, moralize, use sarcasm, float threats and promises and use excessive questioning in attempts to deal with conflicts, without making a clear statement of what the conflict is and how it could be resolved.

'I couldn't possibly take a badly behaved class like you out of school.'

'Any chance of seeing a piece of work out of you before the term ends?'

'The best behaved group will be allowed to go out first.'

Many of the relationships between staff are also highly manipulative.

'I wonder if one of the lady members of staff could take charge of the refreshments on parents' evening?'

'Didn't you go on a counselling course, perhaps you would be the best person to deal with the boy.'

To the headteacher, 'I would like to be able to use the video equipment, but the PE department always seem to be using it.'

It is understandable that teachers resort to manipulative communication simply to get through the average school day. After all, students are not volunteers – education in this country is compulsory and likely to remain so, and the curriculum is not always relevant to what they see as their needs. A degree of manipulation is unavoidable.

* Ask the group members to recall and write down three events from their teaching experience when they were:

1   Aggressive, where they dealt with a conflict by verbally attacking the other person.

2   Passive, where they dealt with a conflict by doing nothing, by being excessively polite, by compromising or trying to smooth away the problem.

3   Manipulative, where they dealt with the problem in a devious way, by moralizing, asking indirect questions, or offering rewards and punishments.

'Now sit quietly, perhaps close your eyes, and summon up the memory of the first situation. Try to experience it as fully as you can. (pause) Now in imagination, try to fantasize how you would have liked to have dealt with this situation. Be as detailed as you can. (pause) Now form groups of three and share the details of your experience.'

Repeat the process with the remaining two events.

The teacher in the counselling role may find that using confrontation creatively can produce positive results. The student in the client role can be confronted with his own behaviour; in particular, the games and defences that are employed to avoid looking at important aspects of the problem. There may be discrepancies or distortions in what is being said, and inconsistencies between verbal and non-verbal communication. The client may be confronted with his potential skills and resources that are not being used. Egan (1982) provided a comprehensive analysis of the skill of confrontation in counselling situations. He described it as an advanced counselling skill which should be used with discretion and only when there is an appropriate trusting relationship and only when the client is ready for it. The confronter in a counselling situation must be aware of his motives and check out that the confrontation is not being made to meet his own needs, to show up the student or to find a distorted outlet for his own feelings.

Many confrontations are designed to get the confronter what he wants, irrespective of the needs of the other person. This is often described as a 'win-lose' situation. That is, one person wins and the other loses. This is invariably true of the aggressive, 'hit-and-run' type of confrontation, but can also be true of the more direct form of confrontation we have recommended, where the direct confrontation is made and there is no intention of negotiating with the other person in order to come to a resolution of the conflict which is beneficial to both parties.

In an extensive study of students and staff in junior and senior high schools in the United States, Delecco and Richards (1974) found that there was little open expression of anger and few attempts to negotiate conflicts openly. The anger which had not been expressed appeared in other destructive forms and the schools became very angry places. A high proportion of the confrontations in schools tend to be of the 'win-lose' type, and the busy teacher could claim, with good reason, that there is not time to allow a confrontation to develop into an extensive negotiation. This is, however, probably a short-term expedient and a serious attempt to negotiate will produce a long-term reduction in conflict.

Johnson and Johnson (1982) provided a comprehensive analysis of the stages of negotiating a conflict, starting with a direct confrontation of the other person. This is followed by jointly defining the conflict in as concrete terms as possible; communicating positions and feelings; communicating co-operative intentions; taking the opponents' perspective; co-ordinating motivation to negotiate in good faith, and finally reaching an agreement. This is clearly a lengthy process and it is understandable that school staff are not willing to give up enough time to negotiate properly. If the time can be found, it is likely that the social climate of the school will improve and bring about a corresponding increase in conventional school work. The most productive application of Johnson and Johnson's techniques would be at a staff training day for the whole group. A shorter form of this approach is found in Nelson-Jones' (1986) CUDSA model.

Conflict is endemic in our education system and yet the skilful use of confrontation is rarely included in teacher training programmes. The inexperienced teacher has only the model of the current practice of experienced teachers which is dominated by aggressive and 'win-lose' confrontations. Training will need to help the student teacher change these unhelpful modes of confrontation in different situations, such as the following three broad categories:

1   In the classroom situation where the teacher is having to deal with discipline problems. Here, the direct form of confrontation we described earlier could become the standard response to conflict situations as they arise. That is, a clear statement of what you think and feel about a situation and a statement about what you need or want from it.

'Jean, the way you keep wandering about the class is really getting on my nerves. It disturbs me and other people in the class. I want you to stay in your seat and get on with your work.'

A statement of this nature does not invite an extended negotiation of the conflict but possibly this could be done at a later time. It does, however, permit a rational response, which is not the case with more manipulative confrontations:

'It looks as though Jean has got itchy feet again!'

'How dare you wander about the class when I haven't given you permission to leave your seat?'

'If you get out of your seat once more, you will be staying behind tonight.'

There are also opportunities for the teacher to challenge inconsistencies in the students' behaviour or point out where they are not using their potential.

'You say you want to pass your exams and increase your chances of getting a job, but you never do your homework.'

'You want to get on the school team, but you are not willing to put in time on training and practice.'

'You never give me an answer when I ask you a question directly and yet I can hear you whispering the right answers to other people.' Or quite simply, 'You have done a lot better than this in the past. What's going on?'

This latter form of confrontation is potentially embarrassing for the student, and the teacher should think carefully before making a confrontation of this nature publicly.

2 In a counselling situation. The invitation to discuss a mutual problem is probably best offered at the end of a lesson, 'Could I have a word with you, Martin?', rather than in the heat of the moment, when it might come out as, 'See me at the end of the lesson and we will deal with this then.'

The forms of confrontation used in a counselling situation can be much softer than those used in the interactions in the classroom. However, the teacher is in a very powerful position in a one-to-one relationship with a pupil. We would agree with Egan (1982) that confrontation should be used sparingly in counselling and great care has to be taken to ensure that the confrontation will move the student on in a positive way and not make him more defensive.

An horrific, but true anecdote is of the deputy head who was interviewing an adolescent boy and his mother, both of whom were grossly overweight. The boy was being transferred from another comprehensive school because of persistent truancy. He had been constantly tormented about his weight. 'By the way, we don't have fat boys here. You'll get plenty of rugger and PE to get that fat off and don't think you will be getting chips for school dinner.' Needless to say, the boy was never seen again.

It is equally important not to carry over the unresolved anger from the classroom into the subsequent counselling situation. If it is, then the interview becomes merely a vehicle for expressing this anger and the teacher is using the situation to satisfy his own needs. The anger can be stated, but perhaps in the form:

'You really made me angry with that disturbance at the end of the lesson. I want to try to sort out what the problem was.'

Having used a form of confrontation, it may then be possible to continue the interview using attending and listening skills and further confrontations may not be necessary.

When the interview has not emerged out of a discipline situation and a student has approached you with a problem, the need to restrain forms of confrontation becomes even more essential and it may require several sessions before an appropriate level of trust has developed. The patterns of teacher behaviour developed to cope with the pressures of the classroom have to be restrained and a new role assumed.

3 Confronting colleagues. Some teachers report that their relation-

ships with colleagues are more stressful than those with students. Our own research (Woodhouse, Hall and Wooster, 1985) suggests that in-service training in communication skills resulted in a reduction in reports of stressful relations with fellow staff.

Both of the main forms of confrontation can be used with colleagues. If another member of staff is making life difficult for you, it is important that the issue is raised directly. Ideally, the confrontation is made with the intention of resolving the issue so that both parties gain and the relationship is improved. Some teachers, however, cannot cope with being confronted and withdraw from future possible conflicts. This is regrettable, but it is less likely that they will behave in a way which will produce the same problem in the future, so at least the confronter has gained. This was true for the woman who took up a post of deputy head in a primary school and found that she was being continually undermined by an older male member of staff who made sarcastic asides about the incompetence of women. On being confronted with his sexist behaviour, he became very quiet and soon took early retirement.

The teacher who has developed good communication skills will soon find colleagues coming to be counselled, particularly new members of staff who are finding it difficult to cope in the classroom. Here, the principles regarding confrontation in counselling situations apply. Only confront when a trusting relationship has developed and then use the skill sparingly.

'You say that you want to get to know your classes better, but you never go on school outings or make any effort to meet the children in your spare time.'

Problems of confrontation become even more sensitive when the two people involved are at different levels in a hierarchy. It is not easy for a member of staff to confront a headteacher skilfully, because the headteacher has power over the teacher's future career. On the other hand, it is not easy for a person in authority to have much respect for a colleague who is over-compliant, and relationships of that nature are probably not conducive to a healthy institution.

The solution for the teacher lies in the middle path of skilful confrontation, avoiding excessive passivity and irrational aggression. It is difficult to avoid carrying over old, negative feelings about people in authority into new situations, in particular, feelings about parents that have never been resolved. A small minority of headteachers will not tolerate any form of confrontation and can only carry out the task of management by decree. A situation like this requires a great deal of self-control on the part of the staff to avoid being drawn into excessively angry responses, which provide an excuse for the authoritarian to become more authoritarian.

A headteacher needs to accept that unresolved feelings about authority are going to be dumped on him no matter how he behaves. In this respect he deserves a high salary for taking this pressure. In certain situations it is inevitable that a headteacher must involve himself in confrontation between either himself and his staff or in mediating between warring factions. In deciding what constitutes a skilful confrontation, the head will have to take account of what his position of authority adds to the situation. This effect will vary from colleague to colleague; some teachers will be able to treat the head as an equal, whereas others will feel oppressed merely by his presence.

This makes the skill of avoiding win-lose confrontations more difficult, and the skills which we have introduced in this chapter will need to be well honed. The worst scenario is where the head has partially learned some of the skills and gives the impression of having listened to his colleagues very carefully and then comes out with a statement to the effect: 'It was very interesting to hear your point of view, but this is what is going to happen.'

* This is a repeat of an exercise given earlier in the chapter, but now the 'observer' is being invited to make comments on a larger number of categories.

  Divide the group into threes with one member of each trio in a counselling role, one talking about 'Good and bad aspects of my relationship with my parents' and the third acting as an observer.

  Give the observer a copy of the following observation sheet.

  As the discussion continues, write down comments on the counsellor's behaviour under the following categories:

1 Body posture.
2 Use of silence.
3 Minimal encouragement.
4 Reflection of content.
5 Reflection of feeling.
6 Expression of feeling.
7 Self-disclosure.
8 Confrontation.
9 Any other comment.

Give the 'talker' ten minutes to talk about his parents while the 'counsellor' uses his skills as he sees appropriate. Then allow five minutes for each trio to share the experience. Repeat the exercise twice to give each member of the trio a turn in each role.

Learning the skills

There are now many books which outline basic counselling skills which, as we have suggested, are central to communication in work and everyday living. These books (Egan, 1982; Okun, 1976; Brammer, 1979; Gazda et al, 1984; Nelson-Jones, 1983, 1986) provided practical exercises for developing these skills, confirming that experiential learning is central to changing behaviour. The skills are often divided into stages, working on the assumption that it is better to become skilled in the earlier stages before moving on to the more advanced stages. The best known of these models is Egan's (1982) three stage model.

1   The first stage involves the skills which are used to help the other person to explore his experience. This stage includes the basic listening skills and the reflection of content and feeling. Here the helper is taking a relatively passive role, apart from paying a great deal of attention to the other person.

2   The helper is putting more of himself into the second stage skills, which would include the expression of feeling, self-disclosure and confrontation. With these skills, the helper is expressing his own thoughts and feelings and presenting himself more as a person than is the case with the first stage skills.

3   The third stage involves the negotiation of a plan of action to try to resolve the issues which have been raised. One way of doing this was developed in chapter two.

This is a gross oversimplification of Egan's model and we have used it to provide some order to the limited number of skills we have discussed. It is likely that a typical helping or counselling relationship will involve the use of the skills roughly in that order, whether in a single session or a long series of sessions.

The training in counselling, communication, inter-personal and social skills is done in a variety of ways. In the case of activities which are often labelled social skills, this is often done in a mechanical and authoritarian manner. This is perhaps because the methods were developed in psychiatric institutions for individuals who demonstrated extremely low ability, or had little control over their behaviour (Trower, Bryant and Argyle, 1978). In this case, a precisely defined item of behaviour would be modelled for the patient and their approximations to this behaviour would be rewarded in the same way as Skinner's rats (see chapter two). This approach has been developed into forms of social skills training using a similar approach, which is often called micro-teaching. As McIntyre (Ellis and Whittingham, 1983) pointed out, training of this nature does not appear to generalize to the classroom situation, though this does not appear to stop teacher trainers from trying to do it.

The same problems apply to forms of counselling training which come under the heading of micro-counselling (Ivey and Authier, 1978). Micro-counselling is, however, carried out in a range of different ways. It may be done mechanistically, where a skill is demonstrated and the trainee's attempt is video recorded. The recording is criticized by the 'expert' and the trainee modifies his behaviour accordingly.

An alternative approach is offered by Egan (1976). Here the training is done in a group which is often divided into triads, in the manner of the last exercise, and the trainees rotate the roles of counsellor, counsellee and observer. Real issues can be used from the trainees' personal lives which gives a high level of involvement in the training. Dividing the group up and then returning to the larger group provides the individual trainee with a wide range of experience and feedback. It also gives a great deal of the responsibility for learning back to the trainees themselves.

In our experience, the optimal training situation involves far more than the introduction and practice of skills and we would recommend two major inputs. Firstly, to intersperse the skills training exercises with exercises which involve fantasy and drawing. This permits the group members to tune in to the more intuitive and feeling components of inter-personal relations. Secondly, to run a non-directive small group or encounter group, in which the group members are invited to explore the relations within the group as they happen, parallel to the training sessions.

In small training groups of this nature, skills can be practised with the full emotional involvement of real interactions. Initially, the group member finds himself de-skilled, confused and discomforted. The learning which emerges from this confused and uncomfortable situation seems to be remembered for long periods of time because of the strong emotional associations provided by the real experience. Joyce (1984) used the term 'dynamic disequilibrium' to describe the discomfort which goes with the teachers' attempts to try out new behaviour. He pointed out that many teachers withdraw from trying out new behaviour because this enables them to avoid the emotional discomfort. The small group training experience makes this sort of avoidance more difficult and there is a greater chance of the trainee working through the difficult situations. Training courses at Nottingham (Hall, Woodhouse and Wooster, 1984) have demonstrated the effectiveness of this combination of inter-personal skills training, the use of fantasy and small group training. (The use of fantasy is developed in chapter five and the use of small group training in chapter seven.)

The importance of working within a group format was confirmed by Higgins, Moracco and Handford (1981). They divided teachers on an initial training course into those who were given human relations training using a group approach, those who were taught skills formally, and a control group. Not surprisingly, both of the experimental groups came out better on scores of empathic understanding, and interestingly the group approach came out better than the formal approach, in spite of the fact that they spent time on exercises designed to develop group cohesiveness.

Although we are gratified that the results of this study confirm our own prejudices, we are not happy with the measures that were used, which invited observers to rate empathic responding on a scale of one to five. This is typical of the 'skills' approach which turns empathy into a quality which the helper either has or has not. If he hasn't got it, then he must be trained in it.

Summary

In this chapter, we have examined some inter-personal skills which could also be described as social, counselling or communication skills. Certainly, a high proportion of counselling skills trainers would agree that these skills as developed by Ivey and Authier (1978) and Egan

(1982) are fundamental to the task of counselling. These writers also have the support of a number of research findings.

We have cautioned against acquiring these skills in a mechanical manner and recommend that they are best learned in a group format, which maximizes the learner's control over his learning, and that a useful arena for trying out new behaviour is a small group experience such as a Rogerian encounter group.

Basic attending and listening skills provide the helper to come to a clearer understanding of how the other person perceives his world. This is central to the notion of empathy, and the use of these skills is likely to result in a more empathic response on the part of the helper.

Connections

The skills developed in this chapter are designed to develop awareness and are consistent with the phenomenological notions outlined in the introductory chapter. The skills provide a practical tool-kit for phenomenology. The ideas developed in Kelly's personal construct psychology underline the importance of using exploratory techniques of this nature in the early stages of a helping relationship. Using this approach within a management structure can result in a significant reduction of stress.

The three sections of the next chapter extend the ideas used here in fine detail. The first section deals with the complexities of the way we use language in communication. The second section examines the part played by imagery and how it can be used to improve communication. The third section emphasizes the importance of non-verbal communication. These three modes of communication can be integrated to provide an holistic approach to human relations in educational settings.

5 Channels of communication

In the previous chapter we were concerned with the mainly verbal skills of counselling and inter-personal communication. We discussed how the helper's interventions could be framed more effectively, and the appropriate use of words. An exception to this was the use of body posture. This is obviously seen by another person, rather than heard. Some people would claim that they can intuit what a person is thinking or feeling by their movements, gestures, facial mannerisms, body posture and so on, and it is this aspect of behaviour that is called non-verbal communication.

Communication can be mediated through any of the senses: hearing, vision, smell, taste, touch, and the internal kinaesthetic experience of feelings. The use of hearing and vision is easy to understand when two people are talking. Smell and taste may also be important, but we will not attempt to deal with them here. Touch and internal feelings play an important part in non-verbal communication.

On the whole in our culture, most attention is paid to language; speaking and listening to what is said. This may be a function of our education system which relies heavily on the spoken and written word. Other means of representing experience are not used so often. Bruner (1966) used the term 'modes of representation' to describe three principal ways of handling experience. He distinguished between 'symbolic' representation, which largely involved language, 'iconic' representation, which largely involved visual imagery and 'enactive', which involved some form of bodily feeling.

A popular update of these ideas is provided by Bandler and Grinder (1979). They suggest that individuals have preferences in the way that they represent experience and that this is revealed by their choice of words.

An auditory person might say, 'I can hear what you are trying to say.'

A visual person might say, 'I don't see what you mean.'

A kinaesthetic (feeling) person might say, 'I feel this is a topic you want to talk about.'

Bandler and Grinder's ideas are entertaining, but there is little in the way of conventional scientific evidence to support their views. They do, however, draw attention to the possibility that there are other ways of representing experience than through language.

Each of the following sections deal mainly with one of the three main modes of representation:

1   The section on the use of language provides an elaboration of the counselling and inter-personal skills outlined in the previous chapter. It is mainly concerned with the spoken word and the practical outcomes of different forms of language.

2   The section on the use of fantasy demonstrates how visualization can be used to help the education process and help the student understand how she relates to herself and other people.

3   The third section on non-verbal communication stresses the importance of communication mediated by the body. With the exception of touch, the receiver is using sight and hearing to take in non-verbal communication, but the sender is using forms of bodily communication.

Although we deal with these three areas separately, the skilful communicator will be aware of cues from all of these channels of communication.

The use of language

There are many different ways of studying language. Best known are the study of the grammatical structure or syntax and the study of meaning, which is called semantics. The practical outcome of what is said is a branch of what is called pragmatics and is the least well-developed aspect of the study of language. Non-verbal communication is an important part of the pragmatics of human communication (Watzlawic, Beavin and Jackson, 1967), though in this chapter we will limit ourselves to the practical outcomes of what is said.

The examples we will give relate to educational situations and how to make your work as a teacher more effective. However, the same principles apply to everyday living and perhaps it is possible to make your personal life more effective as well. This will, of course, involve changing long-standing habits and this can be painful. As we will see later in this chapter, some of our language habits have developed in order to make life safe rather than effective.

Only you, the speaker, can test the effectiveness of what you say against the particular outcomes you would like to bring about. This is like a simple form of psychological experiment. Try one way of expressing yourself and see how the other person responds. In a similar situation, try something different and see if the response changes. This type of experimentation is made more complex because people and situations vary considerably, but it may be that broad patterns emerge that provide guidelines for the future.

If you always ask polite questions such as 'Will you get your books out?', try making a clear statement, such as 'Get your books out.' If you are in the habit of lecturing children in one-to-one counselling situations, try asking polite questions. The rest of this section details possible ways of experimenting with different forms of language.

Unfortunately, most people pay scant attention to the words they are using. Most verbal exchanges consist of well-learned routines which are run off without reflection. Any attempt to change these routines requires considerable effort and practice, perhaps as much as is required to learn a second language. It is useful to be in a situation where another person can give you feedback regarding the way you use language rather like the facilitator in the type of small group experience described in the chapter on working in groups.

It is easy for the teacher to blame the student for not responding in the manner that she expects and, indeed, some students will be unco-operative whatever the teacher may say. It may be, however, that the teacher is inviting the responses she would most want to avoid and is not aware that a possible solution to the problem lies in her choice of words. Although the blame is usually laid at the student's door, both teacher and student are probably locked in a pattern of action and reaction, running off old routines which provoke predictable responses from the other. Mrs Jones claims that she has to keep telling Sharon off because she is always messing about. Sharon argues that she always messes about because Mrs Jones keeps picking on her. It could be argued that the responsibility for breaking out of this vicious circle should largely rest with the teacher, as the more mature person. Usually, it is the student who is exhorted to change.

In the sections that follow we suggest certain ways that you might choose to experiment with the form of language that you use. This is not to say that they are the correct forms. On the other hand, they represent ways of expressing yourself which are often avoided. If this is the case for you, then to practise them is increasing the number of choices available to you. The first set of suggestions are adapted from the techniques developed by Fritz Perls (1969) and Perls et al (1973) in Gestalt Therapy.

Personalizing statements

Most of us have learned, with great skill, to avoid taking responsibility for the statements we are making by choosing not to use the first person. Rather than use the word 'I', several other pronouns are used. Consider the examples in the following exercise and how the change of pronoun changes the impact of the statement.

* Read the pairs of statements to another person. Change over and repeat. Take ten minutes to discuss how you felt and the ways in which you avoid using the first person.

   'One has to control emotion, otherwise one might explode.'
   'I have to control my emotions, otherwise I might explode.'

   'We are finding it difficult to initiate discussion.'
   'I am finding it difficult to initiate discussion.'

   'When you are open about your feelings, you tend to get hurt.'
   'When I am open about my feelings, I tend to get hurt.'

   'It is difficult to relate to you in this situation.'
   'I find it difficult to relate to you in this situation.'

   'Teachers have to keep a certain distance from their students.'
   'As a teacher, I have to keep a certain distance from my students.'

In a television interview, a member of the Royal Family tends to answer questions about important aspects of his life with sentences prefaced with, 'When a person ...'

Several reasons or excuses are given for avoiding the use of 'I'. Academics often argue that they have been trained to write and speak in an objective manner and to avoid personalized statements. This is curious, since the avoidance of 'I', as in the examples given, makes the statement factually incorrect. At best, the speaker only has information about herself and possibly a few other people.

Another common complaint is that the person who always says 'I' sounds self-centred. This suggestion is usually made by individuals who will tie their sentences in knots rather than use the first person; the word 'I' seems to have disappeared from their vocabulary. What we are suggesting here is that the first person is used when it is logically correct.

The use of impersonal statements and the incorrect use of pronouns such as 'you', 'one', 'we', 'they', 'people' and 'it' distance the speaker from the statement that is being made. The implication is that everybody is the same as the speaker when this is patently not true. Instead of taking responsibility for the statement that is being made, the speaker is saying that everybody has the same experience.

A useful device is to ask the speaker to change the sentence using the first person:

'When you go into Mr Brown's class, you always get shouted at. Try saying, "When I go into Mr Brown's class I always get shouted at".' An alternative approach would be 'Don't you mean, "When I go into Mr Brown's class I always get shouted at"?'

The impact is greater when the person actually repeats the words for herself, but it is necessary to judge whether she is likely to co-operate with the suggestion. This demand to use the first person can be so disturbing for some people, including responsible adults, that they literally cannot get the words out of their mouths. They refuse to use the changed form even after acknowledging that it is correct. Perhaps it is best not to push too hard in a situation like this. Some individuals, having grasped this general principle, make themselves positively obnoxious by correcting others all the time.

Certainly there is plenty of support for not using 'I'. Common usage, the media, public figures, teachers, counsellors, parents, all collude to use forms of speech that avoid taking personal responsibility for the content of what is being said. It seems more likely that these forms of speech are habits that we have learned from our parents, rather than any form of academic training. As such they have been ingrained by years of practice and it is unlikely that they will be changed overnight.

This is not to say that it is not worth trying to change. By paying careful attention to what you and other people are trying to say, it will soon become clear that this mechanism dominates everyday conversation. Then try altering your own use of pronouns. You may find, as with the process of changing questions into statements, that what you say takes on a refreshing directness. Listeners will understand what you are saying more clearly and will respond accordingly.

If the situation is appropriate, such as in a counselling situation, then you might suggest to the other person that they change the wording of a particular sentence to use the word 'I'. If this is done sensitively, it can give the other person important insights into their own behaviour.

The depersonalizing process can take subtle forms, particularly in statements that involve feelings:

'It hurts' – 'I am in pain'
'It's hot' – 'I feel hot'
'It's not funny' – 'I don't like what you are doing.'

The process of personalizing statements is also important in lessons which are concerned with discussion about broad moral issues and aesthetic considerations. Again, students often find it a salutary experience to use the first person in this context. This technique not only teaches them what is or what is not their own point of view, but also, that in the final analysis we can only ever speak for ourselves when expressing subjective opinions.

The following example is part of a discussion one of the writers had with a fifth-form O level English group about a modern American novel dealing with racial prejudice in the deep South.

Teacher: What did you feel were some of the more depressing aspects of the novel?

Student A: The part about racial prejudice. I mean, we don't treat them like that and you feel upset that they had to lead such dreadful lives.

Teacher: That's interesting – but can you try saying 'I' instead of 'we' and 'you', because I am sure not everyone here shares that point of view.

Student B: Yes, I don't.

Student A: I'll try, but it's hard. I mean, I don't treat them like that over here and I feel upset that they had to live in those conditions.

Teacher: Did you feel the difference when you used the first person?

Student A: Yes.

Teacher: Can you explain the difference to the rest of the group?

Student A: Well, it felt like I was saying something I really felt. A bit scary really.

Teacher: Try to remember, that in expressing opinions we speak for ourselves, not for everyone else, and that it is important always to own your own beliefs and feelings. Okay, let's go on. . . .

Modes of questioning

The teacher is often placed in the position where she has to initiate conversation or discussion. This is equally true in classroom settings as in counselling, pastoral or discipline situations. It is often necessary for the teacher to initiate discussion by asking direct questions so that the other person can begin to organize thoughts and feelings in a coherent manner.

Asking questions plays a large part in the teacher's ongoing inter-actions with students and yet, as John Holt (1964) suggests, this can be a terrifying experience for the student. As experienced teachers we seem to have forgotten what it was like for us to be 'put on the spot', probed or interrogated. Even in a small friendly tutorial group during teacher training, it can be a negative experience to be asked a question which is likely to demonstrate your ignorance. The experienced teacher seems to have developed an amnesia about her own earlier experiences.

'Why?', 'How?' and 'What?'

In this section we are going to ask you to examine your use of questions beginning with 'Why?', particularly in inter-personal, counselling, pastoral and discipline situations. When something has gone wrong, the 'Why?' questions spring readily to our lips. 'Why did you do that?', 'Why were you late?', 'Why can't you control your class?', 'Why are you feeling upset?'

The main recommendation we make regarding the use of questions is that you examine how often you use questions beginning with 'Why?' and see what happens when you experiment with alternatives. Trying to reform the question with one beginning with 'What?' or 'How?' is a possible alternative, and there are many other ways of achieving the same end.

A 'why' question invariably asks for a person's motives or an analysis of her behaviour when often the person concerned is unclear regarding her motives for behaving in a particular way. There may be a strong moral complaint underlying a 'why' question which goes something like 'Why on earth did you do that?' which is likely to provoke guilt feelings and a heightened resistance to responding.

The 'how' and 'what' questions are asking for more information, and the potential threat is removed if this can be done in a neutral manner. These questions can also imply a moral judgment depending on the tone of voice and the precise choice of words. 'What on earth are you doing?' or 'And how do you propose to do that?' can also imply heavy judgments.

The appropriate use of this form of questioning is particularly important when difficult incidents arise in school. There are probably two major aspects of what is seen to be a discipline problem. Firstly, the student is behaving in a way the teacher does not like; secondly, something is happening emotionally and physically to the student that she may not understand properly. Any attempt to solve the first part of the problem is bound to develop into a struggle of wills, which can only end up as a loss of face for one of the participants. By looking at the second side of the problem, a teacher who is willing to use this form of questioning can add a whole new dimension to the situation, highlighting 'what' is happening to the student rather than 'why'. This allows a much clearer, more rational understanding of the situation, and can enable both the student and the teacher to change or modify their behaviour without having to lose face.

Janet Lederman (1972) provides a moving, semi-poetic account of the use of these techniques with ghetto children in the United States. She elicits clear statements from the children about what they are doing or what they have just done, such as 'Now I am hitting Norma'. When two children are fighting, the response of the protagonist to the question 'What are you doing?' is often 'He hit me'. Of course, this does not answer the question, but it may have a familiar ring to the experienced classroom teacher. Repeating the question will often produce the same response, 'He hit me'. By persevering, you may eventually obtain a more accurate response, which may go something like 'I hit him with my book'. This can be followed by more questions, which, hopefully, will help to make the other person's experience more clear to herself. This may all seem a little silly to someone who has not tried out this approach. There are no guarantees, but many teachers report that this neutral approach often results in the incident fizzling out without any need to take disciplinary measures.

This technique can be developed into quite subtle areas of self-understanding and lead to either a gentle or dramatic shift in the focus of attention.

The following incident involved a strong fifteen-year-old who was prone to violent outbursts of temper. He had been quietly insulted by one of the other students and was about to get up and thump him. One of the writers asked him to say what was happening inside his body and this seemed to stop him in his tracks. He described a tremendous tension building up in his head, which seemed as if it were about to explode. He was then asked to deliberately tense up his head and neck and let it go, several times. After he had done this, he was told to imagine he was breathing deeply into his head and neck. He then seemed quite relaxed and the original problem had apparently disappeared. The class was riveted by the whole event.

It is not easy to detach yourself from your emotional reactions and maintain the necessary control to concentrate on the appropriate form of words when a discipline problem is blowing up in the normal classroom. Teachers invariably experience a threat to their authority, making them react in an emotional manner. This often results in an attempt to impose their own values and expectations onto the situation, which then meets with resistance and sets up a confrontation. The use of a neutral form of questioning is often the last possibility that comes to mind. On the other hand, many of the verbal exchanges between teachers and students have outcomes which are not in the interests of either party and the effort of trying out something new could provide surprising results.

This is not to say that the teacher should never indulge in direct expressions of honest emotion, but perhaps this is best done in the form of a statement rather than a question. 'You really make me angry when you do that', is a much more honest statement of feeling than 'How dare you do that?' This difference will be developed in the next section.

A curious feature of the use of this mode of questioning, particularly when applied to a disciplinary problem, is that the recipient often has the experience of having been punished, even though no punishment has been administered. The person is discomfited by the experience.

We would suggest that this discomfort relates to having a clearer understanding of our own behaviour and the problem of changing. Most personal growth involves breaking old habits and routines which are run off without too much awareness. An awareness of the need to change these patterns can be disturbing. If, however, the upset feelings are related to a burgeoning awareness and acceptance of responsibility for one's own behaviour, they become more acceptable than the feelings that are associated with conventional punishments such as detention, telling off or loss of privilege.

An understandable complaint is that the teacher does not have the time to go into extended dialogue of this nature during the hurly-burly of the working day. However, merely changing the occasional word in a sentence does not require much in the way of time. The extra effort is involved in paying attention and breaking a habit. Compare the following two dialogues and consider which would be more typical of yourself and which is the most civilized.

Student: I'm sorry I've forgotten my homework, sir.
Teacher: But this is the second time in a week. I told you last time you had to buck your ideas up. Why have you forgotten it this time?
Student: Don't know, sir.
Teacher: 'Don't know', of course you know. Why wasn't that book handed in with the rest?
Student: I forgot it, sir.
Teacher: Why did you forget it?
Pupil: Don't know, sir.

And so on.
But now try this:

Student: I'm sorry I've forgotten my homework, sir.
Teacher: Well thanks for coming to see me, but this is the second time

in a week and I asked you last time to be sure to hand all your
work in on time. Otherwise you know, it's difficult for me to keep
track of marking.

Student: Yes, sir.

Teacher: Did you know exactly what the work was about?

Student: Yes, sir.

Teacher: Tell me exactly what you had to do then.

Student: Er, er, er. I've forgotten sir.

Teacher: Did you write the work down in your rough book?

Student: No, sir.

Teacher: Well that could explain it. Where is your rough book?

Student: I haven't got one sir.

Teacher: So you didn't have a note of the homework because you
didn't have a rough book.

Student: Yes, sir.

Teacher: Well that's easily solved. I've an old exercise book you can
use for rough notes until you can get a new rough book. So there
will be no reason for you not to hand homework in on time.

Student: Yes, sir, thanks, sir.

Hopefully these changes have turned the interview into a pastoral care
situation rather than an overemphasis on moralizing and punishment.
Let's try another example:

Teacher: Come in. Sit down, I want to talk to you about your
behaviour in Mr Hunt's class yesterday.

Student: Yes, Miss.

Teacher: Mr Hunt tells me you behaved disgracefully.

Student: Yes, Miss.

Teacher: That you chatted loudly for half the lesson, did no work and
distracted the class around you.

Student: Yes, Miss.

Teacher: Well, what have you got to say for yourself?

Student: I don't know, Miss.

Teacher: Why were you talking?

Student: I don't know.

Teacher: Oh come on! All right, why didn't you get on with the work?

Student: I couldn't do it, Miss.

Teacher: Why couldn't you do it?

Student: It was too hard, Miss.
Teacher: Why was it too hard?
Student: I don't know, Miss.
Teacher: You know if you can't understand the work you must ask the teacher.
Student: Yes, Miss.
Teacher: Well why didn't you ask the teacher?

And so on.

Conducted in a different way the interview could have turned out very differently:

Head of year: Come in John, sit down won't you. I wanted to see you because I'm very worried about some of the things I've been hearing about you – especially from Mr Hunt.
Student: Yes, Miss.
Head of year: Mr Hunt told me that yesterday you behaved very badly in his lesson.
Student: I was only talking Miss.
Head of year: Can you tell me exactly what happened?
Student: When I came in I was talking to my mate and sir told me off – but he didn't tell him off.
Head of year: How did you feel about that?
Student: It's always the same Miss, he always picks on me, he gets on my nerves.
Head of year: Go on, so what happened next?
Student: Well I sat down and I didn't have my book.
Head of year: Did you mention it to Mr Hunt?
Student: No, he would have gone beserk!
Head of year: So what did you do?
Student: Nothing. I just sat there.
Head of year: Just sat there?
Student: Well, I did talk a bit and then this lad behind me kicked my bag over, so I turned round and told him – well you know Miss, and Mr Hunt blamed me again and sent me out.
Head of year: Okay John. Let's go through it again. I can tell you now that Mr Hunt is not 'picking on you' as you think. He was telling me today that he thinks you're a bright boy with lots of potential and he wants to make sure you don't fall behind in your work. He says you often forget books. Is he right?

Student: Yes, Miss, I suppose so.

Head of year: Well we'll see if we can do something about that.

Student: What?

Head of year: We'll try organizing a timetable for you to follow strictly and you can report to me with it daily. Do you think that would help?

Student: Yes, Miss.

Head of year: Are you finding the work a lot to get through?

Student: Yes, Miss, and I was away last week and if you miss any then it's hard to catch up.

Head of year: Okay, I'll tell you what we'll do. I'll ask Mr Hunt to come in and see you about the work you've missed. I know he's anxious to make sure that you keep up and perhaps when you're up to date, you won't have any more problems about being picked on.

Student: Yes, Miss. Thanks, Miss.

Head of year: And when you've spoken to Mr Hunt come back and see me and we'll go through your organization schedule together.

Student (smiling): Yes, Miss, thanks.

Taking this approach to pastoral and discipline situations may result in other important issues emerging which require a more extended counselling response from the teacher. The technique we are dealing with here is a counselling skill and can be equally effective when relating to other members of staff whether on a peer group basis or as part of the pattern of authority within the institution. Used with skill, this neutral form of questioning permits a potent searching interaction without imposing the values, judgments, distorted perceptions and fantasies of the questioner.

Open and closed questions

We referred to the difference between open and closed questions in the previous chapter. The closed question produces a terse or monosyllabic response, whereas the open question permits the possibility of a more extended response. Hargreaves (1982) suggests that this categorization is too simple, and suggests that some apparently closed questions are extended by the respondent. The appropriateness of a type of question depends on what the teacher intends. If you wish to know a student's name, a closed question will achieve this end. If you wish to encourage students to talk more, then an open question will facilitate this, but does not guarantee an extended response. The main problem in this area is that teachers are often not aware of the way they use questions and could be helped by some feedback from an objective observer.

The suggestions made in the previous section provide a more open approach to questioning in counselling and pastoral situations.

The use of statements

The emphasis in the previous section has been on the skilled use of questioning. For some students their only experience of verbal exchanges with teachers is replying to questions, which relate either to the content of the lesson or their behaviour. The words 'interrogation' or 'grilling' could well describe these exchanges.

Perls (1969) suggests that every question covers up an implied statement and that a question is a way of avoiding making a direct statement. This could be a way of defending against the real feeling that would be revealed.

'Why are you so quiet?' may mean 'Your silence disturbs me, I want you to say something about yourself.'

'Why are you running down the corridor?' may imply 'Don't run down the corridor, it is against the school rules.'

'Would you get out your books?' invariably means 'I want you to get out your books.'

It is worth experimenting with changing all your questions into statements for a period of time and seeing what happens. It invariably results in a refreshingly direct form of expression and cuts through a great deal of prevarication which pervades many exchanges. 'Do you want to go out for a meal?' often means, 'I want to go out for a meal and I want you to go with me.'

Often the young teacher expresses her demands in the form of questions and justifies herself by suggesting that it is more polite than using imperatives. Unfortunately the question, 'Will you stop talking please?' invites the answer 'No', whereas the meaning that was implied is closer to 'I want you to stop talking.'

Questions are used by teachers, counsellors and administrators in highly manipulative ways, enabling the questioner to avoid taking responsibility for what she is trying to impose on the other person.

'Are you free next period?' (knowing full well). 'Yes'. 'Oh! Could you take 3T?' Here the responsibility for the decision is partly given to the other person, when, in reality, there is little choice.

More ways of changing language

Recently, a friend was tryng to teach his eight-year-old daughter to dive into the swimming pool. 'I can't go in head first,' came the complaint. 'Try saying "I won't go in head first,"' replied the friend, who had recently attended some sessions on the Gestalt approach to language. 'Don't be silly, I can't go in head first.' 'Just try saying the words, "I won't go in head first".' Angrily, the daughter replied, 'All right, I won't go in head first,' and stormed off in a huff. The instruction had been going on for several weeks, and only two days after this incident, she reported that she had dived in on her own.

There is no way to prove that the events were connected in any way, but the technique of changing 'can't' to 'won't' is one of several ways described in the literature on Gestalt Therapy (Passons, 1975) to help another person be more clear about her experience. The word 'can't' implies that the person has no control over the situation. The word 'won't' implies that the person has some choice in the matter. If the person is choosing, then she has to take responsibility for the choice that is being made.

Most people baulk at the suggestion to make this change and can find it emotionally upsetting to consider the part they are playing in the limitations to their lives. Again, some individuals are unable to get the words out of their mouths, even if it is presented as a simple experiment.

A useful exercise is to consider yourself responsible for everything that happens in your life, rather than blame the headteacher, difficult classes, unco-operative colleagues, a difficult home situation and so on. Some individuals choose to put up with the most appalling life situations, because they imagined alternatives would be even worse. It is as if the person has no choice in the matter.

Consider the following examples:

'I can't control 3B.'
'I won't vary my behaviour in order to be more effective with 3B.'

'I can't make friends with the children in this new class.'
'I won't make friends with the children in this new class.'

'I can't concentrate on my work because Stephen keeps distracting me.'
'I choose to spend more time watching Stephen mess about than concentrate on my work.'

'I can't get to work on time in the morning.'
'I won't lead my life in a way that doesn't make me late in the morning.'

Working with a younger person on a one-to-one basis, it might be worth, on occasions, asking them to repeat what they have said, changing the word 'can't' to 'won't'. To do this constantly, like the person who has to play the counsellor all the time, would make you into something of a pain in the neck, but with judicious timing, this can be an extremely potent intervention.

This is similar to asking a person to change 'have to' into 'choose to'. Again, this suggests that the person has more choice in her life than she cares to admit to herself. The prize example goes something like:

'Why didn't you do your homework last night?'
'I couldn't do it, because I had to play out with me mates.'

However, children are not the only ones to make this sort of statement:

'I would love to come to the meeting tonight, but I have to go to the dentist.'

In both of these examples, there could be a great deal of choice in the situation. For a person who is being counselled, it is particularly important to explore the possibilities for choice, as this is a necessary condition for generating alternative ways of behaving. This is equally important to the mature teacher as to the student in difficulty. The teacher and the student often blame each other for creating a problem situation, when, in reality, they are both locked into a closed system of action and reaction, which could be broken by a creative response on the part of one of the protagonists.

Another variation of the same theme is to ask the other person to examine the use of the word 'but' and see if 'and' wouldn't be a more appropriate conjunction.

'I would like to work for my exams but I get distracted by the early evening TV shows.'
'I would like to work for my exams and I get distracted by the early evening TV shows.'

The 'buts' slip off our tongues so easily that the second version doesn't sound quite right. On the other hand, the 'and' implies that the two activities are not mutually exclusive. There is plenty of time in the evenings to study and watch TV.

'I would like to be nicer to my second year class, but they behave like a bunch of hooligans.'
'I would like to be nicer to my second year class, and they behave like a bunch of hooligans.'

This is an adult version and, once more, the first version implies that there can be no politeness in the face of hooligan behaviour, leaving no choices in the situation. The second version implies that there are two problems, one concerning niceness and one concerning hooligan behaviour. There may be a connection between the two, but the option for change in the situation is being left open.

Another way language can be used to create a change in awareness is to replace 'should' and 'ought' with statements which say 'I want you to . . .'

'You shouldn't wear make-up in school.'
'I don't want you to wear make-up in school.'

'You ought to get to work on time.'
'I want you to get to work on time.'

In the revised form, the speaker is taking responsibility for the statement that is being made, rather than invoking an inferred moral law.

* The following exercise sums up many of the language changes we have suggested so far.
  During the coming week:

1 Never use the word 'why'.
2 Only use statements rather than questions.
3 Change all your 'oughts' and 'shoulds' to 'I want you to ...'
4 Change all your 'I can'ts' to 'I choose not to ...'
5 Always use the first person 'I ...' rather than pronouns such as 'one', 'we', 'they', 'it', and so on.
6 Change all your 'buts' into 'ands'.

It can be useful to enlist the help of someone you live with in this exercise and ask to be corrected you when you slip up. This is a way of getting the other person involved. To be given the role of teacher is an indirect way of getting the other person to pay attention to the same issues.

At the end of the week, share your experience with a colleague or your student group.

Filling in the gaps

The techniques taken from Gestalt Therapy described in the previous section, provide some simple examples of how to change the way that language is used in order to make it more effective. Simple perhaps to understand the theory, but not so simple to put into practice. Often the ideas are rejected before they have been tried out, which is unfortunate because the emotional impact of these techniques cannot be fully understood until they have been tried out in practice; a form of experiential learning.

Our language is, however, very complex and there are many ways in which meaning is clouded, limiting the experience of both the speaker and the listener. This is equally true for the most literate teacher and the most inarticulate student. The use of confusing statements and missing out information is part of everyday language.

These forms of verbal shorthand sound normal to our ears, but when examined in greater depth reveal that language is being used as a form of defence.

'I'm bored' is often the cry heard from adolescents in schools, but for the adolescent or teacher to pursue the cause of the boredom could be a painful experience for them both.

'He can't control his classes.' From whose point of view doesn't he control his classes? Does he never control his classes?

'Her failure at school was due to lack of support from home.' Was there no support from home? Did she fail everything? Did she see herself as a failure?

So, it seems, there is a great deal of information missing from these simple statements. It would not be difficult to make a guess at what these statements intended. Sometimes statements are incomplete because it would be too painful for the speaker to fill in the gaps. Often the speaker is not consciously aware that she is limiting the communication and is defending herself from understanding the situation too clearly.

'The headteacher always argues with me.' Surely it takes two people to make an argument; to what extent is the speaker responsible?

'My bad temper stops me from ever being polite to 3B.' Is bad temper a thing which someone can own, or does it consist of activities the person does?

Bandler and Grinder (1975b) have developed an elaborate system for identifying these ways of limiting communication. They use Chomsky's idea of the difference between 'deep structure' and 'surface structure'. The deep structure is the person's representation of the world in its fullest extent. The surface structure is that part of the deep structure that the person is willing to present to the world and perhaps all that she is willing to present to herself. This has been described as a misapplication of Chomsky's ideas (Watts, 1983), but the techniques for looking at language do appear to be extremely useful in helping another person become more clear about her experience.

Bandler and Grinder discuss three ways in which we limit our communications. These are deletion, distortion and generalization.

Deletion
'When I take 5C on Friday afternoon, I get really angry.'

Who makes her angry and what is she angry about?

'I'm confused by maths.' What in particular is confusing about maths to this person?

'You are a real nuisance.' How is this person a nuisance and to whom?

'That awful child is continually irritating.' What in particular is awful and who is irritated and how?

'I don't want to go into Mr Richardson's lesson.' Why is it difficult to go into this teacher's lesson?

Much of the time, people collude to accept a conversation that has missing information of this nature. To ask for this missing information could create an embarrassing or emotionally charged situation. There are, however, at least two useful ways in which these aspects of language can be examined in educational contexts.

Firstly, as a teacher, it is worth examining your own use of language to ascertain whether more complete statements are a better expression of what you want to say. This can provide useful insights into your own experience and motivation. It may also provide some insight into your own contribution to difficult situations. Clear complete statements can help to solve discipline problems. 'I'm getting annoyed' is an incomplete statement whereas 'Brian, you annoy me when you bang your pencil on the desk' is a complete statement about the annoyance, leaving Brian very clear about his contribution to the situation.

Secondly, one-to-one counselling situations provide an opportunity for the student to explore the emotional limitations of the way in which he uses language.

'I'm scared of going in to woodwork.' What is frightening; is it the other students, or is it the teacher? What do they do to cause the fear? These issues can be dealt with by using the Gestalt form of questioning described in the previous section. 'What makes you scared?', 'What does he do that makes you scared?'

Often, when teachers have been involved with in-service courses which examine these techniques, they start correcting their colleagues over coffee at break-times. You may get away with doing it once or twice and it could be a useful experience for your colleagues. However, if you continually examine what they are saying, you are likely to find yourself sitting on your own.

Forms of deletion are often involved in adverbs ending in -ly.

'Clearly, you need to get down to some serious studying.' To whom is this clear?

'Obviously, Mr Parton doesn't like me.' To whom is it obvious?

'Unfortunately, your attitude isn't going to help us to get on.' To whom is it unfortunate?

'We worked through the steps of the exercise painfully.' To whom was it painful?

The last statement could have been made by a teacher helping a student. It is possible that the student was working in her accustomed manner and all the pain was experienced by the teacher. The statement makes it a shared problem, which may be helping the teacher to avoid her problem of impatience.

Try applying similar questions to the following statements:

'One must take one's colleagues' feelings into account.'

'It is necessary to maintain a degree of reserve in teaching situations.'

'Everybody messes about in French.'

'Every time you get Simon Phillips in your class you have to squash him straight away.'

Distortion

Statements are often distorted by changing what should be an ongoing process into a fixed event. This is done grammatically by changing a verb into a noun. Thus a verb like 'to decide' loses its capacity for change once it has been called a decision.

'My choice of career is making me unhappy.'

'Our decision to introduce setting in maths is causing problems in the timetable.'

In both of these examples 'choice' and 'decision' preclude the possibility of re-evaluation.

This use of nouns is very subtle and is often difficult to identify. Bandler and Grinder suggest a useful exercise of trying to put nouns into an imaginary wheelbarrow. Nouns such as book, spoon, bottle, picture and apple can easily be seen in the imaginary wheelbarrow. Nouns such as decision, feeling, refusal, anger, agreement, confusion, happiness, pain, fear and frustration cannot be imagined in this way. This inability to imagine abstract nouns concretely suggests that they might better be considered as an ongoing process.

'I'm scared of Mrs Banks' bad temper.' What is it that Mrs Banks does that is scary?

'My poor concentration prevents me from completing my assignments.' What is this person doing which is labelled poor concentration?

'I can't go to Junior Club because of my shyness.' What is this person experiencing which is labelled shyness?

'I haven't got much intelligence.' What does this person do that is evidence of lack of intelligence?

'Sharon's impudence causes my anger.' What does she do to make the speaker feel angry?

The questions following the statements illustrate ways in which they can be challenged. The challenge can be taken even further with questions such as:

'What stops you from concentrating?'
'What happens when you do go to the disco?'
'What would happen if you didn't respond to Sharon in an angry manner?'

This use of abstract nouns is perfectly correct in terms of grammar and everyday usage. They can be questioned because they involve a surface structure that does not necessarily represent the person's deep structure. An examination of these abstract nouns may demonstrate to the speaker that she has more choices than she is willing to admit to.

Another subtle form of distortion involves what are called presuppositions. This involves the inclusion of information in a sentence which has to be assumed to be correct for the sentence to make sense. It is a form of semantic blackmail.

'As you are only interested in teaching your subject, I am not giving you a tutor group this year.' The initial assumption may or may not be true.

'If you knew how much work was involved, you wouldn't ask me to do the PTA accounts.'

'Miss, if you knew how much I hated her, you wouldn't ask me to sit next to her.'

'If you had done more preparation in the first place, you wouldn't be having so much trouble now.'

'Since I'm not going to get a job anyway, there's no point in working for exams.'

'If he's going to pick on me like he always does, I'm not going into his lessons.'

The presuppositions in these sentences are easy to identify. They may be perfectly correct descriptions of that person's experience of the world. It may be a deliberate distortion designed to justify the second part of the statement:

'If you are going to indulge in your usual unpleasantness, there is no point in trying to work together.'

It may be that the content of the presupposition is the most important part of the statement. This form allows the message to be given in a more covert manner and relieves the embarrassment of making a direct statement.

'When you have your temper tantrums, I find it impossible to reason with you.'

Another form of distortion is described as Cause and Effect. These are statements that imply that the behaviour of one person causes an inner state or feeling in another person.

'Your continual criticism upsets me.'
'Your continual criticism makes me feel upset.'

Statements of this nature imply that the other person or event has a great deal of power over the speaker and can control her life in some mysterious way. Yet another way of putting responsibility for behaviour onto another person.

'Just walking to school makes me feel sick.'
'Other people's demands take away all of my free time.'
'Your soothing voice relaxes me.'
'You make me angry when you talk in that silly voice.'
'Teaching makes me tense.'

All of these implied causal relationships can be challenged by asking the speaker exactly how the effect is brought about by the cause. The speaker can be asked to check that the cause always produces the effect.

'What is there about teaching that makes you tense?'
'Do you always get tense when you are teaching?'

A more extended form of cause and effect involves the use of the conjunction 'but'.

'I would apply for promotion in another part of the country, but my mother's illness prevents me from moving to a different part of the country.'
'I want to get my homework done, but the rest of the family won't give me any peace.'

These statements may be a reasonable assessment of the situation, or they may be an excuse for avoiding a situation that the speaker is unable to cope with. The statements can be challenged in the usual manner:

'How does your mother's illness prevent you from moving?'
'What exactly do your family do to prevent you getting any peace?'

Yet another form of distortion is described as mind reading. People often make statements that imply that the speaker knows what is going on in the other person's head or knows what she is feeling. These sort of statements can be the cause of a great deal of misunderstanding as they are usually made regarding a third person who is not present and thus not able to confirm or deny the thoughts and feelings ascribed to her.
'Susan doesn't like me.'
'Mr Brown thinks I'm an idiot.'

Generalization
'I find it difficult to work with female colleagues.'
'Miss Soames never listens to what I say.'
'It is impossible to trust anyone in 3T.'

These statements are all generalizations which are only a limited expression of the experiences from which they are drawn. Some generalizations, such as 'All six-foot men are taller than me', are obviously correct, and though they may be of importance to the speaker, the statements do not need to be questioned.

However, the initial statements in this section can all be challenged:

'Is there no woman you have found it easy to work with?'
　'Has Miss Soames never listened to anything you have said?'
　'Can't you think of one person in 3T that you can trust?'

The generalization is often an explanation for not behaving in a certain way. This may be a way of behaving that the person concerned finds difficult or may indeed have never tried. This can be challenged by asking the person concerned to imagine what it would be like to try out the behaviour she finds difficult.

'It's impossible to talk to teachers about personal problems.'
　'What would happen if you did talk to teachers about personal problems?'
　'I wouldn't go on any out-of-school activity with Mr James.'
　'What would happen if you did go on an out-of-school activity with Mr James?'

Another form of generalization puts all of the blame onto the other person, even though the situation demands the active participation of both people.

'Martin Smith is always fighting with me.'
　'Susan Jones is always talking to me.'

Martin and Susan may be fighting with and talking to the respective individuals without their joining in, but it seems unlikely. By suggesting that they are only playing a passive role, the speakers are avoiding the possibility that they are partly responsible for the fighting and talking. A useful shift of emphasis is provided by reversing the statement.

'Are you always fighting with Martin Smith?'
　'Are you always talking to Susan Jones?'

This type of intervention is not necessarily going to solve the problem being discussed, but at least it demonstrates that there is an alternative way of looking at the situation and opens the possibility of the person looking more closely at her own behaviour.

Bandler and Grinder list several different forms of generalization and different ways of challenging them. These forms occur over and over again in the everyday talk of most teachers and students. Few of them are accurate representations of that person's experience, and it may be that a clear awareness of our experience of the world would be too painful, especially if we were bombarded with challenges to our attempts to defend ourselves. On the other hand, the slow erosion of these defensive linguistic tactics could eventually lead to a more open and honest way of interacting with others in your daily life.

Paradoxical statements

Some statements that are made include elements of paradox. Paradox is usually discussed as a logical exercise such as 'All Cretans are liars – I am a Cretan.' Even in this hypothetical form, paradox has a mind-bending quality.

In chapter two we examined the paradox in the statement: 'Take responsibility for your own behaviour' and suggested that the other person could either:

(a) refuse to do it, or
(b) agree to do it, in which case she is doing what you say and hence not taking responsibility for her own learning.

There is no way in which the injunction to be more responsible can be obeyed. The person is wrong if she obeys and wrong if she does not obey. This is sometimes called a negative double bind. A similar problem is produced by asking someone to be more spontaneous.

Sometimes the double bind is not spelled out too clearly as in the statement,

'You never tell me that you love me.'

Implicit is the suggestion that it has to be done voluntarily. Any future response will be seen as a response to the request.

Double binds are often not easy to identify, because half the message is being presented non-verbally. The verbal statement is being contradicted by the non-verbal statement.

The Head of Year may say to the student,

'Of course you can trust me',

when non-verbally it is being made clear that this is not the case. If the student refuses to comply, she will be punished – and if she does comply, her trust might be abused.

These negative double binds can be turned on their heads to everybody's advantage. Usually this involves making the statements which are least expected.

If you are talking to a student who is in some sort of trouble, it might be worth saying,

'You can't trust me completely but . . .'

If she doesn't trust you, then at least she is doing what you asked. If she does trust you, then you are receiving co-operation. Either way, you are probably making an accurate statement, which is also likely to engender trust.

Postscript

The suggestions made in the previous sections for changing the way that language is used serve more than one purpose.

Firstly, they help the individual become more aware of the implications of what she is saying, making her more aware of her existence or 'being-in-the-world' (Boss, 1979). Increasing awareness could be seen as an important part of a definition of education. The guidelines offered by the Gestalt therapist help the person to develop this awareness without an authority figure telling her what her experience is. Many of us have a seriously impoverished awareness of our experience. This self-imposed limitation may be because an increase in awareness might be too painful to bear. If this is so, then the speaker will resist suggestions to change, and there is little point trying to push against the resistance.

Secondly, given this awareness, the individual finds that she has far more responsibility for what happens to her than she may have imagined. Again, this is a rather frightening prospect as existence is much easier when external circumstances can be blamed for life's failures. The section on Locus of Control suggests that there is a personality dimension defined by the degree to which individuals feel that they are personally responsible for what happens in their lives. The writers would make the value judgment that it is a good thing to believe that you have considerable control over your own life.

Thirdly, given this increased awareness and feeling of responsibility, the individual may realize that she has more choices in life. Increasing the choices available to the individual could also be part of a definition of education. A consideration of the possibility of making choices is a hoary old philosophical chestnut. The writers make the assumption that human beings are capable of making choices and do have some control over the course of their lives.

The use of fantasy

Fantasy plays a part in all our lives, whether we like it or not. We day-dream, rehearse negative thoughts about our colleagues, imagine what our holidays will be like, dream, have nightmares and sometimes hallucinate. Indeed, the difference between fantasy and reality is perhaps not as clear as we would like, as Perky (1910) showed in an experiment where subjects had difficulty in distinguishing between an image projected onto a screen and their own mental image of the same object.

So what does this have to do with human relations? If a colleague says, 'I experience my career as crawling along a dark narrow sewer with only a tiny speck of light at the end', she would seem to be communicating much more vividly than if she had said, 'I am finding my work as a teacher difficult'. The use of metaphor powerfully illustrates the strength of feeling contained in the first statement whereas the straight forward meaning of the second is bereft of all feeling content.

We will demonstrate that fantasy and imagery can be a powerful mode for understanding yourself and communicating with other people. In the classroom structured exercises using fantasy can be used to generate a high level of involvement, and help students to get in contact with and express their feelings.

In this chapter we will be dealing mainly with visual imagery. This is not to say that other senses do not play a part in fantasy, and some individuals appear to have preference for auditory or kinesthetic (movement, feeling and touch) forms of fantasy. By evoking several senses in the initial stages of the fantasy, the experience becomes much more vivid.

* Ask the group to relax, close their eyes, take three deep breaths and then read the following script:

   'I want you to imagine you are by the sea – it doesn't have to be a place you know. (pause) Have a good look around. What can you see? What is the shoreline like? What is the sea doing? Are there other people around or are you alone? (pause) What can you hear? What sort of noise is the sea making? (pause) Experience the smell of the sea and the taste of the salt air. (pause) What are you doing – lying – sitting – walking? (pause) Feel the surface you are on – feel the wind blowing from the sea – get a sense of the temperature. (pause) Now try and get the sense that something is about to happen – that someone is coming along the shore to meet you – just allow the fantasy to take its own course – who comes – what is said – what happens? (long pause) When it is right for you, gently come out of the fantasy.'

   Now ask the group to share their experience in sub-groups of five. After fifteen minutes, or when the talking begins to lull, bring the whole group together to share any further aspects of the experience.

A fantasy journey of this nature is often described by the participants as an altered state of consciousness which has not been experienced before and is very different from normal day-dreaming. There are often demands to repeat the experience, because it tends to be very relaxing, irrespective of the nature of the imagery.

Indulging in fantasy is not often seen as an appropriate activity for the classroom. We live in a society that does not encourage looking inward. Day-dreaming is discounted as an adolescent indulgence and yet Singer (1966) showed that normal adults day-dreamed most of the time, even when they were performing complex intellectual tasks. Possibly an examination of our ongoing day-dreams may give us some clues to our current needs and preoccupations that are not being allowed to enter fully our consciousness. Given a good relationship with the teacher or facilitator, a group of students of any age can be asked to share their day-dreams to produce an involved and personal discussion. Some self-disclosure on the part of the teacher tends to make a good starting point.

Psychologists have also tended to ignore fantasy and imagery. Internal experience is not amenable to strict experimental control, and the strong influence of behaviourism which stresses the measurement of observable variables has contributed to this neglect. Singer (1974) charted the history of the study of fantasy and showed how research into this area had been left to clinicians who used fantasy techniques as a form of psychotherapy. This often involved a long fantasy journey. The patient would be given a starting point such as climbing a mountain, or exploring a river from its source. Then she would be asked to describe the fantasy aloud, with minimal help and encouragement from the therapist. This type of experience is now seen as an important part of personal growth (Ferrucci, 1982) and the normal development of any individual. The fantasy we have described here is done on a one-to-one basis and as such is not appropriate for the classroom. The form of scripted fantasy given at the beginning of this section can be used with a classroom group and the quality of the experience tends to be similar.

Do experiences of this nature provide more than a relaxing, pleasant experience? Do the fantasies have any meaning that is likely to be helpful to the person concerned? In an examination of the fantasy journeys of both adolescents and student teachers using a repertory grid technique, Hall (1983) showed that the plethora of images produced by each person was really limited to a small number of broad themes that were unique to the individual concerned. There was one major theme that was common to a large number of the fantasies, which involved images which could be placed on a continuum from 'free' to 'defended'.

Certainly, this research suggested that a series of scripted fantasy procedures produced a limited and organized number of themes, whereas fantasy is normally seen as a vehicle for going beyond ordinary experience, giving the individual limitless possibilities for creative imagery. These themes suggest that fantasy is constrained in similar ways to rational thinking, but in ways that have a logic that is unique to the individual.

The personal testimonies of people who have been through scripted fantasies is powerful and almost universally positive. This type of evidence would not be accepted by a psychologist with a behaviourist orientation and reasonably so, as fantasy involves fleeting, ephemeral phenomena which are easily distorted by suggestion and expectation. Before dismissing these procedures, however, it is important to give them a try and test them in an experiential mode rather than an experimental one.

A major assumption behind the use of fantasy exercises of this nature is that the person is projecting material into the imagery which is psychologically important. As we suggested in chapter three, the truth in the projection is a difficult thing to prove, in particular when it is felt that unconscious processes are being revealed. On the other hand, teachers who have worked with students using fantasy exercises will have no doubt that the students are projecting important aspects of themselves into their imagery. The descriptions of the imagery are often deeply moving and deeply emotional, involving forms of languages and expression that are atypical of their normal school work (Hall, 1983).

The simple exercise used in the introduction of asking a group 'What kind of weather am I?' could be seen as a simple projection exercise. Here is another example:

* Ask a group to sit in a relaxed manner and then take them through the following script: 'I want you to look around the room and choose an object. Any part of the room will do, or anything in it, as long as it is not another person. Now close your eyes, relax, and take three deep breaths. (pause) Now, in imagination, experience what it is like to be your object. (pause) Become the object as fully as you can. (pause) What can you see going on around you? (pause) What does it feel like to be in this situation? (pause) What would you like to say to the world? Just let the words come in imagination. (pause) What is your life like? (pause) When it is right for you, gently come back to the room.'

  Ask the group to share their experience in turn. If someone in the group makes a statement which intuitively seems important, try the question, 'Is there anything like that in your life?' (Oaklander, 1978).

Sometimes a group member will admit that she has been talking about herself when describing the fantasy. Others will deny it. Occasionally, you may be convinced that a person is saying something important, but she disclaims any personal relevance. In a situation like this, it is probably best to resist pressing the person concerned and perhaps examine yourself to see if you are not projecting some of your own thoughts and feelings onto her. An example from one of the writers' experience is that of a group member who, in a fantasy, chose to be a doormat, whom everybody trod upon and ignored. Merely listening to his description triggered off feelings about similar life experiences, yet the inclination was to repress these feelings and insist that the other person confess that he was projecting, which he denied.

In our everyday lives, images slip in and out of awareness very quickly, and exercises can be used to tune into this fantasy experience and to see if it has significant meaning. The simple exercise on 'What kind of weather am I?' can be extended as follows:

* Sit the group in a circle and invite them in turn to nominate another person and use questions of the form, 'Susan, what kind of insect am I?' or 'James, what kind of motor car am I?' Encourage them to be creative in the categories they use. It is always useful for the person in the teacher role to do it first.

    This exercise does require a reasonable set of relationships within the group, as it could lead to swapping mutual insults. It does have a built-in safeguard in that the person may choose who is to give them feedback.

    Afterwards the group can be asked how they felt about taking part in the exercise and about their response to specific comments that had been made. Why were specific people chosen and why were others avoided? It could be gently suggested that some of the comments given were more relevant to the giver than the recipient – a form of projection.

Tuning in to images as they emerge may be saying something about intuition or the ability to tune in to knowledge that cannot be explained in terms of normal rational processes. The following exercise can produce some surprises. The exercise as written is more appropriate for adults, but could be modified to suit younger students.

* Ask the members of the group to form pairs and then take them through the following instructions: 'Sit facing your partner – relax – and try to empty your head and make use of any images that emerge about the other person. Try completing the following

sentence stem using the images that emerge. Try to report them even though they may sound silly.

"When you were a small child you used to . . ."

Complete the sentence stem several times over, taking turns.'

After a few minutes suggest to the group that they repeat the process, but this time to make some guesses about the other person's present life.

'Right now in your life . . .'

Then repeat the process with 'In ten years' time you will be . . .'

Then allow five minutes for the pairs to share their reactions to the experience.

When the group have come together and made some final comments it might be worth asking if anyone felt they were projecting their own material onto the other person.

The reader may still be somewhat cynical regarding the appropriateness of introducing techniques of this nature into the conventional classroom. How can a class, which is difficult to control at the best of times, become amenable to a sensitive exercise which involves closing the eyes and silently following the imagery? It may be difficult to initiate work of this nature, but in the long run, experience has shown that activities of this type will produce a more relaxed classroom. Support for this statement comes from the reports of large numbers of experienced teachers who have attended a range of in-service courses in Human Relations at Nottingham University.

The typical experience of these teachers is that there is often an initial resistance to relaxing and closing eyes. Some schools have carpeted rooms in which the students can lie down. Often this facility is not available, but the students can be asked to put their heads down on folded arms as they sit at their desks. Some students who seem to have retained a form of eidetic imagery can have a vivid fantasy sitting in a normal manner with the eyes wide open.

There seems to be a general resistance to closing eyes in public. There is no point in trying to force compliance and we have found Oaklander's (1978) suggestion to use the phrase, 'You can peep if you want to', to be extremely helpful. It seems to result in a much higher proportion of the group actually closing their eyes.

Alternatively, even very young children can be given the opportunity to opt out of the exercise and sit quietly at the back without interfering in the activity. Teachers have reported that, given this responsibility, children will sit quietly and often report having had vivid fantasy experiences despite themselves.

With classes of disturbed or low achieving students who find it difficult to stay still for any length of time, the students behave in what seems to be a disruptive manner; fidgeting, making noises, moving about and even making comments about the activity. Surprisingly, these disruptions do not appear to disturb the rest of the group and in the subsequent sharing of experience, the disruptive students again invariably report a vivid fantasy. We have found it helpful to avoid the normal disciplinary procedures in a situation like this. Usually a class will adjust to such a novel set of procedures after two or three attempts.

The following anecdotes illustrate that a fantasy experience may be having more effect than might be anticipated. One of the writers invited a group of twelve-year-olds in an inner-city comprehensive school to take part in a fantasy journey. Christina stated that this was a stupid thing to do and sat through the exercise with her arms folded, staring up at the ceiling with a defiant expression on her face. Part of the fantasy involved writing your name over and over again to cover two sheets of blank paper. Three months later Christina's mother came to the school for a parents' evening and reported that Christina had done a strange thing some time ago. She had taken a blank sheet of paper, written her name all over it, thrown it into the fire and said, 'Thank goodness that's over!' It is difficult to know what conclusions to draw from this, but it does suggest that despite her denial, the session was a vivid experience for Christina and the after effects were memorable even for her mother.

We have suggested repeatedly that experiential exercises should end with a sharing of experience for the whole group. The individual who has rejected the experience is often surprised by the feedback given by her peer group and as a result may be more willing to take an active part next time.

The effect of a guided fantasy on the mood of a class group can be very striking. The children tend to become more relaxed, speak more quietly, treat each other more caringly and become more co-operative. The evidence for this is again based on the reports of large numbers of teachers. A science teacher described how he had used a guided fantasy to give his students more insight into the movement of particles in a physics lesson. He was surprised to find that they spent the rest of the lesson talking in whispers – a new experience for that class.

Strangely, he never repeated the experience.

A teacher of rural science took his class through a fantasy in which the children were asked to design their own perfect room, the one they would most like to live in. Finally, they were invited to tidy the fantasy room. Later in the afternoon session, the children tidied up the rural science room, cleaning and putting away the tools, without any prompting from the teacher. Normally they had to be cajoled into tidying up. Again, it is difficult to know how to interpret an outcome of this nature. The suggestion to 'tidy up' appears to have carried over into the post-fantasy period, which was probably made more potent by the relaxed state induced by the fantasy itself.

This state of relaxation induced by a fantasy experience can be achieved in large groups, even a whole school. A teacher involved in one of the Human Relations courses in the School of Education at Nottingham University, and who was also a school counsellor, used a guided fantasy in a school assembly. He introduced it as simulating the state produced by meditation in other religions. The teachers and children were guided through the 'Wise Old Man' fantasy taken from Stevens (1971). After some initial shuffling and disturbance, everyone in the room settled down into a deep silence. Afterwards, the students were asked to discuss the experience with the person sitting next to them. An animated discussion followed which showed a high level of involvement by the students. Several of the teachers who were present commented on the unusual quality of the atmosphere generated by the assembly and also reported that the involved and co-operative mood continued on into the rest of the morning.

A more clinical example of the relaxing effect of fantasy is provided by the teacher who had to cope with a child who was suffering from a severe bout of home-sickness during a school trip abroad. The child concerned was unable to sleep and became very upset. The teacher took him on a short fantasy trip to a pleasant place and the child soon fell asleep and subsequently enjoyed the rest of his trip, without any further bouts of home-sickness. Her colleagues were amazed by this success and subsequently saw her as a person with mysterious powers.

The responses to fantasy journeys vary tremendously from individual to individual. For this reason, we would be opposed to the teacher interpreting fantasy experience for the person who has had the fantasy. An interpretation is probably saying more about the person who is making it, than the person who is being interpreted. In the same way that we project our own needs and feelings into our fantasies, we can also project them into other people's fantasies. If you are prone to interpret other people's fantasies, it might be worth examining the sort of interpretations that you make as they probably provide a clue to your own psychological processes. Freud appears to have had problems with sexual relations and sex plays an important part in psycho-analysis and indeed much of his writing. Sometimes the suggestion is made (Rowan, 1983) that interpretations should be made, but made sparingly. This is probably a much more powerful manipulation than giving interpretations all the time. It is all too easy to play the psychiatrist and impress the 'client' with your ability to see into their psyches. This can lead to a serious abuse of the teacher's position of authority.

On the other hand, the wording of a guided fantasy can be organized to help the person interpret the experience, if this is seen as a useful activity. This can be done by interweaving a neutral form of questioning beginning with 'what?' and 'how?' (see the previous section) to help the person examine aspects of her fantasy in more detail. We will illustrate this in the following fantasy script of 'A Visit to a Wise Old Man', which has often been interpreted as a Jungian archetype, predictably The Animus or Wise Man. Jung's (1959) archetypes imply that interpretations can be made of fantasy and dream experience. Elsewhere, however, Jung (1961) suggested that material produced by the patient should be dealt with in a non-interpretive manner, using questions like, 'What occurs to you in connection with that?', 'How do you mean that?', 'Where does that come from?', 'How do you think about it?' and so on. The interpretations just seem to emerge of their own accord from the patient's replies and associations.

* For the following fantasy journey find a position in which you can relax – if it is right for you, take three deep breaths and close your eyes. Now imagine that you are going up a mountain path. You are walking through the forest in the foothills and you can smell the strong musky scent of the trees. (pause) A clear half-moon lights up the branches and the foliage – the stars stand out clearly in the sky. (pause) The air is warm, but refreshed by a gentle breeze blowing up from the valley. (pause) How do you feel as you gently climb upwards? What are your thoughts? What are your expectations? (pause)

Now turn off from the main path to follow a smaller rocky path

which you know leads to the cave of a wise man. (pause) This route
is steeper and more difficult to climb – soon you begin to get tired
and short of breath. (pause) In the distance you can see a faint
light which shows that you are getting nearer to your destination
and you begin to get a second wind. (pause) As you approach you
can see the wise old man sitting before a fire – the flames send
flickering shadows into the cave and around the surrounding trees.
The old man appears to be aware of your presence and beckons
you to sit by the fire. He passes you a cup of cool spring water to
quench your thirst after the long warm climb. As you both sit in
silence, the old man occasionally stirs the embers of the fire and
you find yourself gently drawn into the trance-like atmosphere.

In fantasy, become the wise old man. (pause) How do you feel?
What are you thinking? What do you think of this person sitting
opposite you? (pause) Now as the old man, begin to talk to the
person who is sitting in front of you. Just allow the words to come
spontaneously. Say things that would be helpful in that person's
life. (pause)

Now become yourself again. How do you feel about what the
wise old man has said? (pause) Now reply to the old man's words.
Just see what comes. (pause) Now ask the wise man a question
that is important in your life. (pause)

Become the wise old man again and reply to the question.
(pause)

Become yourself and sit in silence for a while to examine how
you feel and think about the response to your question. (pause)
Then prepare to take your leave of the old man. As you stand, the
old man reaches into the folds of his clothes and gives you a gift
which is significant for you. You take the gift and examine it
carefully. How do you feel about the gift? (pause) Be aware of
how you say goodbye to the old man. Slowly turn to find your way
down the mountain path. Hold your gift carefully in your hands
and continue to examine it. Become as familiar as you can with
your gift.

As you continue down the path, allow the images to slowly fade
and then gently come back to the room.

Having completed the fantasy, ask the group to share their experience
either in small groups of four to five, or with the whole group. Going
round the whole group can be a long process, and as teacher or group

facilitator you don't have to hear what everybody has to say. Some people give a rich, vivid report of their fantasies and the listeners may feel they are actually sharing the experience. Others give a short factual response. In this case, it is worth asking for more detail in a neutral manner. 'What was it like to become the wise old man?', 'What question did you ask?' and so on. It is rare for questions of this nature not to provide a fuller response. However, it is important not to judge a person who appears to have had a barren experience. The ability to fantasize does seem to improve with practice.

Scripts for fantasies can be written by the teacher. However, two of the best sources of material for scripted fantasies are Stevens (1971) for older students and Oaklander (1978) for adolescents and also very young children. Oaklander worked as a clinical psychologist with disturbed children. Her accounts of the children's responses and the insights they gained into their lives and feelings are a moving testimony to the power of fantasy experience. Psychosynthesis, an institutionalized approach to personal growth, also places a strong emphasis on the use of fantasy. Ferrucci (1982) provided examples of scripted fantasies from this source and Fugitt (1983) provided material for teachers and parents.

As in Jungian psychology, psychosynthesis (Assagioli, 1965) stressed the positive and creative aspects of fantasy experience, contrasting with Freud's implication that fantasy material tapped a sink for experience, feelings, thoughts and infantile wishes that have traumatic and unpleasant associations. Both Jung and Assagioli stressed the transcendent quality of our fantasy experience, in that it appears to go beyond our normal experience and imply that it may provide insights into our spiritual nature.

Jung (1961) also suggested that fantasy provided an outlet for underdeveloped or repressed parts of the person. These represent aspects of the personality which are no longer part of the individual's awareness, or they may represent the 'archetypes' which are part of man's collective unconscious. On a more mundane level, most of us would admit to there being many sides to our personalities.

Perls et al (1973) suggested that every part of a fantasy in some way represented a part or a sub-personality of the person. This is demonstrated in the script of the 'Wise Old Man' fantasy, given earlier, where the members of the group were invited to take on the role of the old man. They could just as well have been invited to take on the role of any of the images that emerged in the fantasy such as the mountain, the moon, the fire, the gift, or even very small parts such as a pebble on the path.

Taking on the role of an image in a fantasy may appear to be a bizarre activity to the uninitiated. However, nearly everyone who tries it out has little difficulty in identifying with the image and soon becomes lost in the activity which takes on a strong significance for the person concerned. Even abstract images can be used in this way. If a person says she is feeling heavy, 'Be the heaviness', or if someone says she feels nothing, 'Be the nothingness.'

It involves a further leap of credibility to suggest that the image in some way represents a sub-personality. The word sub-personality is perhaps unfortunate in that it implies there is some fixed entity inside the person. It is a nominalization and would be better discussed as an ongoing process or an issue that is important to the individual. These ongoing processes or issues appear to have a unique emotional charge. It is not clear whether this is inherent in the image, or whether it develops as the person takes on the role of the image.

The notion of sub-personality does imply that the person is projecting aspects of her personality into the fantasies. Perls suggests that by taking on the roles of these possibly disowned parts of the personality, the individual can come to a better understanding of herself and come to a new synthesis or 'gestalt'.

'There is a part of me that would like to eat a great deal and get drunk, but there is also a part of me that would like to be ascetic, lead a healthy life and fast periodically.' We can all think of polarities of this nature. (Perhaps similar to Kelly's bi-polar constructs.) Perls (1969) presented a similar view and described an important polarity which he called 'top-dog' and 'underdog'. In the example given, the ascetic would be an example of 'top-dog' and the drunk would be an example of 'underdog'. He goes on to suggest that the 'underdog' tends to win out in the end because it represents more basic human needs than the moralizing 'top-dog'.

The notion of projection has come up over and over again in this section of fantasy. Some scripted fantasies have a strong central image, which invite projection even though this is not stated openly. Consider the following two examples:

* Ask the group to settle down, breathe deeper, close their eyes and relax in the usual way.

    'Now imagine that you are an animal in a zoo. Take the first image that comes and examine it in detail. What kind of animal are you? What sort of cage are you in? (pause) What are your surroundings like? Are there people around? How do you feel about them looking at you? (pause) How do you feel as this animal in this cage? (pause) What are you doing to pass the time? (pause) Now in imagination I want you to become the cage and see what this is like. What does it feel like to be the cage? What do you think and feel about this animal that you enclose? (pause) Now, as the cage, see if you have anything to say to the animal. Just permit the words to come in imagination. (pause) Now become the animal and reply – say whatever comes. (pause) Become the cage again and talk back. Become the animal again and reply. (pause) Now as the animal, find a way of escaping from your cage – how do you do it? How does it feel to be out of the cage? (pause) How do the people around react? What do you do? Just let the fantasy develop in any way that you want. (pause) Now in imagination find your way back to the cage. If you manage to get back, see how you feel about being there. (pause) Now slowly permit yourself to come back to the room.'

The next fantasy will involve a drawing, so crayons and a reasonably sized piece of paper will be required for each member of the group.

* 'I want you to use the sheet of paper to draw a tree. Use the paper in any way you want and draw the tree you want to draw – your tree. Take about ten minutes for the drawing.' (ten minutes)

'Can you finish off what you are doing now? You don't have to complete the tree. You know what the tree is like. Now sit comfortably looking at your tree and in imagination I would like you to become the tree you have drawn. (pause) Now take a good look around. What are your surroundings like? What is the weather like? (pause) What do you look like? (pause) What does it feel like to be this tree, in this place, at this time? (pause)

'Now, in imagination, become your trunk. What do you look like? What is the texture of your surface? What are your special features, trunk? (pause) Now, turn your attention inside yourself, trunk. What are you like inside? What is happening inside you? (pause) How do you feel, about your life as the trunk of the tree? (pause) Now in imagination see what you have to say to the rest of the tree, those parts of the tree above you and your roots below. Just let the words emerge spontaneously. (pause) Now in imagination become the upper part of the tree. What do you look like? What are your branches and foliage like – if you have any foliage? How do you feel about yourself – what is life like for you? (pause) What do you think and feel about your trunk? See if you can tell the trunk about these thoughts – just let the words come spontaneously. (pause) Now become the roots of the tree. If your roots are not visible, close your eyes and imagine what it is like to be your roots. What do you look like? What does it feel like to be the roots? (pause) What do you think of the rest of the tree above you? See if you can tell the rest of the tree what you think and feel. (pause) Now see if any part of the tree wants to reply. See how the conversation develops between the different parts of your tree. (pause)

'Now become the whole tree again. How do you feel now, having explored yourself in fantasy? How do you feel about yourself as the complete tree? (pause) When it is right for you, come back to the room and take your time to come out of the fantasy.'

A tree seems to be a potent image for both adults and children. This particular exercise is even more potent when it is done on a one-to-one basis and the person who drew the tree is guided through the fantasy using a Gestalt mode of questioning (Perls, 1969). Having undergone an experience of this nature most adults realize that they have been talking about themselves.

Using a simpler form of this exercise, Hall (1977) reported asking a group of fifteen-year-olds to draw trees. The drawings were then placed in the centre of the group and they talked about the individual trees. The discussion went on for a double lesson and at the end of the session they suggested spontaneously that they had said a great deal about themselves. The following week one of the boys who had not attended the previous session was invited to guess who had drawn the trees. He did this giving a running commentary on the reasons for his choices. The class was captivated by his comments and he guessed them all correctly. The subsequent discussion involved a great deal of personal material and their enthusiasm for the task continued to the end of the lesson. Indeed, when a class becomes involved in this form of exercise, the normal lesson time is often too short. It is interesting to note that the group involved here were considered by other members of staff to be difficult to teach.

Drawing is always an involving exercise if it is used to tap personal material in a creative way. Oaklander (1978) provided many examples of the use of drawing in this manner. Adults and children are usually happy to display their drawings after such an exercise. When the drawings have been pinned to the wall, the group invariably fall into a deep silence as the drawings are looked at. It is as if normal verbal modes of expression have been made redundant. Children in a class will often go back again and again to look at their own and other students' drawings.

A combination of tree drawing and fantasy proved to be a powerful stimulus for an improvement in the quality of writing and in the use of statements involving feeling in a group of twelve-year-olds (Hall and Kirkland, 1984). A mixed-ability class was asked to draw a tree and was then taken through a fantasy similar to the one given above. Afterwards, pupils were asked to write about their fantasy as if they were the tree, and to write in the first person present beginning, 'I am the tree, and I ...' The subsequent writing was compared to a sample of their normal written work. There was a clear difference in quality, but the most striking difference was in the proportion of statements that involved feeling. Here is an example:

> I am the tree and I have no leaves people don't care about me.
> They just swing on my young branches and bend my trunk. I
> have no feelings I just sit there as miserable as could be my roots
> are cold and my twigs are thin and nobody looks at me. I bare
> no fruit and I'm really thin and ugly. The place I'm in is Horrible
> no one to talk to just stuck in the school garden and the children
> I see are horrible to me. They never stop and look at me they just
> say horrible things. I wish I could walk and talk to everyone and
> then I be horrible to them I would. I shout and scream like they
> did to me. The wind just blows me side to side I'm to weak to stop
> it my branches are nearly breaking off. I wish I could be free.

This is a sad and painful account, but is not untypical of the tree descriptions. Their normal writing was flat and dull by comparison. Here is another example:

> I am a tree and I feel sad because my roots are cold, and children
> tie rope on me and swing and snap my branches. I am sad because

know leaves grow on me much. And Know fruit grows on me. And
I am Sad because my bark feels ruff. And I am sad because
children climb me and kick me and it harts. And I am Sad because
I am on my own know one comes and sits under me. And I am
sad because people pull my branches off. And leaves if there is any.
And I am Sad because know birds build next in my branches.
And I am Sad because I have know friends. And I am Sad because
I am old and dieing.

A small minority of the tree accounts were expressed in positive terms,
but the overall picture was one of an expression of sadness, hurt and
anger. Young adolescents often deny that such feelings have anything
to do with their own lives. If, however, they are projecting aspects of
their own existence, it would suggest that the average adolescent is
harbouring a great deal of sadness, hurt and anger. Young adolescents
are not reticent about expressing feelings, but those that are expressed
are generally directed outwards and often relate to likes and dislikes.
The feelings that were expressed a great deal in the tree accounts –
sadness, hurt and anger – are actively discouraged by the adolescent
peer group and by our culture. When anger is expressed by the young
adolescent, it tends to be acted out in a distorted form, such as anti-
social behaviour.

This study was developed (Hall and Greenwood, 1985) with a
larger number of children, four teachers and several fantasy themes.
Again the fantasy-induced writing produced a significantly higher
proportion of statements of feeling, which were overwhelmingly sad.
The teachers concerned were shocked at the outpouring of emotion
and said they now saw the children in a totally different light. They
were also surprised at the improved quality of the writing.

The importance of imagery as an educational tool is now being
recognized in fields as far apart as medicine and sport. In a fascinating
autobiographical account Shattock (1979) described how he used
visualization techniques to cure arthritis of the hip and an enlarged
prostate gland. He even removed polyps from his nose. Shattock had
had years of experience of Vipassana meditation, which enabled him
to concentrate well. He studied the exact physiology of the specific
problems in detail and then designed an appropriate healing image,
such as constricting the blood vessels feeding the polyp, and practised
using the image twice a day for twenty minutes.

The work of the Simontons (Simonton, Matthews-Simonton and

Creighton, 1980) with cancer patients is much more widely known. They encouraged patients to use imagery which simulated white cells destroying cancer cells. This might involve the white cells imagined as piranha fish with sharp teeth consuming the cancer cells. Aggressive images were deliberately encouraged as repressed resentment is thought to be an element in cancer for some people. Sometimes these techniques worked with dramatic results. Often they did not work and the Simontons suggest that success requires the will to live at both conscious and unconscious levels. Results of this nature are sometimes dismissed as mere suggestion. Rather they provide evidence of how powerful suggestion can be, in the same way that expectation can effect educational outcomes. Similarly, having a positive image about yourself will probably contribute to achieving positive things in life.

The evidence for the positive effects of visualization in the cure of cancer has been questioned. However, if mental processes can work to produce disease, as in psychosomatic illness, there is good reason to suppose that mental processes can also work to produce health. Here is a guided fantasy involving healing that you may wish to try out in your group. Even if it has no effect on healing processes, it will produce a stimulating group discussion, which is an end in its own right.

* Permit yourself to relax in a position which is right for you. Take three deep breaths and relax a little deeper. (pause) Now imagine that you are becoming smaller, gradually shrinking in size. You become so small that you are, in imagination, no bigger than a pin. (pause) In a moment I am going to suggest that you enter your mouth and go on a journey exploring your body. See how you feel about the prospect of doing this. (pause) As you go on your journey, don't be too concerned about what you know about the physiology of the body. Just let the images emerge spontaneously.

  Now find a way into your mouth. (pause) Take a good look around. How are you going to set about your exploration. (pause) Just let yourself go and permit yourself to slide down your throat. Where are you now? How do you feel about being here? (pause) Now in imagination begin to explore your body. Just follow the imagery as it develops. (pause) In imagination try and find a way to your heart. Permit the fantasy to find a way there. What is the heart like ? How is it working? (pause) Now in imagination become the heart. How does that feel? What are you doing? (pause) As the heart, what have you got to say to this small person who is exploring the body? Just permit the words to flow. (pause) Now become your small self again and reply – whatever you want to say. (pause) Now continue on your journey, in any way that seems right to you. (pause) In imagination try and find a way to your brain. Permit the fantasy to find a way there. What is the brain like? How is it working? (pause) Now in imagination become the brain. How does that feel? What are you doing? (pause) As the brain, what have you got to say to this small person who is exploring the body? Just permit the words to flow. (pause) Now become yourself again and reply – whatever you want to say. (pause) Now continue your exploration of the body and look for areas where things appear to be going wrong. When you find areas that need attention, examine them in detail. (long pause)

Now in imagination go to that part of the body where there is an army of repair men who mend the damaged parts of the body. Where do they live? What do they look like? (pause) Now have a discussion with them about what needs to be done to repair the body you are exploring. (pause) As they set off to do the repairs, go along with them. What do they do? How does it feel now the repairs have been made? (long pause) When it is right for you, come out of the fantasy and come back to the room.

The use of visualization techniques by professional sportspeople to improve their performance is now becoming a standard training procedure (Syer and Connolly, 1984). Images can be used as a way of rehearsing physical skills and it has been suggested that mental rehearsal can produce more improvement than actual practice (Masters and Houston, 1978). Also an image can be used as a metaphor for the skill involved. A high-jumper might use the image of a soaring bird, a butterfly swimmer might use the image of a porpoise. The images do not have to be as obvious as this. The appropriate image will emerge for the person concerned. One of the writers used the image of a flowing stream when he went out running on his own in the woods. This did not produce any great athletic achievements, but it did seem to add to the pleasure of running. Using images seemed to clear the mind of obsessional thinking which probably interfered with having a clear bodily awareness. This interest from sportspeople in imagery techniques is a significant testimony, as they are usually a hard-nosed group of people who are primarily interested in results.

Scientists are also regarded as down-to-earth people. We mentioned the science teacher who was surprised at the change in behaviour of his class following a fantasy experience. We have also had several reports from science teachers who have used short fantasy experience as a way of providing their students with some visual awareness of processes that are not directly observable in the school laboratory. One example is of a biology teacher who devised a fantasy describing a butterfly landing on a leaf, including the technical terms for the physiology involved. She reported a subsequent improvement in the memorability of the details of the lesson. Other science teachers who have used this technique have reported similar effects. This relationship between imagery and memorability has been known to psychologists for some time (Bartlett, 1932) but its application has been limited to the use of mnemonics to memorize lists of facts.

Are there any dangers in using techniques of this nature? One criticism is that guided fantasy is a mild form of hypnotism. There is an element of truth in this, but this is not a problem apart from the scare-mongering effect of the word hypnotism. Visualization, relaxation and hypnotism all involve similar altered states of consciousness. It seems likely that this is a healthy state to experience, since it avoids the stress of the obsessive cognitive activity, or worrying, that many of us indulge in most of the time.

A more serious danger lies in the way that the fantasy experience is handled by the teacher or facilitator. Some extremely useful guidelines are provided by John Stevens' (1971) book on *Awareness* which has a short section entitled, 'To the Group Leader or Teacher'. His advice is relevant to all forms of experiential learning, but it is particularly pertinent for those who facilitate fantasy experience. He suggested that the teacher should avoid four activities:

1 Judgment. A person's report of her experience should be accepted and acknowledged whatever it may be. This has to be done at both a verbal and non-verbal level. The individual also has to be protected from the judgments of her peers. Judgments usually reflect some discomfort on the part of the person making the judgment and this could be explored sensitively with that individual.

2 Helping. If someone appears to have had an experience that involves what are sometimes described as negative feelings, such as sadness, pain or grief, there is sometimes a tendency to rush in to help

that person suppress the feelings. This is probably because the helper cannot tolerate that particular emotion. There is no evidence that experiencing emotions fully is harmful; if anything, the opposite is true and the repression of feeling is storing up trouble for a later date.

3 'Shoulds'. No one can prescribe what 'ought' to be the outcome of fantasy experience. Images do not have to be happy ones because that was what the teacher intended. There are, of course, 'shoulds' implied in these guidelines, but we would suggest these are the only acceptable ones. It takes a 'should' to get rid of all 'shouldism'.

4 Explaining. It is always tempting to explain another person's experience for them. Some teachers are particularly prone to do this. The extreme form of this is to make an interpretation of another person's experience, an issue we have already dealt with. Clearly, there are other aspects of a teacher's role which do involve detailed explanation. This guideline refers to situations where students are being invited to become more aware of aspects of their own lives as in parts of the pastoral care curriculum.

In conclusion, we would like to make a brief statement about dreaming. The scripted fantasies we have described have a similar quality to dreams, though most of us cannot control our dreams and they are not amenable to external manipulation in the same way as scripted fantasies. If you ask a group of students to share their dreams, perhaps as the teacher giving a lead with your own experience, you are almost certain to have a long, involved discussion. Some students are relieved to discover that others have a similar experience to themselves. Students can be asked to draw their dreams, they can be talked through them and they can be asked to take on the roles of images in them, in the same way as in the scripted fantasies. Students enjoy keeping a dream diary and some students become aware of their dreams for the first time by being asked to pay attention to them. Just at the level of generating an involved discussion, this activity serves a useful purpose. If, as Jung (1961) suggested, dreams are a message from the dreamer to herself, then awareness of dreams may be promoting self-awareness.

Postscript

The type of activities we have described in this section are not usually found in educational textbooks, in spite of the fact that they appear to have positive outcomes. It would appear that academic educational

theorists have had an education that emphasizes rational linear thinking to the extent of eliminating the constructive possibilities of imaginary and fantasy experience. There have been exceptions. Many years
ago, Bruner (1966) was arguing for an increase in education of perceptual skills, including visualization.

The importance of developing the imagination has always been
accepted by the educational establishment but the existence of guided
fantasy is not acknowledged. In a scholarly review of the place of
imagination in education, Sutherland (1971) did not mention fantasy,
not even in passing. It is as if imagination is acceptable if it is being
used to produce material external to the person, but it is not acceptable
as a means of understanding the self. This may reflect a fear on the
part of educationalists to look into their own personalities.

An important justification for the use of fantasy techniques is that
they produce a high level of constructive involvement in the participants. The possibility of developing self-awareness is a bonus. As
an example of this involvement, consider the following anecdote which
involves a thirteen-year-old girl, Joanne, who took part in the research
on themes in fantasy (Hall, 1979) mentioned at the beginning of this
section. The procedures involved generating personal constructs (see
chapter three) and a repertory grid using a rating of twenty images
taken from five guided fantasies. Joanne asked for instructions on how
to guide another person through the repertory test and went home to
generate a list of constructs from her mother. She then asked for the
scripts of the guided fantasies and the forms that had been used for
generating the data. She came back later with a complete set of
ratings, having taken her mother and brother through the same
procedures that she had experienced.

Having learned about herself as a result of the fantasy journeys, she
was motivated to learn about other members of her family, using the
same techniques, and was prepared to spend a great deal of her own
time repeating the task with her mother and brother. This degree of
involvement seems atypical of thirteen- to fourteen-year-old adolescents in secondary schools and indicated the depth of her constructive involvement in the task.

Non-verbal communication

Some years ago, one of the writers was soon to leave his post as
assistant master in an ESN school, where he had taught a class of

fifteen-year-old boys for some two years. During the final week, his replacement arrived to be shown round the school and introduced to the class. After he had left the class, there was general consternation. 'He's not taking us is he?', 'We don't want him.' The writer suggested that they could not know what someone would be like after such a short meeting. 'You can tell he's mean', 'He'll give us a bad time.' They could offer no more detailed explanation. A subsequent visit to the school showed that their fears had been justified. A former colleague reported that the new teacher had developed a terrible relationship with the class. He had been involved in a high level of confrontation and resorted to an extremely punitive regime.

So what had the children noticed that had made them so certain that life would be difficult with him as the teacher? It seems certain that they were picking up non-verbal cues, using a skill which has been lost to most adults educated in a highly rational society. Certainly, the writer was unaware of these cues. Non-verbal communication may play an important part in the process which is often called intuition, particularly the intuitions we have about the people with whom we interact. Teaching is still regarded as more of an art than a science, and an important part of the art might involve being able to tune in to subtle non-verbal cues which defy the systematic analysis of science. In this section, we will examine the ways in which attempts have been made to take a scientific approach to non-verbal communication and its application to teaching.

Most of the writers in this area suggest that there is more meaning conveyed by the non-verbal than the verbal communication. In fact, Birdwhistell (1970) suggested that the verbal component only accounted for a mere seven per cent. In spite of this, non-verbal communication is given scant attention in teacher training in the UK. This is partly because teacher training is dominated by university departments and institutions whose courses are validated by universities. Universities tend to be defensively rational and ill-equipped to deal with issues that are not easily expressed in words. Research into non-verbal communication tends to follow the classical scientific paradigm of observation, and the recording of observations, followed by an attempt to find patterns in the recordings. This approach has failed to give any insights into non-verbal communication such as that used by the class described at the beginning of this section. Most of the research had produced results which would be obvious to any sensitive person. For example, if you wish to communicate with someone, make eye contact, but do not stare too hard and do not look away too much. (Argyle and Cook, 1976.)

The academic and the researcher are practised in communicating in words, so it becomes difficult for them to communicate about non-verbal communication. This is similar to using a digital computer to handle analogical data. This explains why a lecture on non-verbal communication is not much use to teachers in training. What is required is direct experience of non-verbal communication which is provided in a limited way by the exercises included in this section. What the exercises can achieve is to direct the teachers' awareness to non-verbal processes, and this awareness can be used to encourage attending to non-verbal activity in other situations.

Most researchers agree that the meaning of an individual act depends on its context. Books have been written which try to provide a dictionary of non-verbal communication, but these tend to be a dilution of research findings and are often misleading. A student frowning might be concentrating on a difficult problem, but in a different context, she may be distressed as a result of being rep-rimanded by a teacher. Specific gestures do develop a unique meaning in a particular culture, so the possibility is open for misunderstanding between different cultures or even social groups. We gave the example earlier of the children from certain islands in the Caribbean who keep their eyes downcast when they are being told off by a teacher in the UK. For the children it is an act of deference, whereas the teachers may see it as an act of defiance. Even a simple act such as smiling has to be seen in context, as it may reflect pleasure or it may be a cover for embarrassment.

If the meaning of non-verbal communication has to be understood in context, then every item of non-verbal behaviour is potentially different in terms of the possible meaning it conveys. If this is the case, then it can be questioned whether or not any communication in the conventional sense is taking place. Although individuals vary in the way they fit words into their construct systems, there is a great deal of shared meaning regarding the precise definitions of words. This is not the case in the non-verbal domain, although there have been several 'pop' books of doubtful value which try to do this.

With a clear understanding of the context, a non-verbal cue can be very clear. If you lean out of the door in the morning and hold up two fingers to the milkman, he will probably understand that you want two pints of milk. If a teacher sees a student making a similar gesture from the back of the class, she may justifiably feel insulted. If your tutor raises an eyebrow when you express a particular view you might assume that she doesn't agree with what you have said. If a child who is normally extroverted and vivacious talks to you in a flat voice and refuses to look you in the eye, you might assume she is upset.

Another consideration is the length of time that you have known the people involved in the communication. The experienced teacher can silence a class with a raised eyebrow. A married couple might spend the evening together without saying a word, and yet still communicate a great deal. Indeed, silence can be a way of communicating disapproval. The tutor who can only lecture to students and rarely makes eye contact may be giving them a great deal of information about her personality.

The few examples that have been given so far demonstrate that verbal communication can be sent through many different channels. Areas which are a focus for research are facial expression, eye contact, gesture, bodily movement, posture, proximity (how close people get to each other), touch, paralanguage (cues contained in the way the voice is used) and bodily tension. We will now examine these areas which have a research background and speculate as to how this knowledge can be of use to the practising teacher.

Facial expression

Unless a teacher is totally impassive, the expression on her face will vary from situation to situation, communicating approval, disapproval, anger, exhaustion and so on. The students will respond to these cues consciously and unconsciously and may even modify their behaviour to gain approval and avoid disapproval. They may be on the look out for the expression which suggests that they have gone just too far. Certainly, the face is an important medium for the expression of emotion.

Ever since the original paper by Charles Darwin (1872), *The Expression of the Emotions in Man and Animals*, there had been speculation as to whether or not there is a biological basis to the facial expression of emotion. Darwin suggested that expressive behaviour had survival value for the species. Weitz (1979) reviewed the research which had been done on this issue, including comparisons between human and primate facial expressions and the observations of children born both deaf and blind. These children who were handicapped from birth showed the same facial expressions of smiling, anger and affection as did the normal children. This suggests an innate component in the expression of emotion.

Comparisons of humans with animals are often seen as a degrading activity. However, most primary teachers support the notion presented by Zivin (in an unpublished paper reported in Henley, 1977) that children begin to show signs of submission and dominance at an early age. When a conflict situation developed in the playground, one child would present a 'win face', consisting of raised eyebrows, wide-open eyes, firmly jutting neck posture and conspicuously raised chin, whereas the other child would present a 'loss-face', consisting of furrowed brow, slightly squinted eyes, retracted neck, and lowered chin. This is similar to the behaviour of primates who instinctively adopt dominant and submissive postures; the latter reduces the possibility of physically damaging conflict.

Henley also draws some interesting parallels between the use of smiling as an appeasement gesture by primates, and data which suggests that humans in subordinate positions smile more than their superiors when in each other's presence. Thus, in Western society, women smile more than men, children smile more than teachers, and teachers smile more than headteachers in order to maintain position in the hierarchy.

There is a physiological basis to the expression of facial emotion, and, as the emotions usually involve changes in arousal, the musculature has to be used to change the facial expression. Izard (see Wolfgang, 1979) summed up a number of studies which related the facial expression of emotion to internal physiological conditions. Subjects were asked to imagine situations which involved different emotions. These different emotions produced predictable patterns of electrical activity in the facial muscles. For joy, the highest activity was in the depressor anguli oris, the muscles around the mouth that control smiling; for fear, the frontalis, the muscles across the forehead; for anger, the masseter, the muscles across the angle of the jaw; for sadness, the corrugator, the muscles between the eyebrows which can pull the eyebrows together. Perhaps the lines that have become a permanent feature of most of our adult faces in some way represent our emotional histories. As adults, much of this might be acted out in our sleep. The lines are often more clearly etched when seen in the bathroom mirror in the morning.

Many of us seem to carry a specific emotion on our faces even though it may be intermittently broken by changing circumstances and feelings. Certainly, depressed persons carry their depression on their faces, and an examination of the electrical activity of the muscles suggests that it is a mixture of sadness (distress) and anger. Some people look as if they are always about to burst into tears, others as if they are about to lose their temper. When individuals are given feedback about expression of this nature, they are often surprised and may even deny that they have much experience of the particular feeling.

* Divide into groups of three. Present the information given in the previous two paragraphs verbally or on a hand-out. (It might be useful to provide a drawing of a face illustrating the four muscle groups described.)

  'Select one person in each group of three and examine their face in as much detail as you can along the lines I have described (or in the hand-out). Do this aloud, while the person being described remains silent. Do this for six minutes and then allow three minutes for the third person to join in the discussion.'

  Repeat the process with each person in the trio.

This exercise encourages us to look more closely at other people's faces and possibly sensitize us to some of the more subtle nuances of facial expression. It also tends to be highly involving for the participants and encourages discussion on a feeling level. On the other hand, the type of exercise which is often used in courses on social and personal education where students are asked to identify the feelings expressed by the faces on pictures or drawings of people may be of limited value. Students are usually able to identify the emotions correctly, but the drawings tend to be extreme and are not shown in context. This type of exercise is useful to the extent that it draws attention to the possibility of being sensitive to emotional expression.

Exercises of this nature and research which uses this type of picture probably provide a gross underestimate of children's ability to understand facial expression. This skill may already be highly developed at an intuitive level.

An important dimension of emotional expression reviewed by Weitz

(1979) is the relationship between the internal expression of emotion and the external display of it. She quoted the work of Buck (1977) who showed that both children and adults showing little facial expression of emotion had a high level of internal physiological arousal, whereas those who expressed a great deal of emotion on the face had lower internal reactions. It is as if the appropriate expression of emotion in some way relieves the internal emotional turmoil, lending support to the notion that the expression of emotion is cathartic and leads to better health. Certainly, men appear to exhibit less emotion than women, and the subsequent internal stress may explain why they are more prone to stress-related illnesses. Apart from being conducive to better health, we would suggest that the public expression of emotion on the part of a teacher is also conducive to establishing a better set of relationships with both students and colleagues.

Weitz suggested that even though feelings are not being expressed on the face, they leak out in subtle ways, perhaps in other aspects of non-verbal communication or in very brief changes in facial expression which the astute observer can detect. Perhaps children are able to tune into these fine cues even though they may not be able to give a rational explanation of what they have observed.

Eye contact

The eyes are probably the most expressive parts of the face, and many one-to-one interactions involve some degree of eye contact. The avoidance of eye contact or a hard stare tends to make the other person feel uncomfortable. A hard stare is usually experienced as threatening and most of us have had the experience of being told off by a teacher who leaned over the desk and gave us a fixed look. Again it is also disconcerting to be taught by someone who never makes eye contact.

Hodge (1971) suggested that eye contact satisfied a basic human need, since man was the only mammal who had habitual eye contact with the mother during infancy. Through eye contact, the teacher has the opportunity of communicating with every member of a class, even though she may not be able to speak to all the children.

The optimal amount of eye contact depends on the situation. Lovers, or a mother with her baby, will indulge in long periods of eye contact. Colleagues who do not get on with each other tend to look away much of the time. Indeed, the eyes can be used to show affection, but also defensively to establish status. Henley (1977) provided a highly readable review of the research in this area. Humans are compared to primates, some of whom use the stare as a defensive gesture and lower the eyes as a form of appeasement to avoid attack. Within an established primate hierarchy the lower status animals spend more time attending visually to the higher status animals than the reverse. The same process appears to happen with humans. When a new teacher is talking to the head, she will look at her while she is speaking. When the teacher replies, there is a good chance that the head will not feel the need to return the same degree of visual attention. It may appear insulting to suggest that a staff group behave like a troop of baboons, but if you observe the interactions in your own staff group or between student and tutor you may find that the parallels are there. If, as a teacher, you wish to reduce the barrier created by difference in status between you and your students, you may find it helps to give more visual attention to them while they are speaking. Henley goes on to quote studies which show that women look at men more than men look at women, another reflection of differences in status perhaps.

Evidence contrary to the animal behaviour model is provided by the fact that cultures vary in the way they use eye contact in relation to status. Apart from the West Indian children mentioned earlier, American blacks, Puerto Ricans and Japanese tend to avert their gaze when listening to another person out of politeness. Perhaps it is only white westerners who are like baboons. These differences can create confusion when teacher and student come from different cultures. On the other hand, it may be just as well that the teacher does not understand some of the non-verbal cues that are given. An English gesture of contempt is to roll the eyes round the upper half of the sockets. An Afro-Caribbean version is to roll the eyes round the lower half and the implication can easily be missed.

Because of the wide differences in context, culture and status in educational settings, it is difficult to lay down specific guidelines for the teacher regarding eye contact. Perhaps the solution is to become more sensitive to what is happening in specific situations. This requires careful observation of the individuals you interact with, but also feedback from the other person about how you made them feel with the way you use your eyes.

Gesture, movement and posture

These three areas of non-verbal communication will be dealt with together as they are closely related. Our bodies tend to be in continuous motion, even in sleep. Some movements, such as placing the fingers over the lips have a specific meaning in our culture, namely an injunction to be quiet. In some African cultures, the same gesture with the finger slightly turned implies shy embarrassment. Some people appear to be illustrating what they are saying with continuous hand movements. These movements are open to interpretation, such as a sharp, chopping movement being an indication of violence. Some people sit with their legs and arms wrapped tightly around themselves. This may merely be a habit, or it may be an indication of protection from threat.

Thus the meaning in movement or gesture may be intentional or unintentional. A person's body posture may be a reflection of a disturbed internal psychological state, which is clear to another person, but seems normal to the person who has held that posture for a number of years. Indeed, the possibilities for extracting meaning out of movement, gesture and posture are diverse and complex and the potential applications for the classroom teacher are still largely limited to the obvious.

Hand gestures are an aspect of body movement which have been studied in depth. Ekman and Friesen (1972) distinguished between three types of hand gesture:

1 Emblems which can be directly translated into a word or a phrase (such as 'stop' or 'okay'). The meaning of these emblems varies from culture to culture, which could cause some confusion in the multi-cultural classroom, but within a given culture the meanings of the gestures are clear and understood by all involved.
2 Illustrators are hand movements which accompany speech and do not have a specific meaning in themselves. Sometimes the hand movement clearly adds to the meaning of what is being said, such as a wide rounded movement when you are talking about something large and round. Indeed, the hand movements often enhance what is being said and help to gain the listener's attention. Sometimes the hand movements seem inappropriate and distract the listener from what is being said, like someone who is wringing their hands when talking about something pleasant.

3   Adaptors are hand movements which are self-orientated, such as stroking one's hair or scratching. Again, gross forms of adaptor can distract the listener and may keep a whole class amused.

The specific nature of the movement may have as much to do with the listener as the speaker. Condon (Weitz, 1979), using a fine analysis of the frames of films of two people interacting, has shown that the movements of both people are synchronized in very subtle ways. It is as if two people engaged in conversation are moving together in a barely visible dance. It is possible that when an interaction is going badly that this fine synchronization is disturbed. Certainly, we often mirror the other person's posture in a conversation, crossing legs, stroking chins and folding arms at the same time. Again, this could be a measure of the quality of our relationship with the other person. The necessary learning for this unconscious skill may be developed in the early interaction between mother and child.

Henley (1977) also related body movements and position to the power relationship between individuals, again referring to women and children as being 'inferior' to men in western culture. A person in an inferior position will tilt the head, like the gesture of appeasement in some animal species. The superior is able to adopt a more relaxed position than the inferior person, perhaps tilting back on a chair with the hands behind the neck. This is typical of the relative postures of teachers and students. If a student took up the same relaxed posture as some teachers it could easily be seen as an insolent gesture. A relaxed posture adopted by students sitting at the back of the class is often used to express disaffection and boredom. This is another area in which a teacher who is attempting to loosen the authority barrier between herself and the pupil may in fact be reinforcing it with her non-verbal communication.

As with facial expression, bodily movements can, by and large, only be understood in context. So what can the teacher do to become more sensitive to the effects of her movements and become more aware of the ways in which people move around her? Try this exercise as a starting point.

* Divide the group into pairs and ask the pairs to divide themselves into As and Bs. Give the As the following checklist and ask them not to show it to B. Give B a topic to talk about from the list in the Appendix while A makes notes under the following headings.

What movements can you see in the:

head
arms
hands
trunk
legs
feet
any other movements?

After eight minutes stop the exercise. Ask A to share what she has observed and ask her to share what effect the movements had on her. Then reverse roles for a further eight minutes even though the task is known by both participants.

Posture and bodily tension

A more clinical approach to an examination of bodily posture is the hypothesis that the way the body is held reflects inner tensions. Children may have hunched or raised shoulders, tense jaws, twisted spines, hips raised to either side, pelvises swung forward or backward, permanently raised knees, retracted necks, knotted stomachs and diaphragms or clenched fists. The same tensions occur in teachers, usually in a much more chronic form, as the patterns of tension have been held for a much longer period of time. Often the tension becomes so acute that the pain in the muscles becomes unbearable causing a muscle spasm and can only be released by drug treatment. This may produce permanent damage to the tissues. As we shall see in a later section, teaching is a stressful occupation. Schools are probably equally stressful for many students.

In a much neglected study, Fenton (1973) suggested that a high proportion of children in schools have such bad posture that they are establishing habits which are doing permanent damage to the body. He introduced instruction on posture and movement into both primary and secondary schools based on the ideas of F. M. Alexander (see Barlow, 1973). Alexander's notions include recommendations on how to stand, sit, walk and to perform a number of everyday movements. By aligning the body correctly and relaxing the muscles, the possibility of tissue damage, especially in the joints and muscles, is reduced and Fenton reported improvements in psychosomatic disorders such as asthma and stammering. The evidence for the benefits of the Alexander Technique are impressive, but anecdotal, and perhaps the best test is to try it for yourself.

Certainly posture is not an area examined in the typical physical education lesson and the emphasis on good posture smacks of Victorian moralizing. However, the high incidence of back pain, slipped discs and arthritis of the joints would suggest that something is seriously missing in the education of our bodies.

A person's posture may be a metaphor for their inner emotional state. So a distorted posture may be a reflection of emotional disturbance like the children in Fenton's (1973) study. The colleague who is unable to drop her shoulders and unclench her fists is probably working through the day's traumatic events in her mind.

* Try this exercise. Form groups of five, and examine the posture of
  each group member in turn. Ask them to stand in a relaxed
  position against a vertical line on the wall and then look at the
  bodily alignment from the front, back and side. Give feedback
  about the alignment of the head in relation to the spine; whether
  the hips are swung forward or backward; if there is any drooping
  or raising of either hip or shoulder and any other postural features
  that seem relevant. Then help them to adjust their bodies to what
  seems a better position and ask them how it feels to stand in this
  new position.

A central notion of Reich's work (1972) is that as infants we learn to deal with physical and emotional pain by restricting our breathing and tensing our bodies. This learned pattern of bodily tension is picturesquely described as body or character armour. The assumption is made that tensing the body and restricting the breathing reduces the experience of psychological pain. Infants can be seen to do this when they are distressed. After a period of crying, they often tense the body and hold the breath until they go blue in the face. These patterns stay with us into adulthood. When we are involved in a difficult interaction; parts of the body become tense and breathing is reduced, often to the extent that we suddenly have to take in a large gulp of air. If these patterns of breathing and muscular tension are maintained for long periods of time, there is a good chance that they will have a deleterious effect on our physical health.

In the same way that infants develop their own particular comfort habits, like thumb sucking, blanket rubbing and so on, each one learns an individual response to pain. Some may learn to retract their necks, as if to cut off pain from the body; others to tense the stomach or the back muscles, lock the knees or grip the buttocks tightly together. These patterns develop in varying combinations and degrees of chronicity. Reich (1972) argued that we use our bodies as a defence mechanism against emotional trauma. Pain is an unavoidable part of life's experience; even the most carefully nurtured infant goes through teething, weaning, separation anxiety and so on. This armouring is a predictable and necessary part of the infant's attempt to protect herself against the vagaries of a sometimes hostile world. In adulthood these habitual patterns of tension may be redundant, for as adults we have more choice in the way that we respond to emotional and physical pain and Reich would argue that for good physical and emotional health it is necessary for these patterns to be unlearned.

From a human relations point of view, an interaction between two over-tensed, under-breathed individuals is likely to be difficult. If you find yourself in a situation like this, consciously try to relax and breathe more deeply. Remember though, these processes are often not part of our conscious awareness and it may require specialized techniques to deal with the more deep-seated patterns of muscular tension. Lowen (1976) has developed Reich's ideas into a system of exercises called 'bioenergetics', which involves breathing deeply in stressed positions and letting out the sounds which go with the feelings produced. These exercises, which may involve screaming, do not readily fit into a conventional educational establishment. This level of emotional expression may be frightening to the onlooker, and yet the evidence that the full expression of feeling has positive benefits for the individual is fairly convincing. Also, people who have undergone therapy to release their body armour claim dramatic changes in their general well-being.

There is a steady move towards the use of techniques which integrate mind and body, such as the use of imagery in sport and healing described in the previous section. As yet, however, little attempt has been made to integrate feeling and bodily states with rational thinking in conventional education. The denial of feelings in both teachers and students, as if they were irrelevant to the task of education, may be playing a fundamental part in the breakdown of relations in schools.

Yet the possibility of changing the pattern of teaching in educational institutions must be threatening to staff who are only trained and skilled in dealing with cognitive processes.

* Divide the group into pairs and ask the pairs to divide themselves into As and Bs. Give the As the following written instructions and instruct them not to show them to their partners.

    'While your partner is talking, try to become aware of the tension in her body, in the face, the neck, the shoulders, the arms, the chest, the legs, or any other part of the body.

    Also try and be aware of the other person's pattern of breathing, is it shallow or deep, quick or slow? Is it visible at all? Is it audible?

    As the conversation continues, try to adopt the other person's posture, tension and pattern of breathing. Be aware of what this feels like.'

    Give the other member of the pair a topic from the list in the Appendix. After five minutes on the topic, allow five minutes to share the experience. Then reverse roles.

Proximity

You may be familiar with the colleague who thrusts her face into yours when she is chatting. We find ourselves backing away until we are pressed against the wall. In a situation like this, it is not easy to be honest and tell the other person that their proximity is making you feel uncomfortable.

On the other hand, it may be difficult to persuade some children to get anywhere near you. They never initiate a conversation or come up to your desk. You probably have to move over to them or ask them to come to you in order to get them within several feet of you.

Watching people moving around in a crowded school would suggest that everyone is carrying around a piece of personal space. It is as if there is an invisible cocoon surrounding each person, who will move with great skill to maintain this personal space. Infringement of personal space by another will often produce an aggressive response, and the infringement of the space of a high status person by a low status person may result in a rebuke.

The animal ethologists have demonstrated the importance of space in the lives of animals and some popularizers suggest that the same principles apply to human beings. King (1966) showed that chickens commanded more personal space the higher they came in the pecking order. He found a similar pattern in pre-school children. They would keep their distance from other children who had earlier established dominance. A group of students sitting in a circle will invariably leave a larger space for the tutor's chair. If there is a large chair which takes up more space than the others, this is also left for the tutor.

A teacher walking down the corridor appears to cut a swathe through the crowd of students. If a child accidentally bumps into a teacher, she may get a sharp rebuke. Some teachers become very upset when students wander into the staffroom and sometimes react in an extreme fashion. Similarly the headteacher protects her room from both students and teachers, and if the room is more accessible to students than teachers this is likely to upset the teacher group.

Hall (1966) suggested that we are all aware of the correct distances to keep between each other and that this is largely controlled by the person with the highest status. His early research included identifying the differences between cultures. White English and Americans appeared to require more space between them than other cultures, and rarely touched one another. These differences could give the wrong impression; the white Anglo-Saxon teacher may appear stand-offish and arrogant to a person coming from a culture where people get closer together when they communicate. Intuitively we sense when the distance is not quite right and adjust our positions accordingly. The individuals who do not get it right make us feel uncomfortable. If the situation is judged correctly, then it may be possible to manipulate a situation to your advantage. One of the writers is involved in interviewing teachers for extended courses and is often made uncomfortable by the excessive deference displayed by interviewees, some of whom try to get as far away as possible. He was most impressed by the woman who pulled her chair in close, leaned forward and proceeded to ask a series of confident questions about the course. This guaranteed her a place, though her behaviour might have offended some other colleagues.

Indeed, as Henley (1977) pointed out, women generally appeared to occupy less space than men. She suggests that this is yet another of the ways in which men establish their dominance over women both in terms of how they move around their environment and how they control territory. The postures that many women adopt serve to accentuate these differences, sitting with their legs neatly crossed and elbows well in, whereas men sprawl around with their legs open and arms spread out over neighbouring chairs. Women who adopt typically male postures are brought into line both overtly and covertly by both men and women. These processes are operating both among and between students and staff in most educational institutions.

The use of space in school settings is partly determined by the architecture of the building and the arrangement of the furniture. As a teacher you will have little control over the building of walls, although in some open-plan schools, walls are created using furniture where no walls were intended. There may even be competition between neighbouring teachers to establish the maximum territory for themselves. Unless the chairs and tables are fixed to the floor, the teacher has more control over their arrangement, but woe betide the teacher who moves the furniture in a room which another teacher perceives as her territory.

Sommer (1969) examined the relationship between human spatial needs and architecture, including the classroom. He pointed out that the conventional classroom layout of straight rows facing the teacher reinforced the flow of communication from teacher to student. Student participation decreased to the rear and to the sides of the room, where students were more distant and receive less eye contact. Two ways of changing the formal setting are to either reorganize the furniture to suit the particular class activity, or, as the teacher, to move more freely around the classroom. Watching teachers in training does suggest that those who move more freely around the room have a better relationship with the students.

Another aspect relating personal space to architecture is the amount of physical space that is available to each student. Large numbers of students are often crowded into corridors. Older adolescents are often crammed into small rooms with undersized furniture, probably violating their spatial needs. It is not surprising that situations such as these often produce disruptive and anti-social behaviour.

* Ask the members of the group to divide into pairs and to sit facing each other. Give one member of the pair a sheet with the following instructions and suggest that they do not show it to their partners.

  'While your partner is talking, be aware of the space that has been established between you. Try to be aware of who determined the space and how comfortable you feel with it. As the conversation proceeds, slowly move closer to the other person and eventually try and find an acceptable way of touching the other person.'

Give the other member of the pair a topic from the list in the Appendix.

After five minutes conversation, give them five minutes to share the experience. Then reverse roles.

Touch

Touch is a particularly contentious issue, because of the sexual implications of some forms of touch. Indeed, some probationary teachers are given the advice never to touch their pupils. The reasons for this are understandable, but we would suggest that it is not good advice, since it eliminates the possibility of meeting one of the basic needs of most human beings.

Certainly, there is convincing evidence of the importance of touch for the healthy psychological and physiological development of both animals and humans in their early years (Montague, 1978). Controlled experiments have been done with animals (Harlow, 1958) which illustrated the debilitating effects of lack of physical contact. Clinical cases of children who have been neglected from birth demonstrate the same effects (Spitz, 1945), even to the extent of infants dying through lack of physical affection. It would appear that the wonders of modern technology cannot compete with the power of a mother's touch. Research has shown that in Third World countries where hospital resources are limited and incubators scarce, premature babies who were strapped to their mothers' breasts had a better survival rate than those put in the incubators.

So we are dealing with an issue that perhaps should not be dismissed with the crude advice given in the first paragraph. On the other hand, there are definite taboos regarding the use of touch which have to be considered in daily contacts with other people, because of their sexual connotations. Some people, however, are so inhibited that they find it impossible to touch anyone. In the exercise described in the preceding section, in which students are invited to touch their partner, invariably several people fail to make contact, even though they have been given permission by an authority figure. However, most of us know that a light touch on the shoulder is unlikely to cause offence, but it does have to be seen in the context of an ongoing pattern of touching behaviour. If a member of staff is rarely seen without his hands on colleagues of the opposite sex, then it is understandable that comments and objections will be made. Jourard (1966) provided clear diagrams of which parts of the body are touchable, and by whom. This is, however, information which most of us know without research evidence.

The students in school are often clear about which member of staff is the salacious toucher and may even tell you.

'Miss, it's horrible when ... touches you, it makes you go all queer inside.'

Here the child is probably picking up non-verbal cues which reveal the intentions of the toucher. This is not just a problem for male teachers in relation to female students. Any combination of the sexes is potentially problematic. However, this is not a reason for excluding touch from normal healthy inter-personal relations. The salacious toucher is not going to be put off by any blanket regulation.

What we have said so far makes it clear that we are in favour of some form of contact in the classroom. There is, however, no conventional research to support this point of view (Smith, 1979). Most of the research into touch involves adults in highly contrived situations. A typical study of this nature involved a library assistant touching college students on the hand when they checked out their books. Later, they were asked to take part in an evaluation of the library and those who were touched reported more positive feelings about themselves and the assistant than those who had not been touched. It is a large leap from this kind of evidence to use it to justify touching in other situations. Also, the touching in experiments of this nature is contrived, whereas genuine communication may require a more spontaneous form of touching.

As with other forms of non-verbal communication, there are likely to be differences between the intentions of the sender and the experience of the receiver as far as touch is concerned. One of the writers remembers having a visitor in his class who accidentally brushed against a tall adolescent boy. The youth cowered away with his arms protecting his head and said, 'Don't hit me, sir'. It would appear that his experience of touch had not been very pleasant and this was being generalized to any interactions with adults.

Again, Henley (1977) interpreted touching behaviour as a way of establishing dominance. Contrary to popular opinion, men touch women much more than women touch men. This male touching is often in the form of helping the weaker person, easing them through doors, almost shoving the women around in what are intended as gestures of politeness. The woman who objects to this behaviour in a mixed staff group runs the risk of being sanctioned by both male and female colleagues with the cynical use of terms such as 'feminist' or 'women's libber'. In some cases, male touching of this nature is experienced as indecent assault, but to complain could easily be seen as an over-reaction, even though the woman concerned is making a rational use of the confrontation skills described in chapter four.

The same pattern of touching will tend to occur between the head teacher and her staff, and between teachers and students. By and large, the higher status person will touch the lower status person more often. Even within groups with the same status, hierarchies will emerge, much like the pecking orders of the animal kingdom.

Behaviour which transgresses these unwritten rules is likely to create problems in communication. Thus, a child in your class will not necessarily appreciate the intention behind your touch and may intuitively interpret your behaviour as an attempt to dominate, or may feel that she is being patronized.

So, what guidelines can be given to the teacher with regard to the sensitive issue of touching students? Research has been limited, and with conflicting results. Each situation is unique and there are problems of the differing perceptions of reality by the individuals involved in a touching situation. At one extreme, we would see no objection to taking a child and cuddling her for a long period of time, as described by Dockar-Drysedale (1968) in her work with children in care. At the other extreme, if you never touch your students or colleagues, there is a good chance that you are inhibited in your relationships and that this is limiting your ability to communicate. If this is the case, then it may be worth experimenting with some simple forms of touch, such as a hand on the shoulder for a brief moment, or a friendly prod. See how it feels, but don't go too far too soon. In the middle ground between being inhibited and going too far, you will have to rely on intuition, but try to be aware of the motive behind what you are doing.

In some of the pastoral care curricula that are being developed, students are sometimes asked to experiment with touching each other with their eyes closed. We would agree with Hamblin (1983) that this can be an extremely frightening experience for some adolescents and even adult teachers. Having said this, touch is too important an area to be ignored on courses that deal with personal relationships. A group needs to be well briefed for an exercise involving touch, and care needs to be taken to establish that individuals need not take part. A playful exercise, such as arm wrestling, is not likely to cause a problem; the difficulties arise when dealing with sensitive forms of touching. An idea of the problem can be obtained by trying out the following exercise with a group of experienced or student teachers.

* This is not an exercise you can take directly into a school setting, and I would like to make it clear that you can opt out if you want to and sit at the side.

Stand in a space in the room. Relax and take three deep breaths then close your eyes. It would be better if you kept your eyes closed for the rest of the exercise, but if you find this difficult, you may peep if you want to.

Now, with your eyes closed, begin to walk around the room and hold out your hands to protect yourself from other people and the furniture. Try to avoid other people. See how you feel about being separate from other people. (pause) Now, using one hand, try to find another hand to communicate with. When you have found another hand that is right for you, see what you want to communicate to this hand. (long pause) Now find a way of saying goodbye to this hand non-verbally, and without opening your eyes, start to move around the room again. See how you feel about being on your own. (pause) Now find another hand and communicate in the same way. (long pause) Now open your eyes. (If there is an embarrassed reaction to being able to see the other person, ask them about it.) Now try to find the hand that you touched in the first interaction. (long pause) Now form groups of four and share the experience.

After an exercise of this nature, it is important to share the experience. It usually reinforces the notion we have put forward that everyone construes experience differently and that no general rules can be laid down regarding touching behaviour.

Paralanguage

'Don't speak to me in that tone of voice.' Many teachers have used this phrase, which implies that much more is being communicated in the spoken word than the exact meaning of the words. Often when we are trying to cover up our feelings in a bland statement, the feelings leak out in the tone of voice. The importance of being aware of these cues was stressed in chapter four in the discussion on reflection of feeling.

Paralanguage is the term which is usually used to describe those aspects of speech which contain information other than that involved in the meaning of the words. The research into paralanguage is complex (see Weitz, 1979), and has demonstrated that certain qualities of vocal sound are related to specific emotions. If the meaning of the words is scrambled, by cutting and resplicing a tape, the emotional quality of the subsequent sounds still comes through. There is some speculation that paralanguage actually developed first in human evolution, and that sounds developed into words when meaning as communication became more complex. Most pet-lovers would say that this is true of animals, who readily respond to the emotional quality of what is said. Babies are able to communicate their feelings through sound, but most adults are too embarrassed to do this. Emotional expression of this nature is probably inhibited by the sort of conditioning described in chapter two. As adults we may be responding to these cues at a primitive level which is not always part of our conscious awareness.

The way we have consistently suggested that aspects of our behaviour can be brought into awareness is through practical exercises which focus on specific aspects of behaviour. Try the following exercise which focuses on paralanguage.

* Ask the group to divide into pairs and sit facing each other. Give one member of the pair the following observation sheet and ask them to record on the sheet without showing it to the other person.

   As the other person is talking, write down any observations you make regarding the quality of their speech. Use the following categories:

   Loudness
   Pitch

Intonation
Tempo
Pauses
Rhythm
Emotional quality
Any other comment.

Give the person being observed a topic from the list in the Appendix to talk about for five minutes. At the end of five minutes ask them to share the experience for a further five minutes and then reverse roles.

Some teachers sound permanently angry; others apologetic or overly excited. These qualities may be difficult to change because they involve habits of many years standing. The first step is to have some feedback regarding voice quality. As yet, there is little more advice to be given other than to make your voice interesting. There is one other aspect to consider and that is to make your voice congruent with the feelings that are being expressed verbally. If you feel excited about a topic, try and show it in your voice. If you feel angry, let the class know. If you feel amused, smile or laugh. We will deal with the issue of congruence in relation to all aspects of non-verbal communication in the next section.

Putting it all together

So far we have dealt with some of the main aspects of non-verbal communication separately.

Attempts have been made to develop tests which measure several channels of non-verbal communication. One of the best known of these is the Profile of Non-verbal Sensitivity (PONS) Test designed by Rosenthal et al (see Wolfgang, 1979). This is a complex set of procedures which involves the subject watching films and listening to scrambled tapes. These cumbersome attempts to measure non-verbal communication do not appear to have advanced our knowledge in any way which is particularly useful to the teacher. The PONS test measures different aspects of non-verbal communication separately, and perhaps the key to sensitivity is an awareness of the total impact of all the channels and the context in which they are used. The interaction between the channels may provide information which is not in the individual channels, the whole being greater than the sum of any of its parts.

We would suggest that a better way of coming to an understanding of the meaning behind the non-verbal communication is in a group setting where the members are willing to share the messages that appear to be given off. A group of this nature, which we describe in more detail in chapter seven, may provide you with some painful feedback. Usually, a climate of trust has to be established before sharing of this nature can take place. An easier approach is to use exercises such as those described in this chapter, which can be used in the classroom.

Henley (1977) has suggested that non-verbal communication is used to keep 'minority groups' in their place. Minority groups in the UK could include immigrants, women and children. Hanna (1983) provided a fascinating account of the non-verbal communication in an American elementary school where white children were bused into a predominantly black area. Since the black children were on their own 'turf', the white children were in the position of a minority group and the non-verbal communication reflected this.

Henley combines the data from several studies to show that in the interaction between men and women, women tilt their heads on one side, smile more, say less, interrupt less and are touched more than men. Intuitively, this fits the writers' experience and dispels the popular notion that it is women who do most of the touching.

These ideas can easily be tested with a group of student teachers, and even if the results do not support Henley's findings, at least it will have brought the ideas to their attention and then they can be tested out in more naturalistic situations.

* Divide the group into mixed pairs and assign each pair an observer. Give the pair a topic to discuss from the Appendix and ask them to talk for ten minutes while the observers record on the following form:

As the couple are talking, record the following data. It may be difficult to be exact, but do your best.

For what percentage of the time did each person talk?

Man ____ % Woman ____ %

For what percentage of the time did each person smile?

Man ____ % Woman ____ %

For what percentage of the time did each person tilt the head?
Man   % Woman   %

Tick each time:
Man interrupts woman.
Woman interrupts man.
Man touches woman.
Woman touches man.

At the end of the exercise, ask the observers to write up their data on a board and work out the averages for the whole group. First discuss the results in trios and then with the whole group.

Non-verbal communication is often used to make a statement about the relationship. Watzlawic et al (1967) described this as a 'meta-communication'. You may be able to question the content of what is being said, but it is uncommon and would probably be thought impolite to comment on another person's non-verbal behaviour. The teacher asks the students politely to open their books, but implicit in the communication is the injunction that they had better do as they are told. The Head asks a teacher if she is willing to take a group of children on a weekend trip, and implicit in the communication is the injunction to remember that the Head plays an important part in the teacher's future career.

Meta-communications do not merely have to do with power. The teacher can indicate non-verbally whether she likes or dislikes a particular student. Usually, the students are skilled at picking up these cues. A tutor discussing work with a student can make it clear that as far as she is concerned the interview is finished, using yawns, glances at her watch and even silences to freeze out the student. At the same time she may be responding meaningfully to what the student is saying.

This raises the issue of congruence between what is being said verbally and what is being communicated non-verbally. This was introduced in chapter four where we suggested that statements of feeling were often contradicted by the tone of voice in which they were made, and the suggestion was put forward that congruence between these two aspects of communication made an important contribution to an open interaction. There is no point as a teacher in telling a student that she can trust you, when non-verbally you are indicating clearly that this is not the case. There is a good chance that the student will be responding to the non-verbal cues. To be congruent is an easy piece of advice to give, but impossible to carry out if you are not aware of the non-verbal signals you are giving off. Even going through the exercises given in this chapter is not likely to produce much in the way of change. In our view, the best training situation for producing change in this area is the type of unstructured group described in chapter seven, which forces the individual to face the consequences of her verbal and non-verbal communications.

Postscript

Non-verbal communication has been a developing area for a considerable period of time, and writers have been saying for at least two decades that the breakthrough in understanding is about to arrive. It is interesting to compare the reviewing articles contained in whole issues of *Theory into Practice* (1972, 1977) and the article by Smith (1979). The confidence about the breakthrough appears to be receding. One of the reasons for this may be the failure of the traditional scientific paradigm, which isolates individual variables, to deal with the interaction of several variables at one time. The statistical techniques which have been developed to deal with interacting variables assume that they can be summed on nominal scales, ignoring the explosive possibilities of the mixture.

The practising teacher is left with some rules of thumb, but no specific advice for specific situations. These rules of thumb are summed up by Galloway (1977) as follows:

1 Non-verbal communication plays an important part in all relationships, which the participants recognize and understand. This is, of course, true of all relationships in educational settings.

2 The main way of expressing emotion is through non-verbal communication.

3 Non-verbal communication acts as a meta-communication and makes a statement about the relationship. If a teacher allows her uncertainty to show through when giving commands, the class will invariably respond to the meta-communication.

4 The information given by non-verbal communication is difficult to control and is often a statement of the person's true feelings.

Unconscious processes may be leaked out. A permanently clenched fist may be an indication of unacknowledged anger.

5   It is difficult to be aware of your own non-verbal communication, because it is not common to be given feedback on the effect you have on other people. Initial training may be the last time a teacher is given information of this nature. Ironically, the students in class may be more forthcoming, but their motives might not be in your interest.

6   A teacher and her class quickly learn a set of non-verbal responses to facilitate the activities of the class. Some are quite obvious, such as raising hands to ask a question, and others more subtle, such as a raised eyebrow to gain silence.

The sensitive teacher could justify saying that she knew all this already. However, unless she has had extensive feedback from sympathetic friends, there is a good chance that there are large areas of her non-verbal repertoire of which she is unaware. If the social scientists have not come up with some clear answers, what is there left? Perhaps as adults we need to rediscover the intuitive processes of childhood, like the children described at the beginning of this section. This will help us to read other people's non-verbal communication, and will help in understanding the cues we are sending. Perhaps exercises which are designed to hone up intuition and which are shared mutually in pairs will be helpful. Try this exercise adapted from Bandler and Grinder (1979).

Ask the group to divide into pairs and to sit facing each other. Ask them to choose who is A and who is B. Then give the following instructions:

'I want you all to think of two events in your life, one of which you would describe as very positive and one you would describe as very negative. (pause) Now A, select one of the life events, but do not say which one it is. Hold hands, and B observe what is happening to A as we continue. A, close your eyes and remember the event. Don't see yourself in the experience, be in the experience. What is happening? What can you see? What do you hear? What do you feel? Really become aware of the feelings. Try and turn them up. (pause) Now let go of the memory and perhaps disengage hands.'

Then ask the pair to repeat the experience, using A's second experience. Talk them through it in the same way. When they have finished, ask A first to guess which was the positive and which was the negative experience. Then ask A to hazard a guess at the actual details of the memory. Then ask them to discuss the exercise in their pairs, and finally get an indication of how accurate they were from the whole group.

Ask them to reverse roles and repeat the procedure.

Conclusions

Each of the sections in this chapter has been concerned with communication, but not with the literal meaning of the words that may have been involved in an interaction. The section on the use of language examined the practical outcomes of the use of different language structures and the ways in which these structures can be changed to produce different outcomes and possibly to make a teacher more effective.

The section on the use of fantasy examines how forms of imagery can be used to enable the individual to come to a better understanding of herself and to convey information which cannot be expressed adequately in the literal meaning of the words. The use of fantasy in educational situations other than creative English and art will require careful handling to overcome the prejudice that fantasy is merely an indulgence for the idle.

The area of non-verbal communication is one in which teachers often show an immediate interest. This interest tends to wane when they discover that they are not going to be given a set of interpretations for specific forms of non-verbal behaviour. However, if the claims for the relative importance of non-verbal communication are correct, then it should play a greater part in the initial and in-service training of teachers.

Each of these areas needs to be tested out in practice in order to establish which are the optimal choices for the individual. The exercises provided will go some way to achieving this, but the experimentation has to go out into real life situations such as dealing with colleagues and working with classes of students. Eventually, all three modes of communicating can be combined with skill. Instead of asking the usual ineffective question, make a statement in the form of a fantasy, using a congruent body posture and tone of voice.

'When you interrupt me in that silly way, I feel I am going to blow my top.'

Connections

A great deal of what has been written in this chapter is an extension of the section on defence mechanisms in chapter three. Forms of language are used to avoid facing issues which might be painful. Fantasy can be used to avoid a more painful reality, but also provide a means of bringing unconscious processes into awareness. Non-verbal communication can also provide clues to issues that are not being dealt with consciously.

An understanding of the pragmatics of language and non-verbal communication provides an extension to the counselling skills. The use of imagery as a counselling skill is less widely known, but with creativity on the part of the teacher, it can be an effective tool. Imagery plays an important part in the relaxation techniques described in the next chapter and it may be that there are physiological connections between the process of attending to imagery and being relaxed. However, passive relaxation is not likely to reduce stress as effectively as an improvement in communication skills. Both of these issues will be addressed in the next chapter.

6 Stress and relaxation

Stress

Is teaching a stressful activity? Most teachers would give an emphatic 'Yes' to this question. Several surveys have been carried out inviting teachers to state which aspects of their work cause stress (Dunham, 1981; Kyriacou and Sutcliffe, 1978; Fletcher and Payne, 1982). Among other causes, relationships with both colleagues and students were seen as sources of stress. In an investigation that involved in-service courses for training experienced teachers in the skills of self-disclosure (Woodhouse, Hall and Wooster, 1985), conflicts with staff emerged as a much more important set of problems. The term 'burn-out' has become popular in the American literature (Alschuler, 1980b) and provides a vivid metaphor for the effects of a long period of teaching under difficult circumstances.

Most teachers know intuitively what they mean when they are talking about stress and use the word freely. There are, however, problems about using the word stress in the teaching context, as it is a word borrowed from engineering to describe the effects of an external force on an inanimate material. Here the material has no control over either the way the stressor operates or how it reacts to the stressor. This would also be true of a human being if she were restrained and exposed to extreme heat, cold or electric shock.

Experiments of this nature were performed on rats by Selye (1976) who demonstrated that the mobilization of the body's resources to cope with continuous stressors of this nature eventually damaged the internal organs and the animals died. He described a cycle that the animals went through as the 'General Adaption Syndrome', which may also be relevant to humans. He distinguished three stages. The first stage he called the alarm reaction, where the organism has the physiological reactions which go with high arousal or emotionality: a release of adrenalin, high blood pressure and pulse rate, tense muscles and the release of hydrochloric acid into the stomach. In the second stage, the stage of resistance, these physiological symptoms subside, but the body is still using up considerable energy to cope with the stressor and the body's resources gradually become depleted. Resistance to disease is lowered and if a second stressor is added, the organism may go into the third stage, the stage of exhaustion, which may result in death.

Most of us can cope with a short period of stress and we are probably aware of the increase in arousal involved. If a child is cheeky, we might become angry, but after the event, the anger subsides. If we are continually involved in discipline problems, there may be a long-term heightened level of arousal, which is barely noticeable because it is always there, but nevertheless is gradually depleting our resources. This may eventually lead to a breakdown in our ability to cope, and if a second stressor, such as a serious domestic problem, is added, the chances of breakdown are increased.

We suggested that stress in human beings is not merely a passive response to the effects of stressors. A teacher can change her behaviour, which will produce corresponding changes in the students' behaviour. This new situation may then be less stressful. Equally important, she can change her perception of a situation, which will determine whether or not the situation is one that needs to be responded to in an angry manner. Students talking may be seen either as a failure in discipline, or a high level of student involvement in the set task. Most writers (Cox, 1983) accept a transactional model of occupational stress, which assumes that the person's perception of a situation plays an important part in whether or not it will be stressful.

The noise level in most classrooms is low in actual decibels, and the level of stress induced by that noise will depend on your expectations of what ought to be happening. A much higher level of noise, such as in a swimming pool, is unlikely to be stressful if you do not have the responsibility of keeping the swimmers quiet. Thus different teachers will respond to different situations with varying degrees of stress. The ambitious teacher will probably find the current lack of promotion prospects difficult to cope with. A teacher with unresolved issues in relation to his mother may find it stressful to be given instructions by a female deputy head. The strict disciplinarian will have problems in coping with any talking in the classroom which he has not sanctioned. There are not many teachers who do not get upset when a student refuses to do what she has been told. There is evidence (Smilansky, 1984) that 'better' teachers are more willing to admit to stress and the next exercise will provide the opportunity to do this.

* Ask the members of the group to recall their recent teaching experience, even if it is only a short teaching practice, and to write down two events that they found particularly stressful, one in relation to students and one in relation to colleagues.

   Then take them through the following instructions:

   'Close your eyes, take three deep breaths and relax. (pause) Now summon up an image of the first stressful event. Be in the event. Don't see yourself in it. (pause) What is happening? What are you doing? What is being said? (pause) Now become aware of how you are feeling in your body. Intensify the feelings. (pause) Now open your eyes and write down how your body reacted to this first stressful situation.'

   Repeat the process with a second stressful situation.

   Tell the group to divide up into sixes but to do it non-verbally and insist they remain silent for the rest of the exercise. Provide each group with an assortment of coloured crayons or felt-tip pens and a six-foot length of blank wallpaper. Ask one member in each group to lie on the paper so that the outline of her body can be drawn. Then ask the groups to draw in their own physical responses to stress onto the outline on the paper. They can all work together, but insist that they work silently.

   When the activity seems to be drawing to a close, ask the groups, still non-verbally, to pin their drawings to the wall and allow the whole group five minutes to look at them. Then go back into the groups of six to share the experience verbally.

There is a good chance that an exercise such as this, using fantasy and drawing, will elicit more descriptions of the physical responses to stress than a verbal discussion. This is because we are often unaware of the fine detail of the body's reactions. For the same reason, the effects of stress on the body develop without our noticing, and illness may catch us unawares.

Research using the Holmes and Rahe (1967) *Schedule of Recent Experience* suggested that most of the key events in life are potentially stressful, such as the death of a spouse, losing a job or taking on a mortgage. They also include activities which are usually seen as positive, such as getting married, having a child, being promoted or going on holiday. They even include Christmas as a stressful event. Different events were given different weightings, but individuals who had a high score including several of these events were almost certain to have a serious illness within the next eighteen months.

It is impossible to establish a direct causal link between the stress of teaching and subsequent illness. The reports that teachers give of the symptoms of stress tend to be more vague and general. The comprehensive school teachers in the study of Kyriacou and Sutcliffe (1978) gave feeling 'exhausted' and 'frustrated' as the main symptoms of stress, and feeling 'very tense' as contributing most to the 'awareness of stress symptoms'. Presumably, if this exhaustion, frustration and tension were continued over a long period of time, the teachers concerned would be in Selye's stage of resistance and are at risk as far as illness and physical damage are concerned.

The American literature on burnout identifies further psychological outcomes of prolonged continuous interaction with people in an emotionally charged atmosphere. Schwab (1983) summed up the research in this area and identified three main symptoms: emotional exhaustion, negative attitudes to clients, and a loss of feeling of accomplishment in the job. With this goes an increased incidence of leaving teaching, going sick, an increase in the use of alcohol, and more marital and family conflict.

So, from the point of view of the students, the teachers and their families, it is important to find a way of reducing the stress in teaching situations. There are several ways in which this can be attempted, and these include trying to change the education system or the individual school, changing the way that you respond as an individual to students and staff, trying to change the way you respond emotionally to situations and changing your perception of situations.

1 It is rarely possible for the individual teacher to have much effect on the education system as a whole, or indeed the way her own school is organized. It is not the norm in UK schools for staff to have a democratic say in the running of the school. One well known school, Countesthorpe College in Leicestershire, recently had its democratic constitution suspended by the Head. On the whole, schools in this country are managed in a highly autocratic manner by the head teacher, who has considerable personal autonomy. They vary greatly in the degree they permit staff to join in decision-making.

There cannot be many schools which model the suggestions made by Iwanicki (1983), which summed up the organizational conditions which were likely to minimize stress in schools. These included:

(i) having clear goals which are acceptable to the staff
(ii) no distortion in the flow of communication among staff
(iii) the optimal equalization of power using collaboration rather than coercion
(iv) having a cohesive staff who wish to stay and contribute to the development of the organization.

The improvement of communication skills at all levels of the organization, particularly the skills of dealing with confrontation, could play an important part in achieving these conditions. Lloyd (1984) provided a fascinating case history of the first one hundred and twenty days of her attempt to use inter-personal skills in a humanistic framework in her new headship. Unfortunately, the majority of school staff in management positions have not had the appropriate training.

2 Changing the nature of ongoing inter-personal relationships. The individual teacher may feel that she has no say in the running of the organization, but usually she has considerable autonomy in the way she behaves in the classroom, and plays an important part in the extent to which her relationships with both students and staff are stressful.

Research at Nottingham, combined with in-service training, has provided some clear indication of how the stress levels in teaching can be reduced (Woodhouse, Hall and Wooster, 1985). This essentially involves the type of training recommended at the end of chapter four. This involved six days intensive experiential work, alternating between structured skills training and an open, small group in which changes in behaviour could be practised. Aspects of fantasy were introduced to try to generate a more creative response to situations. The ninety teachers involved were asked to keep a diary of events in school which took place prior to the course and which they had found stressful. For each incident, they were asked to state:

(i) action you took
(ii) outcome
(iii) possible alternative action you might have taken
(iv) after effects (stress, hangover).

Of the 327 incidents recorded, 187 involved students and 140 involved members of staff. Three-quarters of the incidents with students involved punishment or the threat of punishment. Surprisingly, one-third of the incidents with staff also involved punishment, usually a report to a senior member of staff. The forms of punishment may have provided short-term solutions, but they took their toll in the form of increased stress, damaged inter-personal relations, alienation, anxiety and personal suffering. The in-service course aimed to encourage alternative responses to problem situations. The teachers concerned were provided with situations in which they could take responsibility for their own behaviour and be more direct and open in their communication.

A similar diary was kept in the period following the course, and forty-two of the teachers were subsequently interviewed. Forty of these made statements to the effect that increased directness at work had produced a lessening of stress and improved relationships.

All of the interviewees reported the open, small group as a potent source of learning, but also reported the small group experience itself as stressful. It seems reasonable that learning to deal with stress can only be done in a stressful situation, but in a supportive environment old habitual ways of responding can be set aside and new ones tried out.

3   Changing the way you respond emotionally to situations. The advice to 'stay calm' when you are in a difficult situation is usually not very helpful, mainly because most of us do not have that degree of control over our emotional reactions. We end up by merely controlling the outward expression of the feelings, while they go on churning inside. As we have suggested, this may not be a healthy thing to do and eventually you may deceive yourself that you are calm and relaxed and lose awareness of the ongoing internal stressful reactions.

There are a number of training techniques for reducing your emotional reactions, such as relaxation techniques, biofeedback, yoga and meditation. They all have similar effects in that they help the body into a resting or parasympathetic state as opposed to the sympathetic state when the body's resources are mobilized for fight or flight. A good sign that you are in a relaxed state is that there may be a tingling on the surface of the skin, particularly in the face and hands, as the blood is permitted to flow to the more peripheral parts of the body.

Biofeedback techniques involve taking one index of emotionality, such as blood pressure, pulse rate, sweating of the palms, muscle tension or the pattern of electrical activity in the brain (Brown, 1975). Small machines are commercially available which will measure these responses and feed back the information to the person concerned with a sound or a light. Sweating of the palms lowers the resistance of an electric current passing across the skin (galvanic skin response). A machine with an electrode attached to two fingers can feed back a bleep which increases in frequency as the fingers become more moist. The subject can be instructed to reduce the frequency of the bleep. Most people can do this with practice, though they may not be able to explain what they have done. The reduction of any one measure of arousal tends to produce a corresponding reduction in the other measures of arousal.

Yoga and meditation are best practised with a good teacher as there are dangers associated with both sets of techniques. There are many relaxation tapes on the market, but there is really no substitute for the natural voice. We will examine some different approaches to enabling a group to relax at the end of this chapter. It requires no expert knowledge to teach a staff group to relax in the lunch hour or after school. Adolescents particularly like being taken through a relaxation schedule.

Being able to relax is helpful for your general well-being and probably improves human relations generally. Within the total institution of a school, however, the use of relaxation techniques tends to be a palliative and is not working on the basic causes of stress which lie in your own behaviour or in the organization of the school.

4 Changing your perception of situations. Since the stress in any given situation is largely a function of how we perceive that situation, then changing the perception is likely to reduce the stress. Our perceptions, however, are not easy to change as they are often related to strong conditioned emotional associations. If a student refuses to do as she is told, this may be a blow to the teacher's self-concept, and generate feelings of anxiety and shame. It is not a great help to know that all your colleagues get the same response from this student. There are clear expectations from parents, teachers and students regarding the manner in which a student should behave in the presence of a teacher.

Even in schools for emotionally disturbed children the children are coerced into behaving much like the students in a normal school in order to maintain these expectations.`

Our perceptions of situations are powerfully reinforced by worry. Thoughts go round in our heads about what might happen, about how awful things might be and how things are likely to go wrong. Fisher (1984) suggested that a reasonable amount of mental rehearsal of future events could be useful in order to anticipate a range of possible choices. On the other hand she does suggest that excessive worry is a major source of occupational stress. 'Will I be able to control all those children on the school trip?', 'What does the head-teacher want to see me about?', 'Will Mr James shout at me when I tell him he will have to lose a free period?'

It is all too easy to 'catastrophize' future events and to rehearse mentally the worst scenario possible. Many times the real event bears no relationship to these imagined fears.

Being able to effect any of these four broad approaches to dealing with stress implies a degree of control over your life. If you are in a position to change the institution you work in, then you have a high degree of control over your life. Perhaps that is why teachers who feel they play an important part in the decision-making of the school, also have a high level of job satisfaction. If all your attempts to change the institution are blocked, you may have to limit yourself to palliative activities such as changing your perceptions, or learning how to be more relaxed.

A relationship between teacher stress and locus of control, as measured by questionnaires, has been demonstrated by Kyriacou and Sutcliffe (1979) and McIntyre (1984); teachers who reported higher levels of stress tended to also report less control of their lives. This is in line with findings of Miller (1980) who, on the basis of tightly controlled experiments, argued that to be 'in control' of a situation made it more predictable and hence less stressful. The use of questionnaires to elicit levels of stress experienced by teachers is open to question. Smilansky (1984) found that 'better teachers' reported higher levels of stress. This may be because the teachers who were confident about their work were more willing to admit to stress, even though it could be seen as a sign of weakness.

The relationship between the reduction of stress and the development of more control in teaching situations is demonstrated much more vividly by Woodhouse, Hall and Wooster (1985). Here teachers were provided with a situation where they were able to practise alternative ways of responding to situations which they had identified as being stressful. Since they now had more choices available, they perceived themselves as having more control over their lives in general and also found their teaching less stressful. The following exercise will give you an opportunity to identify the degree of control you have in teaching situations which involve stress.

* Thinking back over your own teaching experience, identify four stressful events; two which involved students and two which involved colleagues. Describe these incidents as concretely as you can on the following form:

	1	2	3	4
Incident				
Action you took				
Outcome				
Cause of incident				
Possible alternative action you might have taken				
Short- and long-term emotional reaction				

Now divide the group into fives and ask them to spend five minutes discussing the events identified by each member of the group. Pay particular attention to the section on possible alternative responses.

What we have said so far implies that becoming emotionally aroused results in stress and is therefore harmful. There is a sense in which this is true, in that any use of the body is contributing to its eventual wearing out. On the other hand, we do need an optimal amount of activity in order to keep healthy. If we have been inactive for a long period of time, we will seek out situations which will make us aroused. Individual needs for arousal will vary, with some people seeking out a hectic life and others a quiet one.

Problems arise when the stress is continuous, especially when it is maintained by worry. Going along with the emotionality of teaching situations and dealing with situations effectively as they arise, could well provide a move to an optimal level of stress and at the same time make teaching a much more satisfying activity.

Relaxation

Just the sight of the students at the school gate may result in your shoulders hunching up. Later, when you repress the urge to shout, your jaw might tense. A negative exchange with a colleague and the neck might retract, while resisting the urge to hit a student leaves you with a clenched fist for a long period of time. These tensions seem to build up during the day and are often taken home at the end of the afternoon.

Muscular tension is a natural response by the body when it is under threat, and the body is mobilized to either flee from the threat or attack and destroy it. In most teaching situations, there are often threats, usually to self-esteem and occasionally to physical safety. Running away or destroying the threat is rarely appropriate, and the teacher is left frozen in this position of flight or fight and the tension remains. A congruent expression of your feelings in a stressful situation may be sufficient for the muscular tension to be released. Some of us may have to learn to relax.

Benson (1976) used the term 'relaxation response' to describe the release of muscular tension. This is the opposite of what happens in the fight-flight situation and involves a shift from the dominance of the sympathetic system to the parasympathetic system. Apart from the release of muscular tension, the breathing slows, heart rate and blood pressure decrease and the blood flows into the peripheral parts of the body such as the skin rather than the muscles, giving a tingling feeling in the hands and face. The pattern of brain-wave activity changes from predominance of the frenetic beta waves that go with thinking and activity, to the long, slow alpha waves which occur in relaxation, and also in meditation and hypnosis.

There are many ways of verbally inducing relaxation in individuals or groups (Mason, 1980) which either involve directing attention to what is happening in the body, or using a fantasy. We looked at the relationship between relaxation and fantasy in the previous chapter and here we will concentrate on the approaches which direct attention to a 'here-and-now' awareness of bodily processes. The wording is not particularly important, though it does help to include some suggestions about relaxation and to use a deeper, slower voice.

We will give three forms of relaxation that are best done in a prone position on a soft surface, followed by some suggestions on how to relax standing up, which is a better simulation of a typical teaching situation. The normal position for relaxation is to lie on the back, with the arms out at an angle to the body, the palms uppermost, the legs slightly separated, and with the feet relaxed and turned out.

Progressive relaxation involves going round different parts of the body, usually the muscles. Progressive relaxation can be done actively by tensing and releasing muscles as you move around the body, or passively, as in the following example:

* Find a comfortable position for relaxation. Take three slow, deep breaths and then permit the breath to slow down to a natural rhythm. Close your eyes and take your attention to the point where the neck meets the line across the shoulders. Allow the tension in this area to just melt away. As you breathe out, have the sense that the tension is melting away with the breath. Permit the shoulders to fill with relaxation.

  Now take the sense of relaxation down into the long strong muscles of the upper back. Breathe out the tension. Permit the relaxation to penetrate deep into the muscle groups. Let go.

  Now permit the sense of relaxation to move down into the shorter over-worked muscles of the lower back. Breathe out the tension. Have the sense that the curve of the back is sinking a fraction down to the floor.

  Allow the relaxation to move down into the pelvis and the buttocks. Have the sense that the whole of the pelvic area is gently being filled with relaxation and that the legs are being released from the hip joints. Breathe away the tension.

  Now permit the relaxation to move down into the long, strong muscles of the thighs. Gently release the tension with the outbreath as the muscles in the thighs relax and let go.

Now take the sense of relaxation down through the delicate structures of the knees and into the calves. Breathe away the tension in the calves, allowing the relaxation to move down into the feet. As the legs relax and let go, just let them lie there on the floor, with nothing to do right now.

Now go back to the shoulders and be aware of the relaxation in the shoulders. Allow the sense of relaxation to move down into the strong muscles of the upper arms. Gently breathe out the tension as the upper arms relax and let go.

Permit the relaxation to move down through the delicate structures of the elbows and down into the forearms. Breathe out the tension in the forearms and as they relax and let go, permit the relaxation to flow down through the cube bones of the wrist. Breathe out the tension in the palms, the fingers, the thumb and the thumb joint. Just let the arms lie along the floor, with nothing to do right now.

Now become aware of the relaxation in the neck once more and permit the relaxation to flow up into the head. Breathe out the tension in the scalp, allowing the relaxation to flow over the forehead to soften the face. Permit the tense muscles of the face to relax and let go, releasing the tension in the angle of the jaw. Let the tongue hang in the mouth. Let the eyes hang in their sockets. Just allow the head to lie on the floor, like a heavy ball.

There are several ways of helping a group to come out of a deep relaxation. The following is one example:

And now bring your attention back to the breath and breathe just a little deeper – and – when it is right for you – bring some feeling back into the fingers and toes, but don't rush away from the sense of being relaxed. And then, when it is right for you, give yourself a good stretch down each side and take your time to come gently back into a sitting position.

As the group facilitator, have a good look round the room when everyone appears to have sat up, in case anyone who is a good hypnotic subject is still in a trance state. Usually a firm grip on the wrist will bring them back to the room.

The second approach to relaxation comes from the system known as autogenic training (Luthe and Schultz, 1965) and involves giving yourself instructions to relax.

* Find a comfortable position for relaxation. Take three deep breaths and close your eyes. Take your attention to your right arm and repeat over to yourself, 'My right arm is heavy. My right arm is heavy.' Then take your attention to your left arm, and repeat over to yourself, 'My left arm is heavy. My left arm is heavy.' Now take your attention to your right leg, repeating, 'My right leg is heavy.' Repeat left. Now go to the area around the neck and shoulders and repeat, 'My neck and shoulders are heavy.' Now the muscles down the length of the back. 'My back is heavy.'
  Now return to your right arm and say over to yourself, 'My right arm is warm and relaxed and the muscles lengthened along the floor.' (Continue going round the same series of parts of the body using this phrase.)
  Now repeat to yourself, 'My whole body is warm and heavy, the muscles are relaxed and extended along the floor.'
  (At the end of the sequence, bring the group gently back to the room.)

This is a fairly repetitive script to read, whereas the next relaxation sequence permits endless creativity on your part. It is based on the techniques of the hypnotist Milton Erickson (Erickson and Rossi, 1980) which have been popularized by Bandler and Grinder (1975a).

* Find a comfortable position for relaxation. Take three deep breaths and close your eyes.
  Perhaps right now you are aware of sounds outside the room as the breathing settles down to a natural expansion and contraction of the diaphragm, as the body breathes itself. Perhaps now, you are aware of the temperature of the air against any exposed skin and the gentle brush of the air as it moves. As the pulse rate slows a little, the blood flows more slowly and more freely. The capillaries dilate and there is a sense of tingling in the peripheral parts of the body.
  And now, become aware of the unique smell in the room as the muscle groups gently begin to relax and let go, the muscles become warm and heavy and relaxed and extend along the floor. Be aware

of the taste in your mouth and the amount of saliva in your mouth –
as the deeper knots of tension gently unfold and the relaxation
moves down to deeper and deeper levels of relaxation, releasing
the muscles which support and work the internal organs.

Perhaps, become aware of the feel of your clothes against your
body and the pressure of the body against the floor – knowing
that the floor doesn't just end there, but goes down – down – deep,
deeper down – down – deep down all the way to the centre of the
earth. Knowing that this is a safe place to relax, explore the limits
of relaxation, moving down to levels of relaxation deeper than you
have known before. The relaxation penetrating deep into the
marrow of the bones – deep into the nucleus of every cell in the
body. Relaxing – rejuvenating – healing – changing – bringing the
many systems of the body into a new balance, a new symmetry.

In this last sequence, the person relaxing is being asked to pay attention to ongoing sensory experience. This gives the confidence to accept
the suggestions about relaxation which follow. 'You are lying on the
floor – and the body is relaxing.' Also, embedded in the text, are
phrases, such as 'relax and let go', and 'move(s) down to deeper levels'
which can be accentuated slightly to become hypnotic suggestions.

The embedded suggestions occur in everyday conversation though
they are not normally intended. If, as a teacher, you use many
statements of the nature, 'Don't misbehave', 'I want you to stop
messing about', the students may be unconsciously choosing to hear
'misbehave' and 'mess about' and react accordingly. This is another
good reason for emphasizing the positive aspect in what you are saying
as often as you can.

The relaxation sequences as presented here are short, but still very
effective. For longer and more varied forms of instruction, the reader
is referred to Mason (1980). However, the teacher is not often in a
situation where she can lie down and relax so the following suggestions
are about how to relax in a standing position. Again it is useful to
practise this in a group, so that the members can give each other
feedback about their posture.

* Stand with the feet directly in line with the shoulders and the feet
  parallel. Check that the knees are not locked and the buttocks are
  relaxed. Bend the knees a fraction. Allow the arms to hang with
  the backs of the hands facing forward. Have the sense of lifting

between the shoulder blades and that the shoulders are expanding out and down over that lift. Permit the pelvis to hang at the end of the spine, like a dish filled with water. For most people this involves hingeing the pelvis slightly forward, though the reverse might be true for others. Now imagine that the head is being lifted by a string attached to the top of the head, so that the neck extends and the chin is tucked slightly in. Check that the face, the jaw and the hands are relaxed and breathe slowly and deeply into the diaphragm.

This is a great deal to remember and is unlikely to spring to mind in a difficult discipline situation. After practice in a safe environment, try planning to use these instructions at a particular time in a difficult lesson and see what effect this has on your performance and the way you relate to your students.

It may be helpful to have some key words, which enable you to check out the various parts of the body for tension. 'Breathing, face, neck, shoulders, hands, thighs' and so on. This gives a breathing space between the occurrence of a stressful incident and an automatic reaction which makes the situation worse. It will also help you to maintain relaxation during the day.

Offers to take sessions in relaxation and stress management in the lunch hour or after school are often taken up enthusiastically by colleagues. These passive forms of relaxation make a good starting point as there is usually a quick pay-off. Further gains will come from helping colleagues to self-disclose about their experience of stress and to practise the skills of effective communication and confrontation. These approaches to the management of stress are also important for the students and are being included in some social and personal education programmes.

Summary

There is no doubt that many teachers experience their work as a stressful activity. Although it is probable that stress is largely a function of how the teacher perceives the situation she is in, the pressure of the expectations of students, parents and colleagues are very strong. There is little doubt that the excessive physiological activity of prolonged stress will eventually lead to illness and this underlines the importance of stress reduction training in the form of improved communication skills and relaxation training. This in its turn enables the individual teacher to control her own stress levels more efficiently.

Connections

If the experience of stress depends in part on the teacher's perceptions of situations, then individual constructions of reality will be important. The emotional response to stress is probably a classically conditioned one and the ability to change behaviour to control this response will reflect an internal locus of control. Stress invariably occurs where there is a threat to the self-concept, and illness may be a defence against extended periods of high levels of arousal.

Relaxation provides an alternative conditioned physiological response to situations. Communication skills, particularly those of expressing feeling and dealing with confrontation creatively, can play an important part in the reduction of stress. These communication skills are probably best facilitated in groups. This will be developed in the next chapter.

7 Developing relationships in groups

The experience of most students in secondary schools is of working in isolation, often in competition with the other members of the classroom group. Even when groups are formed, they are frequently set in competition against each other, as in competitive sports. Competition between groups often occurs within the classroom perhaps to earn housepoints, but the individual members of the groups are still working on their own. The suggestion that the first table or row to complete a particular exercise can leave the classroom first is not helping the group concerned to develop the skills for working together.

The primary school is often described as a place where groupwork is encouraged and, indeed, a visit to most primary schools in the UK will reveal children sitting around small tables. The idea of working in groups in the primary school was particularly encouraged in the Plowden Report (1968) which made a major contribution to the move away from serried ranks of desks. However, a close examination of what is actually happening in the primary school reveals that even though the children may be organized into co-operative working groups, most of them are in fact working individually. This was reported independently by an HMI Primary Survey (DES, 1978), the Oracle Research Project (Galton and Simon, 1980) and Lunn (1984), providing a very large sample which revealed this pattern.

In secondary schools, as the work for examinations begins to dominate the curriculum, the possibilities for co-operation diminish and even seating arrangements, by and large, militate against the possibility of groups working together. Co-operative ventures do take place in the secondary school, but they are certainly not the norm. This extended experience of isolated and competitive work has a profound effect on students which extends into adult life. On our courses in

Human Relations at Nottingham, we encourage students to read each other's essays and to work together on projects for their written work. Many of these students have been experienced teachers for many years and yet most of them have considerable difficulty in showing a fellow student what they have written. Some never manage it even after a year of working together. They report that it would seem like cheating to write in an area after they had read someone else's work on the same subject. This is, of course, what academics do all the time.

* Ask the whole group to consider the possibility of reading each other's essays. Ask them how they feel about receiving feedback from their peers. If a reasonable number are willing to try this out, arrange a second meeting for the group later in the term to share the experience.

Recently, there has been a renewed interest in the relative usefulness of co-operation, competition and individualized learning in the class-room. In such studies, co-operation refers to a situation where members of a group work together to achieve a common goal; competition refers to a situation where, if one student wins, the other must lose: individualized learning refers to a situation where students' goal achievements are unrelated to each other.

Generally, the results show that where the teacher organizes the lessons so that the students have to work co-operatively, there is an increase in effectiveness in both task-related and socio-emotional areas, compared with the competitively organized lesson.

1   The task-related matters include, productivity, creativity and efficiency.
2   The socio-emotional factors include satisfaction, intrinsic motivation, positive self-concept, helpful attitudes towards staff, willingness to express ideas and feelings, willingness to become involved in learning activities, prejudice reduction and liking of peers.

Students who prefer to study on their own tend to be less open in the expression of ideas and feelings and tend to have lower self-esteem.

These general statements are distilled from several studies and are summed up by Slavin et al (1985). It would seem that a co-operative climate in the classroom is educationally superior to a competitive one and yet there is evidence, at least in America and Australia, that most students perceive school as being competitive and that most students become more competitive the longer they are in school. In other words, while co-operation is educationally more effective, competition is more frequently emphasized.

* Divide the group into sub-groups of six and supply each group
  with a pack of 100 file cards. Give them the following instructions.
    'I would like you to work co-operatively within your groups to
  build a three-dimensional structure – as if you were designing a
  building. During the construction, keep the hand you normally
  use behind your back. The cards can be torn.'
    After ten minutes, and time to admire the structures, bring the
  whole group together and invite them to share how they felt when
  they were performing the task.

So, having established the advantages of co-operative learning, how can the teacher set about helping her classes to become co-operative groups? The development of co-operative groups has been taken seriously by industrial trainers, where productivity has always been a serious concern. Whatever the motivation for maintaining schools as inefficient institutions, the general pattern of organization tends to produce a competitive climate. There are many textbooks on group-work in schools, but until recently, little has been written on group processes in the classroom. An exception is Schmuck and Schmuck (1975) who identified, on the basis of research findings, the necessary conditions for the establishment of a healthy, productive classroom group.

These conditions included:

1   Having supportive inter-personal relationships in that the staff have positive expectations of their students and the students have positive expectations of each other.
2   Leadership is shared, in that the staff co-operate with the students in decision-making regarding what is to go on in the classroom, giving the students an increased sense of control over their lives.
3   Friendship is widespread. Classes with a diffuse friendship pattern have a more positive climate.
4   There is open communication. Students who mix more with each other tend to like each other better.

All of these conditions interact, and an improvement in any one of them is likely to bring about an improvement in the others. Positive expectations, the development of a more internal locus of control and open communication are issues which have already been considered, and a number of exercises have been introduced which are designed to produce changes in these areas.

Lagging behind the work in the United States, a number of schemes have been developed in the UK which use experiential exercises to help students become more aware of themselves and how they relate to others and to increase their repertoire of social skills. Some of the best known schemes are Developmental Group Work (Button, 1974, 1981, 1982) and an offshoot of this scheme, Active Tutorial Work (Baldwin and Wells, 1979). The latter, in particular, is being used in what are frequently called tutor periods first thing in the morning. Often staff who are not committed to work of this nature, but have a tutorial role, are being asked to follow an organized scheme of exercises in a short period of time, with competing activities such as taking the register and general administration. Leech and Wooster (1986) provide useful resources for working with the students with special needs.

A far more effective approach is to have a specific slot on the timetable so that activities of this nature become part of the curriculum. This is the case with Personal and Social Education (Pring, 1984) which seems to us to be one of the best labels for the activities we are trying to categorize. A good example of a serious attempt to introduce work of this nature is the Leeds Partnership Scheme. This was initially set up for the more disaffected students in comprehensive schools and involved the students negotiating their own curriculum with the teachers, including a high proportion of personal and social education. Realizing the importance of work of this nature, some schools extended the scheme to students of all abilities and in some cases involved as much as half the timetable.

The same experiential exercises are being used in subjects such as health education and drama. Also, there is a burgeoning awareness that bringing the group together and dealing with the feelings component can encourage a much higher level of involvement in any aspect of the curriculum. The same set of experiential learning structures are included in courses which have a vocational orientation. The Lifeskills developed at the Careers and Counselling Development Unit (CCDU) at Leeds provides an excellent set of resources and there have been patchy developments in schemes such as YTS and Technical and Vocational Educational Initiative (TVEI). Similar exercises are finding their way into new developments such as Peace Studies and political education.

It does not appear to matter which aspects of the traditional curriculum are integrated with processes of this nature. Any classroom group involved in activities which encourage the students to communicate more with each other, to be more open and share their experience, seems to produce an improved self-concept and a more co-operative group. This demonstrates that dealing with the classroom group process should come before the effective learning of content. Throughout this book, we have been emphasizing process rather than content – the processes being the personal and inter-personal issues involved in educational contexts.

The nature of the timetable in most comprehensive schools makes it difficult to evolve co-operative working groups in the classes. Lessons are short and students move from teacher to teacher several times in one day. The gains made by one member of staff may be undermined by another who is not sympathetic to meeting the social and emotional needs of the students. The slots on the timetable allocated to work of this nature may be short and infrequent and the staff not trained for inter-personal work.

On the other hand, if the pastoral team are committed, given time to work on inter-personal concerns and the same team do a substantial part of the subject teaching for the same group of students, there is a good chance that the climate of the classroom groups will begin to change. It might be argued that the timetabling of a scenario of this nature would be impossible. It would certainly be difficult and would probably depend on the extent to which the hierarchy wanted it to succeed.

These same problems of timetabling do not apply in primary schools and schools for slow learners where classes of students spend most of the week with one teacher. Psychologists of a Piagetian orientation might argue that students of this age have not reached an appropriate intellectual level to develop social skills that involve empathy – the ability to see the world from the other's point of view. The following small-scale studies suggest that this is not the case.

Wooster and Carson (1982) examined the effects of a programme of social and communication skills on a class of 26 eight-year-olds. The students were described by their teacher: 'These are the most difficult group of children I have ever taught.' The group included six itinerants and ten children from broken homes. Their behaviour exhibited spitefulness, rejection, bickering, tale-telling, sulking, irresponsibility, isolation and a fear of new experiences. Measures of reading ability and self-concept revealed a pattern of low achievement and low self-esteem. Some parents had even threatened to withdraw their children from what was a very destructive social climate.

The class had had several changes of teacher when they were taken over by one of the writers of the report. At that time, she was in the middle of a course on counselling skills and this had included exercises in communication and self-concept building. Her aim was to pass on to the children the skills she had learned, providing a form of what Alschuler et al (1977) described as 'psychological education'.

Initially, brainstorming was used to deal with a number of organizational problems, such as leaving the classroom open at playtime, getting in and out of assembly quietly, and rearranging the furniture in the classroom. This permitted a high proportion of children to take part in the decision-making and to express a point of view without it being judged.

The classroom discussions were formalized using the approach developed by Ballard (1982) in his 'circle time' in which students were encouraged to listen carefully to what the others were saying and to respond supportively. The discussions were complemented by self-concept development exercises (Canfield and Wells, 1976) and exercises involving physical contact and sensitivity training (Castillo, 1974; Simon and O'Rourke, 1977; and Colwell, 1975). After two terms, there were dramatic and statistically significant gains in reading and in self-concept scores.

In this short space of time, the class had moved to a more co-operative climate, taking more responsibility for the discipline and problem solving in the class. They were providing a great deal of mutual support and they were helping each other to maintain a positive view of themselves. No special effort had been made with their academic development, but this seemed to improve at the same time as their personal and social skills.

A similar study involving a class of slow-learning students was set up by Wooster and Leech (1985). The class was given a course in social and personal education for one day a week for ten weeks. At the end of the ten week period, the students were more friendly and attended better at a statistically significant level. The researchers designed an interesting measure for changes in friendship. In one of the sessions the students coloured a picture of an island. They wrote their own name in the centre, which represented the chief's hut. Around this they were to mark on the names of their classmates, deciding how far away their huts were to be. This might even be on a neighbouring island across shark-infested water. The exercise was repeated at the end of the course. This produced an activity that had a value for both the learning process and evaluating the programme.

In an evaluation of the use of Developmental Group work in middle schools in Exeter, Thacker (1985) reported a number of positive gains on the basis of eleven one and a quarter hour sessions. The teachers were seen by colleagues to become less forceful, calmer, more child-centred and viewed children in a more positive light. The students reported that they got on better with the teachers, who shouted less and allowed the students to join in discussion more. The report provided interesting case-history data of change in individual students.

In the primary study described above 'circle time' played an important part in the programme. This set of techniques designed by Ballard (1982) aimed to encourage students to participate in discussion sessions. It is intended for groups of six to twelve, but the same principles apply to sharing experience in the whole classroom group. The groups are given topics to discuss which are bound to relate to the experience of all the members of the group, such as, 'My favourite time of day', or 'Something which turns me off'. Every member of the group is invited to take a turn and the other group members are trained to respond with reflection of feeling. This encourages an emphasis on statements of feeling in the group discussions. This approach promotes a high level of self-disclosure and much supportive attention is paid to these disclosures involving participation from all the group. Ballard provides a long list of possible topics, which can easily be elaborated by the creative teacher. With a short period of training, a teacher could provide an extended effective curriculum.

At the end of any session which has involved personal and social issues, the class can be brought into a circle and asked, 'What was your experience of this session?' The use of reflection of feeling will encourage statements of feeling rather than the airing of views. When students say what they think about what has been done the teacher could reply, 'Yes, but what was your experience?' 'How did you feel when that was happening?' Younger students tend to respond more readily to a request for statements of feeling. A small minority of teachers seem to be so cut off from their feelings that they can only respond at an intellectual level. One of the advantages of sharing experience with the whole class is that it helps the individual to become aware of and to tolerate a wide range of different experience.

There are then a number of developments in schools which are encouraging students to learn more about themselves, to become more co-operative and to develop their social skills. Davies (undated) made a trenchant analysis of much of what is described as social and life skills in the new pre-vocational courses. He argued that the students are being trained merely to conform to and slot into what is effectively an iniquitous society; that the training is more in the interests of employers and the agents of social control than the students themselves. This could well be true of some of the work which is currently being done in further education, but of course it is also true of most conventional secondary education. The key variables are probably the values and training of the facilitator.

Many teachers have found it difficult to move from a teaching role to that of a facilitator of learning. Many teachers in both secondary schools and colleges of further education have been asked to switch from the subjects they have been trained to teach to forms of social and personal education. This is often done with little or no training and the only resource may be a book of exercises to work from. At the very least, the facilitators themselves should be asked to work through similar types of exercises to those that they are expected to use with their students. If they find it difficult to cope with exercises of this nature, then perhaps they should return to their original teaching specialism.

Our own experience, and the evaluation of such courses (Hall, Woodhouse and Wooster, 1984), implies that a powerful training experience for working with personal and inter-personal issues is a small group of ten to fifteen participants working with a facilitator on the 'here-and-now' relationships within the group. This experience does seem to provide the necessary struggle for making the shift from teaching to facilitating. We will deal with this training process in the next section.

In a situation where social skills training is being conducted by a non-judgmental and non-directive facilitator and the students themselves are truly involved in the decision-making about the learning process, it is unlikely that the outcome will be a move to conformity and social control. The students are being invited to widen the repertoire they have in social situations.

The small group experience

The use of unstructured small groups as a form of training for the helping professions tends to produce a highly polarized reaction. Most of the participants are very enthusiastic about their experience and claim that they have learned a great deal about themselves and changed their behaviour. Some display an enthusiasm which resembles religious conversion. A few are violently opposed to activities of this nature, usually those who have been forced to take part, or who have left a course before it has ended. We have known individuals who left confused and bewildered, but over a year later began to realize the value of what they had done. Some participants consider the experience a waste of time and even harmful.

Discussion of these activities is made more difficult by the fact that there are many different types of group which appear superficially similar, but which are actually based on different theories and have different modes of facilitation. An important distinction is between groups which are designed to provide therapy for individuals who are finding it difficult to cope with life, and groups which are designed to improve the competence (Argyris, 1968) of individuals working in professional situations. For the development of competence, far more responsibility for learning can be given to the group members. Here we are concerned with the development of competence, though it is inevitable that the process will also involve personal growth.

Groups which fit this description and the existential/phenomenological emphasis presented in this book, include the T-group as developed by the colleagues of Kurt Lewin (Benne, 1964) and the encounter group as described by Carl Rogers (1969). In these groups, the task is to examine the way the members interact with each other and the way the group is working as a whole. Thus, the ongoing 'here-and-now' activity within the group.

So, what happens? Usually the group members meet at a specific time in a room furnished with a circle of chairs. The task may have been explained in the course literature, or it may be stated briefly by the facilitator at the beginning of the first session. The facilitator is likely to take a back seat as far as initiating activity is concerned. She merely comments on what she perceives is happening in the group. The timing and content of these interventions depend very much on a personal and an intuitive judgment.

This lack of formal structure invariably throws the group into confusion and individual members become unskilled. There is often a desultory attempt to learn names and a strong need to introduce a topic for discussion, such as persuading group members to talk about their jobs or how the task can be applied to their work. Some members want to introduce structured exercises to help the group along. Most of these attempts fail because they do not have the support of the official group leader.

In this initial period, the facilitator can point out alternative ways of communicating, such as:

1   Using the first person where it is appropriate so that a comment such as, 'It is impossible to talk in the group without a proper topic' becomes, 'I find it impossible to talk in the group without a proper topic.'
2   Talking directly to another group member, rather than talking about them to another individual or the whole group.

'I don't think Paul should be allowed to sit there and contribute nothing to the group.'

'Paul, I don't think you should be allowed to just sit there and contribute nothing to the group.'
3   Pointing out incongruities between verbal and non-verbal communication.

'Jean, you say that you are angry with Paul's silence and yet your voice is expressing no emotion at all.'

'Gary, you are talking to Anne and yet you are making no eye contact.'

The anxiety generated by the lack of structure is dealt with in a variety of defensive manoeuvres. Some members withdraw into silence. Others make aggressive attacks against other members, particularly the facilitator. Often group members are too anxious about authority to attack the facilitator directly and displace these feelings onto the silent members or group members who have tried to take a leadership role. One of the difficult aspects of the facilitator's role is to assist the group members to work through these feelings about authority, even though her natural reaction may be to defend herself against them.

It is not uncommon for the group to lapse into silence. These silences are described by the members in different ways: tense, relaxed, reflective and even spiritual. The silences may last for long periods of time. They are an important source of learning, because they enable the group members to pay careful attention to their feelings without the distraction of continual chatter. It also enables the members to learn to tolerate silence, which is an important skill for facilitating discussion groups with students.

Much of the group discussion is carried on at an intellectual level and ongoing feelings are not expressed openly. Nevertheless, a 'here-and-now' awareness of feeling can be encouraged by the facilitator, with comments such as, 'And how do you feel about that?' and by modelling, 'Dick, I feel upset about the way you always talk about Ron in the group and never say anything directly to him.'

Some group members use the word 'feel' when they are expressing ideas, and this can be pointed out to them. 'I feel that it would be a good idea for us to have a topic to discuss.'

Invariably, the group members come to the conclusion that it would be useful if they shared their perceptions of each other. When a group member does this for the first time, the group becomes intensely involved in what is going on. Often, the negative feelings have to come out first before there can be any genuine expression of positive feeling. Some group members are so frightened of the expression of negative feeling that they will do anything to stop this from happening.

'You shouldn't have expressed your anger at Jason like that, it must have been very hurtful.' The facilitator might suggest that the speaker is actually concerned about the possibility of receiving negative feed-back herself. Paradoxically, group members who have had an open exchange of feelings often end up liking each other. As the group becomes more aware that expressing feelings is not as difficult and dangerous an activity they once felt it to be, feedback is given more spontaneously. Instead of condemning other people, members learn to make specific comments on behaviour.

'I don't like the way you always cut me off when I am trying to speak', rather than, 'You really get on my nerves.' And, 'I really admire the way you ask just the right question to get other people talking', rather than, 'I think you are terrific.'

It is really important to work through the mistakes in giving this sort of feedback in an experimental situation, rather than make mistakes in the staffroom which may be held against you permanently.

At some point, most groups will get round to discussing the way that sex differences affect interactions within the group. This is a difficult subject to broach because of the embarrassment normally associated with any mention of the word sex. There is also confusion between physical sexual attraction and issues relating to gender, where past experiences with the opposite sex affect behaviour.

With regard to physical attraction, some group members will only talk to others to whom they are attracted. Conversely, others find it impossible to talk to those that attract them.

Similarly, gender issues may limit the choices that members have in relating to the opposite sex. Some women withdraw in the presence of forceful men, and some men are frightened by assertive women. Most important gender issues are acted out in a very real way in the small group.

These problems are relevant to both the relationships between teachers in the staffroom and between teachers and students in the classroom. The small group provides an opportunity to become more aware of these issues and for trying out alternative behaviour.

Racial differences are also important, but these are rarely discussed within the group. The group may claim that a member's race, and particularly colour, are unimportant, and yet their non-verbal behaviour contradicts this. After the initial social chit-chat within the group, the person of a racial minority is seldom spoken to and if she speaks, rarely gets a response. After a few sessions of treatment like this she may lapse into silence. If the facilitator points out this pattern it may be hotly denied, but confirmed by the individual who is often glad that the issue has been raised. If the person is both a woman, and from a minority group, then she has a double handicap. Similar patterns of rejection are acted out dramatically in the staffroom.

The problem is exacerbated when the individual has difficulty in speaking English. This is often dealt with by pretending that the problem and therefore the person does not exist.

The group sessions range from periods when nothing much seems to be happening, to times when extreme emotions are expressed. Group members may explode with anger, burst into tears, become very elated or affectionate. In most professional working situations, feelings tend to be suppressed.

It is sometimes argued that this is necessary for the smooth running of the institution; that outbursts of emotion, whether pleasant or unpleasant, are disruptive. However, as we have shown in the previous chapter, this suppression can result in serious psychological and physiological damage, as well as providing a very unnatural atmosphere in which to work. The small group provides a situation in which members can learn what is an acceptable level of emotion to display and also how to function efficiently when strong emotions are being expressed.

We prefer a style of facilitation which does not involve making interpretations of the group members' behaviour, such as, 'The group is setting up Sally as an earth mother to meet its dependency needs.'

This may or may not be the case, but unfortunately the facilitator's words are often treated as infallible and given an authority that they do not warrant. The facilitator can ease this problem by using a vocabulary which implies that what she says is merely her point of view.

'Joan, I get the impression that you would find it very difficult to talk to Peter directly.'

'I have the feeling that there is a lot of resentment towards me for not providing a clear structure.'

'My fantasy is that several members of the group wish they weren't here.'

If the facilitator makes a mistake, she can own up to it, rather than try to rationalize her earlier statements. So the facilitator can be seen to be fallible. In their struggle with problems of authority, the group members sometimes treat the facilitator like a god and the facilitator might foster this image in order to maintain the understandable ego-boost it provides.

So, what do the participants in such a group learn and, in particular, how is it useful to the teachers? There is no easy answer to this question, as each participant has a different history of experience in social situations and each will be working through a different personal agenda. When teachers have been through a learning experience of this nature, a large majority report having had a positive experience but find it difficult to be precise about how it has changed their behaviour in their working lives. This may be because aspects of the learning are taking place at an intuitive or non-verbal level, which is difficult to verbalize. However, when interviewed in depth, concrete instances of learning begin to emerge which can be directly attributable to the small group experience.

We have collected data over a number of years which indicates that specific changes do occur in the teaching situation (Hall, Woodhouse and Wooster, 1984) and have data, Bowes (1985), which suggests that this learning is still effective and vivid five years later. It must be stressed that the small group experience was embedded in courses for teachers which also include training in counselling skills and experiential learning structures which involved fantasy and non-verbal work. However, a majority of the teachers interviewed reported that the small group experience was the most vivid part of the course and they could even remember verbatim some of the conversations which took place five years later. The following themes emerged most frequently:

1   Attitudes to colleagues in authority had changed. They were able to treat members of the hierarchy more as equals.

'I was able to go to the Head and discuss the possibility of moving more towards pastoral work. Prior to the course I wouldn't have spoken to him voluntarily.'

2   Many teachers reported that they had come to a new understanding of what 'listening' meant.

'I find I am listening to the children for the first time in my life and have a genuine concern for what they have to say.'

'Since I did the course, several colleagues have come to me with their problems. It seems I am developing a reputation as a person who listens.'

3   Attitudes to discipline and classroom control have changed. There was evidence of a move from a teaching role to a facilitative role.

'My whole attitude to the children has changed and I let them have a say in what we are doing.'

'I don't seem to get het up about what is going on in the classroom. I am much more relaxed and tolerant and the whole atmosphere is softer.'

4   The expression of feeling was accepted. If a colleague or student became angry or upset, there was less need to become emotional oneself.

'When the complaints and bitchiness start in the staffroom, I find I don't get sucked into it.'

'If a pupil starts to cry, I find I can accept it and just let it happen and not try to comfort them out of it.'

5   There is a greater tolerance of silence.

'When there is a pause in the class, I don't have to rush in and fill it.'

'When I am counselling a child I can just sit there with them, even though they are not saying anything.'

6   The course members became more assertive in their relations with colleagues and students.

'When I am asked to do something I don't want to do, I make sure I get in my point of view before I go along with it. The first time I tried this, the request was withdrawn.'

'A senior member of staff kept calling me "My dear". When I told him that I found it demeaning, he started treating me as more of an equal.'

7   There were many reports of the group experience producing changes in the participants' personal lives.

'I was able to talk to my teenage daughter for the first time.'

'I found my husband and I spent hours talking after the course . . . I felt we were really open and honest with each other.'

It seems likely that gains in the quality of personal life will have a positive effect on performance in professional life.

These reports are biased in the sense that they come from teachers who volunteered to come on courses of this nature in the first place. An additional bias comes from the fact that a small proportion refused to return questionnaires or to be involved in an interview. For some, this refusal to take part in evaluation may just be due to lack of time, but there is probably a minority who feel that groupwork of this nature was a waste of time or even harmful. When course members describe the group experience as harmful, they are usually referring to other people's experience, not their own. When these 'other people' were asked, they often reported the experience as being highly productive.

Rogers (1969) and Gibb (1970) discussed the problem of rumours about the harmful effects of small group training and how colleagues who had been on courses had suffered personally and had had problems readjusting to their work. An examination of individual cases showed that these rumours were invariably unsubstantiated. There is no evidence that training of this nature produces any more psychological disturbance than any other aspects of normal living and probably less than conventional education (Hartman, 1979). There are clearly powerful gains for people working in the helping professions, particularly teachers.

Lieberman, Yalom and Miles (1973), in a massive evaluation of encounter groups in California, presented a more negative picture regarding casualties. In their study, they included some of the more dramatic forms of personal growth groups and they found that the highest rate of casualties came from groups with highly charismatic leaders. This does not fit the style of facilitation advocated by Rogers or that we would encourage. In the Lieberman et. al. study, among the most helpful and least harmful were those which had no leader, but followed taped instructions, which provided minimal guidelines for moving the group along. This perhaps says something about the importance of the leader in group work of this nature. The central skill of the facilitator may be in not interfering too much with the learning process of the group.

A more detailed examination of small-group training can be found in Egan (1970) and Rogers (1969).

Group dynamics

One particular approach to group work has developed out of the work of the Tavistock Institute for Human Relations and in particular from the ideas of Bion (1961). As well as working in small face-to-face groups of up to fifteen members, courses using this model may include large groups and inter-group exercises.

The focus of these courses is on authority and leadership. These issues are deeply embedded in the school system. When the traditional pattern of dependency on authority is removed, there is often an emergence of irrational dependent behaviour on the part of both staff and students.

The main emphasis in all of these events is on what is happening in the group, rather than what is happening to the individual. Again, the groups have no specific task, other than to study what is happening in the group in the 'here-and-now'. This permits the members to increase their awareness of processes that operate in most working groups, but which are not normally attended to because of the daily tasks that the group may be trying to get through.

An important emphasis made by the consultants in groups using the Tavistock model concerns leadership and authority. The consultant does not permit herself to socialize with the group, refuses to answer direct questions and avoids being drawn into conversations. She only comments on the group process. This often stirs up strong feelings about authority, which are then projected onto the consultant. These feelings invariably reflect a high level of dependency on the consultant.

When it becomes clear that the consultant has no intention of telling the group members what they should be learning or how they should set about it, the leadership tends to switch erratically round the group. This takes two forms:

1 Leadership which is designed to attack the consultant or other group members, and
2 Leadership which is designed to escape from the task, such as organizing an early exit for coffee, or discussing events outside the group.

A much more curious phenomenon is the group's involvement in the setting up of a paired interaction, which often has a sexual charge. It is as if the group is looking to the pairing to produce a solution to the group's problems, almost like the birth of a Messiah.

These group processes have been encapsulated in Bion's (1961) model that groups try to cope with the anxiety and fear of its members by operating under what he calls 'basic assumptions'. These are, dependency, fight/flight, and pairing. When the group is working efficiently on its task, then there is no need for these basic assumptions to be operating. Usually, it is necessary for the normal tasks of a group to be stripped away before these processes can be seen operating.

In our experience, groups using this model stir up the most primitive feelings in the group members. No attempt is made by the consultants to resolve these feelings, and participants sometimes leave with strong negative feelings for both the consultants and the model. Of all the group approaches, it does provide the best opportunity for dealing with irrational dependency on authority. This enables the individual to develop her own authority and control over her own life.

Small group training and education

How can these forms of group training be applied within the educational system? In the UK, there are few teacher training institutions which include work of this nature in their programmes, either for initial training or for in-service work. If a member of college staff is interested, the group work is done with volunteers outside the normal programme of courses. It has been done in this fashion for some time and it is well worth reading the early reports by Ottaway (1966) and Richardson (1967). There has been an increase recently because of the development of in-service courses in counselling skills, some of which include a small group experience.

The courses which are part of the Human Relations programme at Nottingham University involve individual teachers coming from their schools to spend from five days to a year's secondment working in courses where the small group is seen as a central training experience. Now that several hundred teachers have attended these courses, many return to their schools to the support of other colleagues who have shared the experience. In some schools, whole year tutor teams are in a position to share their feelings openly, to listen to each other and take responsibility for their part in the decision-making of the work group. Other teachers return to a situation where they have no support and may even face a hostile response to their attempts to develop a more humanistic approach to relationships within the school. In a situation like this, any attempt to become more personally autonomous and to encourage autonomy in students becomes a lonely business.

The headteacher is a key figure in enabling the development of human relations training to work within the school as a whole. This would require staff to work in small groups within the school and possibly working towards a situation where staff and students are involved in the same groups. Rogers (1983) described situations in the United States where whole institutions and even groups of institutions were involved in training of this nature. In spite of considerable evidence of success, all of these experiments foundered because of the lack of involvement and often open hostility of top administrators.

In this country, Richardson (1973) has described how the total institution of the school can be developed, using a model based on Tavistock-style group dynamics. Miles and Fullan (1980) reviewed evidence which suggested that the use of small group work could have important benefits for a school staff if it was integrated with group and organizational issues. An emphasis on personal growth alone appeared to be self-defeating. They suggested that spending less than twenty-four hours of organizational development work for each member of staff opened up problems that were not resolved properly and, again, this could be self-defeating.

In this country, secondary schools usually set aside five days in the year for in-service training with the whole staff. Often, this opportunity is wasted by bringing in 'experts' to give 'inspiring' lectures and, at most, half a day is set aside for work of a practical nature. This is pitifully inadequate for the use of experiential techniques and suggests that the organizers are not genuinely interested in meaningful change within the institution. Perhaps the best thing that could happen on training days of this nature is to help the staff to get to know each other a little better.

Can a classroom teacher use small group training of this nature with a conventional class? There is an initial logistical problem in that most classes involve more than the fifteen group members which is usually recommended as the top limit for a group of this nature. However, it is not impossible for a teacher to arrange to teach a smaller group occasionally. In this country, there is an unfavourable attitude to introspective activities and the introduction of group work of this nature would be frowned on by both staff and students.

There is, however, a detailed account (Grainger, 1970) of the use of Tavistock-style group dynamics sessions being used with whole classes in a Leicestershire High School. These were conducted in lesson time which was normally used for discussions as part of their English programme. Grainger told the classes, who sat round in a large circle, that the task of the group was '... to study its own behaviour as it happens in "the here and now"'. He insisted on certain rules, which included a ban on physical harm, damaging property and making excessive noise. The circle was not to be broken and children who did not wish to attend had to give a day's notice.

These sessions were soon nicknamed 'The Bullring', which became the title of Grainger's book. The children learned that they could do anything they wanted within the rules. Initially, there was a great deal of dependent behaviour, the students looking to the teacher to provide topics for discussion. Later the children dealt with their anxiety by indulging in fight and flight. Some children withdrew by becoming silent and others indulged in conventional forms of playing-up behaviour, such as throwing paper darts, which was probably an attack on Grainger's authority. As the sessions progressed, there did seem to be evidence that the students were becoming increasingly aware of the processes that were going on in the group and began taking responsibility for their own behaviour. Their own reports suggest a great deal of confusion and probably reflect the kind of struggle we have referred to as being necessary for effective learning. Children often reported that they had wasted their time, but that they wanted the 'Bullrings' to continue. When questioned in depth, there was clear evidence of specific learning about behaviour in groups. The behaviour of the children is remarkably similar to that of adults in the same sort of situation.

Grainger makes the important suggestion that groupwork of this nature can play an important part in the moral education of the students. He argues that the students are able to try out and examine the effects of new behaviour in a real situation. In this situation, the students have the opportunity to deal with their own thoughts, feelings and actions that are involved in incidents as they arise. This surely must be more effective than discussion of hypothetical moral choices which may have no relevance to the students concerned. Pring (1984) stressed the importance of 'respect for persons' as an important part of moral development which also has a central place in social and personal education. In Grainger's descriptive account there is evidence of the development of respect for both the teacher and the other students in the class. These changes of behaviour, feeling and thinking were developed independently of the authority figure (the teacher) which implies that the children were learning to be independent of convention and the indoctrination of didactic teaching.

Grainger's work provides evidence that work of this nature can be done in a conventional classroom, that it can be a potent source of learning and that it probably does less harm than conventional schooling. It would, however, be strongly advisable to have the approval of the Head and the support of other colleagues before developing groupwork in a school because of the strong prejudice against any activity which permits students to become more independent of their teachers and decide for themselves what they are going to learn. There is the suggestion in Grainger's book that colleagues were blaming the 'Bullrings' for misbehaviour in their classes. The irrational criticism that did not filter through was probably far more vitriolic.

A further problem lies in the training of teachers to take a facilitative role with groups of students. Because of the ethos of most school situations, it is difficult for a member of staff not to be directive, not to try and manipulate changes in behaviour, avoid judgments and interpretations. The general principles outlined by Rogers (1983) are probably the most appropriate, and he provided evidence that training based on these principles made for a better teacher, even in conventional terms. The most potent form of this training, as we have suggested, is for the teacher to experience small-group training for herself.

Having experienced the training, but finding herself in a situation where the institutional ethos does not permit the use of these forms of training in its full form – that is most schools in fact – there are many ways in which the training can be used to good effect. Listening, reflecting content and feeling, confronting and giving feedback skilfully, initiating interactions, enquiring about feelings, tolerating silence and self-disclosing are all skills that can be honed up in small-group training and which contribute to a more effective classroom climate.

Summary

The human dynamics of the classroom undoubtedly have a profound impact on the effectiveness of academic learning and social skills. Teachers and students can both be trained in the skills of relating more effectively and how to work more co-operatively, providing an enormously improved classroom climate.

Unstructured small-group training provides a free-wheeling, real-life opportunity for teachers to practise new ways of behaving and to extend their repertoire of choices in the way they relate to colleagues and students. Because this form of training involves real people in real situations, feelings are often strong and the experience is highly memorable.

Group dynamics training in the form developed at the Tavistock Institute provides an opportunity to study the conscious and also the less accessible processes that affect behaviour in groups.

Connections

Many of the exercises used in courses on personal and social education involve inter-personal and communication skills. These are very similar to counselling skills. To teach counselling skills to a classroom group is likely to have a beneficial effect on the social climate of the classroom group.

A group does appear to be the best situation in which to learn inter-personal skills (Egan, 1976) as the peer group can provide a range of models and feedback which is likely to be an improvement on the resources of any one expert.

This is also true of the more spontaneous experience of small-group training. Listening, attending, reflecting content and feeling, self-disclosure, confrontation and the effective use of different forms of language are all skills which can be tried out in the small group. Although learning in this situation is usually perceived as stressful, it does appear to produce a long-term reduction of stress in the pro-fessional setting.

During the course of a small-group experience, the members often reveal clear examples of defence mechanisms. The peer group, in their feedback to individuals, can help the group members to become more aware of the ways they defend themselves. The process of giving feedback is made more complex by the possibility that the person who is giving feedback is projecting aspects of herself onto the other person.

Similarly, the small-group training experience can provide a vivid illustration of the differences in the way that individuals construe their experience, particularly their experience of other people.

8 Conclusion

The material and exercises provided in this book are designed to help teachers become more aware of how they behave in face-to-face situations and provide practical possibilities for change. The issues dealt with have been integrated in a unique manner. The criterion for inclusion is usefulness, that is, what theory, research and experiential work can lead to changes in awareness and behaviour.

We are making the assumption that the important changes in awareness and behaviour have to be mediated through experience, and that only the learner can decide what is important in a particular experience. Hopefully, the exercises will have provided a gentle introduction to experiential learning and will have given the text a vividness which is difficult to generate at a purely cognitive level. It is probably advisable to use gentle structures in the teacher training context, since as a trainer you may be dealing with groups who are not volunteers. Expanding awareness can be an unsettling business, and the more advanced work can be carried out in optional courses. If you have already been involved in experiential learning then you will be in a strong position to judge the effectiveness of the suggestions we have made.

This emphasis on experiential learning is in line with a subtle shift which is now taking place in schools and colleges. Many teachers are becoming involved in forms of human relations training to prepare them for the pastoral curriculum, in social and personal education, Active Tutorial Work and Developmental Group Work. Others have been involved in counselling skills training to help them in their pastoral roles. A high proportion of teachers who have undergone experiential training in these areas are very enthusiastic about what appears to be a totally new approach to learning and relationships in school. They report that this enthusiasm spills over into their teaching of the more conventional subject areas and the experiential techniques are adapted to relate these subjects more closely to the students' lives. Indeed, the teaching of conventional subjects appears to become more efficient as a result of improving the relationships within a class and enabling them to become a more co-operative group.

By working with whole class groups to deal with personal and social issues, there is a shift in emphasis in the approach to pastoral care. There is less emphasis on dealing with individuals who have 'problems', usually of a disciplinary nature, and a shift towards the development of the school or class as a therapeutic community. Hopefully, this will produce a reduction in conventional discipline problems and when they occur, the peer group will play a part in the resolution of these problems.

This positive approach to classroom discipline has been taken much more seriously by writers in the United States such as Alschuler (1980a) and Jones and Jones (1981). They advocated many of the suggestions made in this book, such as working on the relationships within the class, developing positive self-concepts and working on behaviour problems using self-negotiated management strategies. Discipline is often seen as something which is done by the teacher to the students. Here we are suggesting that discipline is something that the students develop within themselves and within their groups. The importance of self-discipline has often been presented as an ideal for students in schools, with no clear indication as to how this can be brought about. The introduction of humanistic and experiential approaches in education is providing a technology to achieve this end. Enlightened teachers have been working in this mode for many years, but it is only recently that a humanistic/experiential approach has been formalized into parts of the curriculum, and that these ideas and training are being introduced to a larger number of teachers.

The notion of students working towards self-discipline is central to moral education. Pring (1984) emphasized the need to become an autonomous person, one who could work out the appropriate way to behave for himself. This he sees as the highest level of moral development, and he sees social and personal education as playing an important part in this development. He tends to emphasize the cognitive side of moral education, insisting that some aspects of morality can be taught. In our experience, most children come to important moral conclusions for themselves in the experiential learning setting. This provides them with the opportunity to look at social behaviour directly, experience the associated feelings, draw rational conclusions from the ensuing discussion and plan for future action.

We would argue that experiential learning provides the bedrock for moral education, since it begins with the student's immediate experience in the classroom where it produces a high level of attention and is highly memorable. The broader social issues related to this immediate experience can be developed in other parts of the curriculum, such as in literature and the humanities.

The most influential writers on moral education have tended to be philosophers or psychologists with a strong involvement in cognitive development. This may explain why they play down the importance of unconscious processes in moral action. Most older students will be able to provide the 'right' answer to a hypothetical moral dilemma and understand that the intentions behind a specific action will play an important part in its moral evaluation. In the introduction, we developed the notion of intentionality to include unconscious motivation. Most mature professionals will also be able to answer the hypothetical moral question and yet their behaviour in situations which involve status, power, promotion and the like, may bear no relation to the rationally thought out moral prescription. Indeed, if the behaviour conflicts with stated moral beliefs too sharply, the person concerned may have to produce a rationalization to justify his behaviour.

We have written about the use of fantasy and non-verbal communication as a means of understanding the unconscious processes that may distort behaviour and relationships. The term unconscious is often seen to refer to processes which are inaccessible and can only be dealt with in an extended analysis with an expert therapist. A few experiences with scripted fantasy will usually demonstrate that hidden aspects of the personality can be quickly brought into consciousness. We would prefer Perls' (1976) notion of lack of awareness rather than that of the unconscious. Some aspects of our existence may be on the edge of awareness and it may only require some feedback from another person to extend that awareness. This is particularly true in the area of non-verbal communication, where behaviour which is out of our awareness is in full public view. The emphasis in work on non-verbal communication has been on reading other people's signals. Perhaps it is more important for the teacher to be more aware of her own non-verbal communication.

The direct exploration of imagery and feeling is missing from most educational situations and yet to do this appears to produce highly memorable and vivid experience. The resistance against developing the use of imagery in the classroom comes from the expectations of both students and teachers regarding what are appropriate activities for the classroom. The possibilities for change have to come from the teacher.

Imagery, feeling and unconscious processes do seem to be linked, and may have a common physiological basis, as they all seem to involve states of consciousness which are qualitatively different from that involved in rational linear thinking. Whether these differences are adequately explained by the split-brain hypothesis is still an open question. Certainly those activities which have been described as involving right-brain processes are not given a high priority in our schools.

Lastly, we would like to stress the importance of the group process and the need to trust the group. Many teachers see discipline, and social and moral problems, as issues they have to control. Lecturing and moralizing about behaviour have a long tradition of failure. Situations where the decision-making regarding personal, social and moral issues can be worked on by the group as a whole provide a potent training ground for moral development. Real issues are being used as a source of learning rather than hypothetical questions, simulations and role-play.

A great deal of important research has been carried out describing the nature of human relations in educational settings. The technology of producing effective change in these relationships is still in its infancy, but there is growing evidence that the experiential/humanistic approach has a great deal to offer.

Appendix

The following list of topics can be used in the exercises given in this book. They can also be used as discussion topics which will encourage self-disclosure in a group of students.

1   Talk about your earliest memories.
2   What are your first memories of being at school?
3   What was it like for you to change from primary to secondary school?
4   How did you get on with the opposite sex in secondary school?
5   What sort of problems did you have to face when you went to college or university?
6   What sort of things do you dream about?
7   Talk about the problems you have with a difficult colleague.
8   What was it like to have your place in the family – eldest, youngest, middle or only child?
9   What situations make you embarrassed?
10 How do you feel about what is happening in your life right now?

References

Adams-Webber, J. R. (1979), *Personal Construct Theory: Concepts and Applications*, Chichester: Wiley.

Alschuler, A. S. (1980a), *School Discipline: a Socially Literate Solution*, New York: McGraw-Hill.

Alschuler, A. S. (1980b), *Teacher Burnout*, Washington: National Educational Association.

Alschuler, A. S., Ivey, A. E. and Hatcher, C. (1977), Psychological education, in C. Hatcher, et al (Eds), *Innovations in Counselling Psychology*, San Francisco: Jossey-Bass.

Argyle, M. and Cook, M. (1976), *Gaze and Mutual Gaze*, Cambridge: Cambridge University Press.

Argyris, C. (1968), Conditions for competence acquisition and therapy. *Journal of Applied Behavioural Science*, 4, 2.

Aspy, D. N. and Roebuck, F. N. (1977), *Kids Don't Learn from People They Don't Like*, Amherst, Mass.: Human Resource Development Press.

Assagioli, R. (1965), *Psychosynthesis: A Manual of Principles and Techniques*, New York: Hobbs Dorman.

Axelrod, S. (1983), *Behaviour Modification in the Classroom*, 2nd Edition, New York: McGraw-Hill.

Baldwin, J. and Wells, H. (1979), *Active Tutorial Work Books 1-5*, Oxford: Basil Blackwell.

Ballard, J. (1982), *Circlebook*, New York: Irvington.

Bandler, R. and Grinder, J. (1975a), *Patterns of the Hypnotic Techniques of Milton H. Erickson, MD*, Cupertino, Calif.: Meta Publications.

Bandler, R. and Grinder, J. (1975b), *The Structure of Magic I*, Paulo Alto, Calif.: Science and Behaviour Books.

Bandler, R. and Grinder, J. (1979), *Frogs into Princes*, Moab, Utah: Real People Press.

Barlow, W. (1973), *The Alexander Principle*, London: Gollancz.

Bartlett, F. C. (1932), *Remembering*, Cambridge: Cambridge University Press.

Bateson, G. (1979), *Mind and Nature*, Hounslow: Wildwood House.

Becker, E. (1973), *The Denial of Death*, New York: Free Press.

Benne, K. D. (1964), History of the T-group in the laboratory setting, in

L. P. Bradford, J. R. Gibb and K. D. Benne (Eds), *T-Group Theory and Laboratory Method: Innovation and Re-Education*, New York: Wiley.

Benson, H. (1976), *The Relaxation Response*, London: Collins.

Bion, W. R. (1961), *Experiences in Groups*, London: Tavistock.

Birdwhistell, R. L. (1970), *Kinesics and Content*, Philadelphia: University of Philadelphia Press.

Boss, M. (1979), *Existential Foundations of Medicine and Psychology*, New York: Aronson.

Bowes, M. E. (1985), *An Evaluation of In-Service Courses in Human Relations*, Unpublished M.Ed. Thesis: University of Nottingham.

Boydell, T. (1976), *Experiential Learning*, Manchester Monographs: Sheffield City Polytechnic.

Brammer, L. M. (1979), *The Helping Relationship*, Englewood Cliffs, New Jersey: Prentice-Hall.

Brandon, D. (1976), *Zen and the Art of Helping*, London: Routledge and Kegan Paul.

Brophy, J. E. and Good, T. L. (1974), *Teacher-Student Relationships: Causes and Consequences*, New York: Holt.

Brown, B. B. (1975), *New Mind, New Body*, New York: Bantam Books.

Brown, G. I. (1972), *Human Teaching for Human Learning*, New York: Viking Press.

Bruner, J. S. (1966), *Towards a Theory of Instruction*, Cambridge, Mass.: Harvard University Press.

Buber, M. (1947), *I and Thou*, Edinburgh: Clark.

Buck, R. (1977), Non-verbal communication of affect in pre-school children: relationships with personality and skin conductance. *Journal of Personality and Social Psychology*, 35, 225–236.

Burns, R. B. (1982), *Self-Concept Development and Education*, London: Holt, Rinehart and Winston.

Button, L. (1974), *Developmental Group Work with Adolescents*, London: University of London Press.

Button, L. (1981), *Group Tutoring for the Form Teacher, Book 1*, London: Hodder and Stoughton.

Button, L. (1982), *Group Tutoring for the Form Teacher, Book 2*, London: Hodder and Stoughton.

Canfield, J. and Wells, H. C. (1976), *100 Ways to Enhance Self-Concept in the Classroom*, Englewood Cliffs: Prentice-Hall.

Carkhuff, R. R. (1969), *Helping and Human Relations*, New York: Holt.

Castillo, G. (1974), *Left-Handed Teaching*, New York: Praeger.

Chelune, G. J. (1979), *Self-Disclosure*, San Francisco: Jossey-Bass.

Colwell, L. C. (1975), *Jump to Learn: Teaching Motor Skills for Self-Esteem*, San Diego: Pennant Educational Materials.

Combs, A. W. (1965), *The Professional Education of Teachers*, Boston, Mass.: Allyn and Bacon.

Condon, W. S. (1976), An analysis of behavioural organization. *Sign Language Studies*, 13, 285–318.

Corey, G. (1977), *Theory and Practice of Counselling and Psychotherapy*, Monterey: Brooks/Cole.

Cox, J. (1983), *Stress*, London: Macmillan.

Crandall, V. C., Katkovsky, W. E. and Crandall, V. J. (1965), Children's beliefs in their control of reinforcements in intellectual achievement behaviour. *Child Development*, 36, 91–109.

Curle, A. (1973), *Education for Liberation*, London: Tavistock.

Darwin, C. (1872), *The Expression of the Emotions in Man and Animals*, London: Murray.

Davies, B. *From Social Education to Social and Life Skills Training: In Whose Interests?* National Youth Board, Occasional Paper 19.

De Charms, R. (1972), Personal causation training in schools. *Journal of Applied Social Psychology*, 2, 95–113.

De Charms, R. (1981), Personal causation and locus of control: two different traditions and two uncorrelated measures, in H. M. Lefcourt (Ed), *Research with the Locus of Control Construct. Vol 1, Assessment Methods*, New York: Academic Press.

Delecco, J. and Richards, A. (1974), *Growing Pains: Uses of School Conflict*, New York: Aberdeen Press.

Dember, W. N. (1969), *The Psychology of Perception*, New York: Holt, Rinehart and Winston.

DES (1978), *Primary Education in England: A Survey by HM Inspectors of Schools*, London: HMSO.

Dockar-Drysedale, B. (1968), *Therapy in Child Care*, London: Longmans.

Dunham, J. (1976), Stress situations and responses, in National Association of Schoolmasters (Ed), *Stress in Schools*, National Association of Schoolmasters.

Dunham, J. (1981), Disruptive pupils and teacher stress. *Educational Research*, 23, 3.

Dweck, C. S. (1975), The role of expectations and attributions in the alleviation of learned helplessness. *Journal of Personality and Social Psychology*, 31, 674–685.

Egan, G. (1970), *Encounter: Group Processes for Inter-personal Growth*, Belmont, Calif.: Brooks/Cole.

Egan, G. (1975), *The Skilled Helper*, Monterey: Brooks/Cole.

Egan, G. (1976), *Inter-personal Living*, Monterey: Brooks/Cole.

Egan, G. (1982), *The Skilled Helper: Model, Skills and Methods for Effective Helping*, Monterey: Brooks/Cole.

Ekman, P. and Friesen, W. V. (1972), Hand movements. *Journal of Communication*, 22, 353–374.

Ellis, R. and Whittingham, D. (1983), *New Directions in Social Skills Training*, London: Croom Helm.

Erickson, M. H. and Rossi, E. L. (1980), *Experiencing Hypnosis: Therapeutic Approaches to Altered States*, New York: Irvington.

Fenton, J. V. (1973), *Choice of Habit*, London: Macdonald and Evans.

Ferrucci, P. (1982), *What We May Be*, Wellingborough: Turnstone Press.

Feusterheim, H. and Baer, J. (1975), *Don't Say Yes When You Want to Say No*, New York: Dell.

Fisher, S. (1984), *Stress and the Perception of Control*, Hillsdale, N.J.: Lawrence Erlbaum Associates.

Fletcher, B. C. and Payne, R. L. (1982), Levels of reported stressors and strains amongst school teachers: some UK data. *Educational Review*, 34, 3.

Fransella, F. and Bannister, D. (1977), *A Manual for Repertory Grid Technique*, London: Academic Press.

Freire, P. (1972), *Pedagogy of the Oppressed*, Harmondsworth: Penguin.

Fugitt, E. D. (1983), *He Hit Me Back First*, California: Jalmar Press.

Galloway, C. M. (1977), The challenge of non-verbal research. *Theory into Practice*, 10, 310–314.

Galton, M. and Simon, B. (Eds) (1980), *Progress and Performance in the Primary Classroom*, London: Routledge and Kegan Paul.

Gammage, P. (1982), *Children and Schooling: Issues in Childhood Schooling*, London: Allen and Unwin.

Garber, J. and Seligman, M. E. P. (Eds) (1980), *Human Helplessness: Theory and Applications*, New York: Academic Press.

Gazda, G. M., Asbury, F. S., Balzer, F. J., Childs, W. C. and Walters, R. P. (1984), *Human Relations Development*, 3rd Edition, Boston: Allyn and Bacon.

Gibb, J. R. (1970), The effects of human relations training, in A. E. Bergin and S. L. Garfield (Eds), *Handbook of Psychotherapy and Behaviour Change*, New York: Wiley.

Gladstein, G. A. (1977), Empathy and counselling outcome: an empirical and conceptual review. *The Counselling Psychologist*, 6, 4, 70–79.

Gordon, T. (1974), *TET Teacher Effectiveness Training*, New York: Wyden.

Grainger, A. J. (1970), *The Bullring*, Oxford: Pergamon.

Greenspoon, J. (1962), Verbal conditioning and clinical psychology, in A. J. Backrock (Ed), *Experimental Foundations of Clinical Psychology*, New York: Basic Books.

Hall, E. T. (1966), *The Hidden Dimension*, New York: Doubleday.

Hall, E. (1977), Human relations training in a comprehensive school. *British Journal of Guidance and Counselling*, 5, 2.

Hall, E. (1979), *The Structure of Fantasy*, Unpublished Ph.D. thesis, University of Nottingham.

Hall, E. (1983), Patterns of meaning in guided fantasy. *Journal of Mental Imagery*, 7, 1, 35–50.

Hall, E. and Greenwood, E. (1985), *The Effects of Fantasy on the Expression of Feeling and the Quality of Writing by Young Adolescents*, Unpublished paper presented to the 2nd International Imagery Conference.

Hall, E. and Kirkland, A. (1984), Drawings of trees and the expression of feelings in early adolescence. *British Journal of Guidance and Counselling*, 7, 1.

Hall, E., Woodhouse, D. A. and Wooster, A. D. (1984), An evaluation of in-service courses in human relations. *British Journal of In-Service Education*, 11, 1, 55–60.

Hamacheck, D. E. (1978), *Encounters with the Self*, New York: Holt, Rinehart and Winston.

Hamblin, D. (1983), *Guidance: 16–19*, Oxford: Blackwell.

Hanna, J. L. (1983), Black/white non-verbal differences, dance and dissonance: implications for desegregation, in A. Wolfgang (Ed), *Non-verbal Behaviour: Perspectives, Applications, Nonverbal Insights*, Lewiston, N.Y.: Hogrefe Inc.

Hargreaves, D. H. (1982), *The Challenge for the Comprehensive School: Culture, Curriculum and Community*, London: Routledge.

Harlow, H. F. (1958), The nature of love. *American Psychologist*, 13, 673–685.

Hartman, J. J. (1979), Small group methods of personal change. *Annual Review of Psychology*, 30.

Henley, N. M. (1977), *Body Politics*, Englewood Cliffs: Prentice-Hall.

Herbert, M. (1981), *Behavioural Treatment of Problem Children: A Practice Manual*, London: Academic Press.

Higgins, E., Moracco, J. and Handford, D. (1981), Effects of human relations training on education students. *Journal of Educational Research*, 75, 1, 22–25.

Hinckle, D. (1965), *The Change of Personal Constructs from the View Point of a Theory of Construct Implications*, Unpublished Ph.D. thesis, Ohio State University.

Hodge, R. L. (1971), Inter-personal classroom communication through eye contact. *Theory in Practice*, 10, 264–267.

Holmes, J. H. and Rahe, R. (1967), *Schedule of Recent Experience*, Department of Psychiatry: University of Washington, School of Education.

Holt, J. (1964), *How Children Fail*, Harmondsworth: Penguin.

Hopson, B. and Scally, M. (1980), *Lifeskills Teaching Programmes No 1*, Leeds: Lifeskills Associates.

Hopson, B. and Scally, M. (1981), *Lifeskills Teaching*, London: McGraw-Hill.

Ihde, D. (1979), *Experimental Phenomenology*, New York: Paragon.

Ittleson, W. H. and Kilpatrick, F. P. (1951), Experiments in perception. *Scientific American*, Vol 185, August.

Ivey, A. E. and Authier, J. (1978), *Microcounselling*, 2nd Edition, Springfield: Charles C. Thomas.

Iwanicki, E. F. (1983), Towards understanding and alleviating teacher burnout. *Teaching into Practice*, 12, 1, Winter.

James, W. (1890), *The Principles of Psychology*, New York: Holt, Rinehart and Winston.

Jersild, A. T. (1955), *When Teachers Face Themselves*, New York: Teachers' College, Columbia University.

Johnson, A. W. and Johnson, F. P. (1982), *Joining Together*, 2nd Edition, Englewood Cliffs, New Jersey: Prentice-Hall.

Jones, V. F. and Jones, L. S. (1981), *Responsible Classroom Discipline*, Boston: Allyn and Bacon.

Jourard, S. M. (1964), *The Transparent Self*, Princeton, New Jersey: Van Nostrand.

Jourard, S. M. (1966), An exploratory study of body-accessibility. *British Journal of Social and Clinical Psychology*, 5, 221–231.

Joyce, B. R. (1984), Dynamic disequilibrium: the intelligence of growth. *Theory into Practice*, 23, 1, 26–34, Winter.

Jung, C. G. (1959), Archetypes and the collective unconscious. *The Collected Works of C. G. Jung*, Vol 9, London: Routledge and Kegan Paul.

Jung, C. G. (1961), *Memories, Dreams and Reflections*, Aniela Jaffé (Ed), New York: Random House.

Kelly, G. A. (1955), *The Psychology of Personal Constructs*, Vols 1 and 2, New York: Norton.

King, M. G. (1966), Inter-personal relations in pre-school children and average approach distance. *Journal of Genetic Psychology*, 109, 109–116.

Kolb, D. A. (1984), *Experiential Learning*, Englewood Cliffs, N.J.: Prentice-Hall.

Korzybski, A. (1958), *Science and Sanity*, Lakerville: International Non-Aristotelian Library.

Kyriacou, C. and Sutcliffe, J. (1978), Teacher stress: prevalence, sources and symptoms. *Journal of Educational Psychology*, 48, 159–167.

Kyriacou, C. and Sutcliffe, J. (1979), A note on teacher stress and locus of control. *Journal of Occupational Psychology*, 52, 227–228.

Lange, A. J. and Jakubowsky, P. (1976), *Responsible Assertive Behaviour*, Champaign, Illinois: Research Press.

Laughlin, H. P. (1970), *The Ego and its Defenses*, New York: Appleton-Century-Crofts.

Lederman, J. (1972), Anger and the rocking chair, in J. Fagan, and I. L. Shepherd (Eds), *Gestalt Therapy Now*, Harmondsworth: Penguin Books.

Lee, D. (1976), *Valuing the Self*, Englewood Cliffs: Prentice-Hall.

Leech, N. and Wooster, A. D. (1986), Personal and social skills: A practical approach for the classroom, Exeter: M.R.E.P.

Liberman, R. P., King, L. W., Dirisi, W. J. and McCann, M. (1975), *Personal Effectiveness*, Champaign, Illinois: Research Press.

Lieberman, M. A., Yalom, I. D. and Miles, M. B. (1973), *Encounter Groups: First Facts*, New York: Basic Books.

Lloyd, A. (1984), *The First 120 Days*, Unpublished M.Ed. dissertation: University of Nottingham.

Lowen, A. (1976), *Bioenergetics*, London: Coventure.

Lunn, J. B. (1984), Junior school teachers: their methods and practice. *Educational Research*, 26, 3.

Luthe, W. and Schultz, J. (1965), *Autogenic Training*, New York: Grune and Stratton.

Maslow, A. T. (1962), *Towards a Psychology of Being*, Princeton, N.J.: Van Nostrand.

Mason, L. J. (1980), *Guide to Stress Reduction*, Los Angeles: Peace Press.

Masters, R. and Houston, J. (1978), *Listening to the Body*, New York: Delacorte.

McIntyre, T. C. (1984), The relationship between locus of control and teacher burnout. *British Journal of Educational Psychology*, 54, 235–238.

Miles, M. B. and Fullan, M. (1980), Organization development in schools, in P. B. Smith (Ed), *Small Groups and Personal Change*, London: Methuen.

Milgram, S. (1974), *Obedience to Authority*, New York: Harper and Row.

Miller, G. A., Galanter, E. and Pribram, M. H. (1960), *Plans and the Structure of Behaviour*, New York: Holt.

Miller, S. M. (1980), Why having control reduces stress: if I can stop the roller coaster, I don't want to get off, in J. Garber and M. E. P. Seligman (Eds), *Human Helplessness: Theory and Applications*, New York: Academic Press.

Montague, A. (1978), *Touching*, 2nd Edition, New York: Harper and Row.

Murgatroyd, S. (1985), *Counselling and Helping*, London: Methuen.

Murphy, G. (1975), *Outgrowing Self-Deception*, New York: Basic Books.

Nash, R. (1976), *Teacher Expectation and Public Learning*, London: Routledge and Kegan Paul.

Nelson-Jones, R. (1982), *The Theory and Practice of Counselling Psychology*, London: Holt, Rinehart and Winston.

Nelson-Jones, R. (1983), *Practical Counselling Skills*, London: Holt, Rinehart and Winston.

Nelson-Jones, R. (1986), *Human Relations Skills*, London: Holt, Rinehart and Winston.

Oaklander, V. (1978), *Windows to our Children*, Moab, Utah: Real People Press.

Okun, B. F. (1976), *Effective Helping: Interviewing and Counselling Techniques*, North Scituate: Duxbury.

O'Leary, K. D. and O'Leary, S. G. (1977), *Classroom Management*, Oxford: Pergamon.

Ottaway, A. K. C. (1966), *Learning through Group Experience*, London: Routledge and Kegan Paul.

Passons, W. R. (1975), *Gestalt Approaches in Counselling*, New York: Holt, Rinehart and Winston.

Patterson, C. A. (1980), *Theories of Counselling and Psychotherapy*, New York: Harper and Row.

Perky, C. W. (1910), An experimental study of imagination. *American Journal of Psychology*, 21, 422–452.

Perls, F. S. (1969), *Gestalt Therapy Verbatim*, Moab, Utah: Real People Press.

Perls, F. S. (1976), *The Gestalt Approach and Eye Witness to Therapy*, Palo Alto, Calif.: Science and Behaviour Books.

Perls, F. S., Hefferline, R. and Goodman, P. (1973), *Gestalt Therapy*, Harmondsworth: Penguin.

Phares, E. J. (1957), Expectancy changes in skill and chance situations. *Journal of Abnormal and Social Psychology*, 54, 339–342.

Phares, E. J. (1984), *Introduction to Personality*, Columbus: Charles E. Merrill.

Phelps, S. and Austin, N. (1975), *The Assertive Woman*, San Luis Obispo: Impact Publishers.

The Plowden Report (1968), Children and their Primary Schools. *A Report of the Central Advisory Council for Education*, HMSO.

Pope, L. M. and Keen, T. R. (1981), *Personal Construct Psychology and Education*, London: Academic Press.

Pring, R. (1984), *Personal and Social Education in the Curriculum*, London: Hodder and Stoughton.

Ravenette, A. T. (1977), Grid techniques for children, in D. Child (Ed), *Readings in Psychology for the Teacher*, London: Holt, Rinehart and Winston.

Reich, W. (1972), *Character Analysis*, New York: Touchstone.

Richardson, E. (1967), *Group Study for Teachers*, London: Routledge and Kegan Paul.

Richardson, E. (1973), *The Teacher, the School and the Task of Management*, London: Heinemann.

Rist, R. (1970), Student social class and teacher expectations. *Harvard Educational Review*, 40, 411–451.

Rogers, C. R. (1951), *Client-Centered Therapy*, Boston: Houghton Mifflin.

Rogers, C. R. (1961), *On Becoming a Person: A Therapist's View of Psychotherapy*, Boston: Houghton Mifflin.

Rogers, C. R. (1969), *Encounter Groups*, Harmondsworth: Penguin Press.

Rogers, C. R. (1983), *Freedom to Learn for the 80s*, London: Charles E. Merrill.

Rosenthal, R. and Jacobson, L. (1968), *Pygmalion in the Classroom*, New York: Holt, Rinehart and Winston.

Rosenthal, R. (1976), *Experimenter Effects in Behavioural Research*, 2nd Edition, New York: Irvington.

Rosenthal, R., Hall, J. A., DeMatteo, M. R., Rogers, P. L. and Archer, D. (1979), Measuring sensitivity to non-verbal communication: the PONS test, in A. Wolfgang, *Nonverbal Behaviour: Applications and Cultural Implications*, New York: Academic Press.

Rotter, J. B. (1966), Generalized expectancies for internal versus external control of reinforcement. *Psychological Monographs*, 80 (1, Whole No 609).

Rowan, J. (1983), *The Reality Game*, London: Routledge and Kegan Paul.

Rowe, D. (1978), *The Experience of Depression*, London: Wiley.

Rubovits, P. C. and Maehr, M. L. (1973), Pygmalion black and white. *Journal of Personality, Sociology and Psychology*, 25, 210–218.

Rutter, M., Maughan, B., Mortimer, P. and Ouston, J. (1979), *Fifteen Thousand Hours*, London: Open Books.

Schmuck, R. A. and Schmuck, P. A. (1975), *Group Process in the Classroom*, 2nd Edition, Dubaque, Iowa: William C. Brown.

Schwab, R. L. (1983), Teacher burnout: moving beyond 'psychobabble'. *Teaching into Practice*, 12, 1, Winter.

Sears, R. R. (1936), Experimental studies of projection: 1. attribution of traits. *Journal of Social Psychology*, 7, 151–163, 180.

Seligman, M. E. P. (1975), *Helplessness: On Depression, Development and Death*, San Francisco: W. H. Freeman.

Selye, H. (1976), *The Stress of Life*, New York: McGraw-Hill.

Shattock, E. H. (1979), *Mind Your Body*, London: Turnstone.

Short, G. (1985), Teacher expectation and West Indian underachievement. *Educational Research*, 27, 2 June.

Silberman, C. E. (1973), *The Open Classroom*, New York: Vintage Books.

Simon, S. B. and O'Rourke, R. D. (1977), *Developing Values with Exceptional Children*, Englewood Cliffs, New Jersey: Prentice-Hall.

Simonton, O. C., Matthews-Simonton, S. and Creighton, J. L. (1980), *Getting Well Again*, New York: Bantam.

Singer, J. L. (1966), *Daydreaming and Fantasy*, London: George Allen and Unwin.

Singer, J. L. (1974), *Imagery and Daydream Methods in Psychotherapy and Behaviour Modification*, New York: Academic Press.

Skinner, B. F. (1968), *The Technology of Teaching*, New York: Appleton-Century-Crofts.

Skinner, B. F. (1974), *About Behaviourism*, London: Jonathan Cape.

Slavin, R., Sharon, S., Kagan, S., Herty-Larowitz, R., Webb, C. and

Schmuck, R. (1985), *Learning to Co-operate, Co-operating to Learn*, New York: Plenum Press.

Smail, D. (1984), *Illusion and Reality: the Meaning of Anxiety*, London: Dent.

Smilansky, J. (1984), External and internal correlates of teachers' satisfaction and willingness to report stress. *British Journal of Educational Psychology*, 54, 84–92.

Smith, H. A. (1979), Non-verbal communication in teaching. *Review of Educational Research*, Fall, 49, 4, 631–672.

Sommer, R. (1969), *Personal Space: The Behavioural Basis of Design*, Englewood Cliffs, N.J.: Prentice-Hall.

Spender, D. (1982), *Invisible Women: The Schooling Scandal*, London: Writers and Readers.

Spitz, R. A. (1945), Hospitalisation: an enquiry into the genesis of psychiatric conditions in early childhood, in A. Freud, et al, *The Psychoanalytic Study of the Child*, New York: International Universities Press.

Stevens, J. O. (1971), *Awareness: Exploring, Experimenting and Experiencing*, Lafayette, California: Real People Press.

Stipek, D. J. and Weisz, J. R. (1981), Perceived personal control and academic achievement. *Review of Educational Research*, 51, 1, 101–137.

Sutherland, M. B. (1971), *Everyday Imagining and Education*, London: Routledge and Kegan Paul.

Syer, J. and Connolly, C. (1984), *Sporting Body: Sporting Mind*, Cambridge: Cambridge University Press.

Thacker, J. (1985), Extending Developmental Group Work to junior/middle schools: an Exeter project. *Pastoral Care*, February.

Thorenson, C. E. and Mahoney, M. J. (1974), *Behavioural Self-Control*, New York: Holt, Rinehart and Winston.

Torbert, W. R. (1972), *Learning from Experience: Towards Consciousness*, New York: Columbia University Press.

Trower, P., Bryant, B. and Argyle, M. (1978), *Social Skills and Mental Health*, London: Methuen.

Tucker, I. F. (1970), *Adjustment: Models and Mechanisms*, New York: Academic Press.

Walter, G. A. and Marks, S. E. (1981), *Experiential Learning and Change*, New York: Wiley.

Watts, F. (1983), Magical therapy – just a bag of tricks. *Changes: The Psychology and Psychotherapy Journal*, 1, 2, February.

Watzlawic, P., Beavin, J. H. and Jackson, D. D. (1967), *Pragmatics of Human Communication*, New York: Norton.

Weitz, S. (1979), *Non-verbal Communication*, 2nd Edition, New York: Oxford University Press.

Westmacott, E. V. S. and Cameron, R. J. (1981), *Behaviour Can Change*, London and Basingstoke: Macmillan Educational.

Wheldall, K. (1981), *The Behaviourist in the Classroom*, Birmingham: Educational Review Offset Publications No 1.

Wilson, C. (1966), *The New Existentialism*, London: Wildwood House.

Wolfgang, A. (1979), *Non-verbal Behaviour*, London: Academic Press.

Woodhouse, D. A., Hall, E. and Wooster, A. D. (1985), Taking control of stress in teaching. *British Journal of Educational Psychology*, 55, 119–123.

Wooster, A. D. and Carson, A. (1982), Improving reading and self-concept through communication and social skills training. *British Journal of Guidance and Counselling*, 10 (1).

Wooster, A. D. and Leech, N. (1985), *Personal and Social Education for Slow Learning Children: a Research and Development Project*. Paper presented at the International Congress on Special Education, Nottingham, England, July, 1985.

Index